The Chinese Cookbook

The Chinese Cookbook

Yamei Tsai

BARRIE & JENKINS

COMMUNICA-EUROPA

© Editions Guy Authier 1977

First published in France in 1977
as *La Cuisine Chinoise*

First published in Great Britain in 1978 by
Barrie and Jenkins Ltd
24 Highbury Crescent London N5 1RX

ISBN 0 214 20506 1

Typeset by Computacomp (UK) Ltd
Fort William, Scotland

Printed in Great Britain by
REDWOOD BURN LIMITED
Trowbridge & Esher

CONTENTS

ABOUT CHINESE COOKING

'Have you had your rice today?'

This is a very common greeting in many areas of China, taking the place of the habitual 'hello' or 'how are you?'. Everyday usage of such an expression demonstrates, in part, the role famine and privation have played in Chinese history. Moreover, its continued usage throughout periods of abundance reflects the profound consideration the Chinese express for their national cuisine.

Such appreciation, which first developed on a regional level, eventually expanded to an overall national pride. Today this esteem is international. Chinese cookery ranks equally with French and, even more important, it is now recognised by the experts as being one of the most highly nutritive and healthy cuisines of the world. For these reasons, it is being adopted throughout many western countries. Indeed, one day the entire world, in appreciation of Chinese cuisine, may use the salutation: 'Have you had your rice today?'!

What, exactly, is Chinese cookery? It is an ancient art, often misunderstood and not well enough known in its great simplicity. Over 5,000 years ago, the Emperor Fu Shi introduced agriculture and domestication of animals to the primitive Chinese culture, elements which gave rise to the birth of the culinary arts. From their earliest beginnings, these arts were profoundly influenced by two factors basic to Chinese life: philosophy and privation.

While in western cultures, dishes and fashions in cookery have changed throughout the centuries, in China the contrary has been true. Due to constant privation, the Chinese were obliged to adapt obtainable ingredients to a method of cooking dictated by chronic lack of fuel. The important factor became the cooking technique itself, rather than the ingredient. A keen interest in the taste, texture and appearance of prepared food was first expressed by the great Master, Confucius, born over 2,500 years ago. A sensitive connoisseur, Confucius established special rites and rules of cooking methods, taste and table manners. His wisdom was applied religiously and handed down from century to century. Indeed, many of his principles are still valid today. We are all quite ready to agree with Confucius that: no discoloured or badly cooked food should be eaten; all meat should be correctly cut; one should buy fresh rather than pre-cooked food.

A second philosopher of far-reaching influence was Lao-Tze who, for his part, was interested in the spiritual rather than the

MAP OF CHINA

HONAN

SZECHWAN

SHANGHAI

FUKIEN

TAIWAN

CANTON

physical qualities of food. His disciples, searching for the secret of longevity, carried out research on plants and herbs and so discovered the importance, healthwise, of the very cooking techniques already practised by necessity.

Thanks to the traditions and rules firmly established by Confucius and Lao-Tze, we today prepare recipes which are one to two thousand years old! Lack and privation were the conductors, and philosophic thought the transmitter, which have carried down to us such recipes as 'Empress Chicken'. Accordingly, the two fundamental differences between Chinese and other cuisines are its methods, ancient yet modern, and its philosophy or symbolism. Above all, it is through learning the methods, in all their simplicity, that the first step is taken toward thoroughly understanding Chinese cookery. Then, as the methods are mastered, will the more complex philosophy and symbolism that surrounds our cuisine become comprehensible.

Of course there are other, lesser elements which help to compose a total definition of Chinese cooking, the most interesting of these being its great diversity. Due to the vast stretches of the great land of China, the cuisine which developed was quite distinct and even dissimilar, from one region to another. In fact, 76 divergent 'schools' of cooking were formerly identified. Today, however, due to modernization of transportation, refrigeration and so on, these 'schools' have intermingled until only five are now counted, and certain experts are already declaring there to be only four.

The school of Peking and the north has its origins in the cuisine of the emperor who ordered the best chefs of all of China to prepare special delicacies for the court. The succulent Peking Duck with its little wheat cakes is the most famous of these superlative dishes. Wheat, the basic food of Northern China, produced the renowned egg noodles from which the European noodles are the descendants. Equally from the north comes the much enjoyed Chinese Hot Pot or 'Fondue' as well as many delicious little dishes prepared in delicate sauces. The school of Szechwan is located in the south western part of China, a mountainous region far removed from sources of salt. For this, as well as climatic and agricultural reasons, the province of Szechwan has developed highly seasoned dishes and sauces. The school of Shanghai/Fukien, a coastal area, is sometimes identified as two separate schools. It is renowned for its fish specialities and innumerable exquisite soups. The cuisine of Fukien offers a variety of most subtly flavoured, sautéed dishes. The school of Honan, an area located in the centre of the triangle formed by Peking, Szechwan and Shanghai, has combined the tastes of these three regions, preparing food in heavy sauces, rich in soy sauce and sugar. The Cantonese school of cooking, representing the south of China, is the most widely known internationally. This is partly due to the fact that the greatest majority of overseas Chinese come from the province of Canton. They have brought with them their sweet and sour, sautéed and highly coloured dishes, so much in vogue in the west.

Generally speaking, the oriental restaurants of the United Kingdom and Europe offer a considerable selection of dishes from each of the distinguished regional cuisines, for the Chinese love to combine and juxtapose different tastes and textures. You will find in this book family and restaurant recipes from each of the outstanding schools, so that you may enjoy the abundant variation of Chinese cuisine.

COOKING UTENSILS

Chinese utensils, strange and complicated in appearance, are often obstacles for beginners who do not understand their usage yet believe them indispensable. The assertion that one cannot 'cook Chinese' without a wok or chopsticks is a myth. European utensils replace perfectly well their Chinese counterparts. Moreover, the recipes of this book have all been tested, with success, using a simple set of European cookware. However, Chinese utensils are beginning to appear more often in oriental stores, expositions and bazaars throughout the United Kingdom and Europe and, therefore, merit certain explanation.

The wok (also called Kuo), a sort of all-round cooking pan, is ideal for nearly all methods of Chinese cooking: braising, sautéing, frying, stewing and steaming. It is wide and deep, with rounded sides and bottom. Woks come in several sizes, the 12" (30 cm) and 14" (35 cm) in diameter being the handiest for home use. Should you decide to procure a wok, do be sure to season and maintain it properly. When new, wash with a detergent and hot water. Dry with

absorbent kitchen paper or place it for several interior with a cooking oil. Place it over a hot fire for one minute. Rinse immediately under hot water, dry the wok and oil it once again. Place it a second time over the hot fire for one minute, rinse again under hot water and dry. If the absorbent paper remains clean, your wok is ready to use. If it is still dirty, repeat the process until no trace of black is to be seen. After cooking in the wok, scrub it with a non-scratch soft brush, then rinse under hot running water. Do not use a strong detergent. Dry with absorbent kitchen paper or place it for several seconds over a hot fire, then re-oil lightly. A good storage place for the re-oiled wok is the oven.

Modern woks are sold with separate circular collars which serve to support the rounded base over gas or electric burners. Formerly, the rounded base fit directly into the Chinese cooker. While much is to be said in favour of a wok, it may be replaced in all its functions by western skillets and saucepans. Heavy, round-bottomed iron frying pans are recommended as prime substitutes.

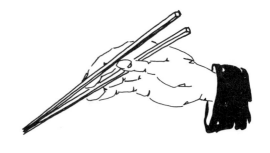

The gracious bamboo steaming baskets seen in oriental exhibitions and Chinese shop windows are placed in the wok which holds the boiling water. These bamboo baskets are put on top of each other, so that several different foods can be steamed at the same time. The western aluminium steamers, however, can be used instead of the Chinese variety and their cleaning and upkeep are far more manageable. Furthermore, any large stewing saucepan or pressure cooker supplied with a steaming basket can be adapted to this use. Take care, if using a

pressure cooker, to prevent it from sealing by placing a dish towel between the cooker and its lid. It is also very easy to make your own steamer. Punch several holes in the bottom of an empty food tin. Place the tin, bottom side up, in a large saucepan containing 3" to 4" (8 cm to 10 cm) of boiling water, then the dish or bowl of

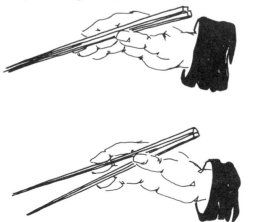

food to be steamed on top of the tin, making sure the dish can take the heat without breaking. Cover tightly with a lid and there's your steamer.

Our chopsticks are used not only for eating but for cooking as well. With them we beat, mix, turn, stir, toss and whip. However, all these operations can be carried out just as effectively with forks, spoons, beaters and whips. If you do wish to try chopsticks, use those made of bamboo; they are more practical than the plastic or ivory variety, for the food does not slip from them so easily.

The Chinese cleaver, which resembles the French chef's knife, is extremely important in our cookery. Chinese mothers traditionally give young daughters a good cleaver which will last a lifetime. My cleaver follows me everywhere in my suitcase as is the case with many Chinese cooks. It is the perfect instrument for every kind of cutting: slicing, cubing, shredding, mincing and so forth. Nevertheless, a good European kitchen knife, well sharpened, can handle the cutting preparation of most Chinese food.

The other principal Chinese cooking utensils, all of which have their western equivalent are: copper ladles with long or short handles, brass strainers, shovel-like spatulas, wooden spoons and, of course, scissors and chopping boards.

In olden days, the Chinese had no ovens.

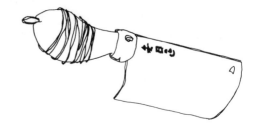

Women bought oven-cooked food from specialized merchants. It has been, in large part, the overseas Chinese who have adapted their recipes to modern, individual ovens, still not found in all Chinese homes. The 'fire pot' or Mongolian brazier used for special table cooking, is replaced by the hibachi or electric frying pan commonly used in the west.

Thus, as you can see, there really is no mystery concerning our utensils. You already have, in your own kitchen, all that you need to begin your Chinese cooking experience.

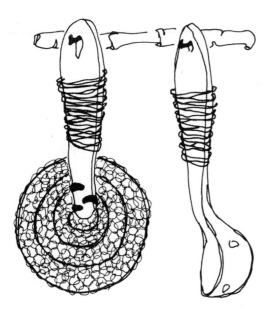

PREPARATION
AND COOKING TECHNIQUES

Chinese cookery is very easy and simple if you observe several basic rules. Indeed, it is so simple that it soon becomes like the Peking Opera: 'One changes, adapts and improvises, depending upon what one has on hand'!

The first basic rule is to finish all preliminary preparation of food and sauces before embarking upon the cooking process. The importance of this rule cannot be stressed strongly enough to those who are in the western habit of putting the meat or vegetables on to cook before preparing the appropriate seasonings and sauces. On the contrary, in Chinese cookery, all cleaning, the cutting, the marinating, the mixing of the sauces, seasonings and thickenings must be completed and the ingredients placed at hand before turning on the stove. By following step by step the recipe directions in this book, the separation of these two procedures (preparation and cooking) becomes natural and easy.

The second basic rule of Chinese cookery concerns the proper cutting of ingredients. With very few exceptions, all ingredients are cut to bite-sized dimensions, or smaller, due to the necessity for rapid cooking and the use of chopsticks. In addition, ingredients composing the same dish are cut into even, equal sizes so that cooking time and appearance will be uniform. For example, if the pork is cut into matchstick-thin strips, all the other ingredients of the dish – carrots, onions, and so on – should also be cut into matchstick-thin strips.

There are four cuts basic to the preparation of Chinese food:

DICE/CUBE/SQUARE

Small and large cube cutting is common to occidental cookery and should cause no difficulty. Diced, the ingredients are cut from $\frac{1}{8}'' \times \frac{1}{8}''$ (2.5 mm × 2.5 mm) to $\frac{3}{8}'' \times \frac{3}{8}''$ (7.5 mm × 7.5 mm). Cubes are $\frac{1}{2}'' \times \frac{1}{2}''$ (1.25

Cube

cm × 1.25 cm) in size, while squares or what is called bite-sized are approximately $1'' \times 1''$ (2.5 cm × 2.5 cm). For perfect cubes, first cut the ingredient into strips, then crosswise into segments.

STRAIGHT SLICE/DIAGONAL SLICE

The straight-cut slice (used on tender vegetables such as the cucumber) is the same slice as that used in western cookery. For fibrous and hard vegetables such as the carrot, the slicing should be done on the diagonal. It looks prettier, the cooking surface is enlarged and taste improved. The width of all slices, whether on the diagonal or straight, should be no larger than ¼" (7 mm).

In Chinese cookery, slicing is the cutting method the most frequently used for meats. Paper-thin slicing can be easily accomplished if fat and tendons are first removed, then, the meat

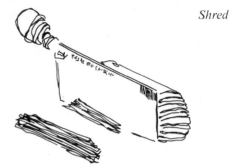

Shred

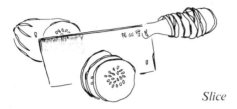

Slice

half-frozen. The slicing should always be done against the grain, in 1" to 1½" (2.5 cm to 4 cm) lengths and no larger than 1/16" to 1/8" (1.5 mm to 3.5 mm) in width. If possible, slice the meat on the diagonal.

OBLIQUE

This cut is typically Chinese but very easy to learn. It is practised on tough and fibrous vegetables such as the carrot and is used principally for dishes which call for long cooking. First slice the vegetables on the diagonal about 1½" (4 cm) from its end. Then, turn the vegetable half way around and slice it once again on the diagonal 1½" (4 cm) from the end, continuing on in the same manner until completed.

Oblique

SHRED/MATCHSTICK/STRIP

Of the four basic cuts, this is the one which is the most extensively used by the Chinese. Shreds, matchsticks and strips are generally 1" to 1½" (2.5 cm to 4 cm) in length. The width of the shreds will be 1/8" (3.5 mm) or less, of the matchstick-thin strips ¼" (7 mm) and strips above that. To cut into shreds, matchsticks or

strips, first slice the ingredients thinly. If the ingredient is a hard vegetable, use a potato peeler for the job. Then, cut the slices into shreds. For pliable vegetables such as cabbage, use a grater or grinder for shredding.

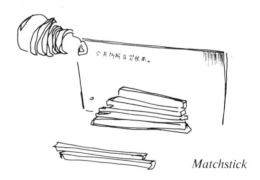

Matchstick

The third basic rule of Chinese cooking is to follow precisely the cooking techniques indicated. In addition to insuring successful results, Chinese cookery, correctly done, is the most healthy of all cooking techniques for it retains the vitamin and mineral content of the ingredients while offering an enormous

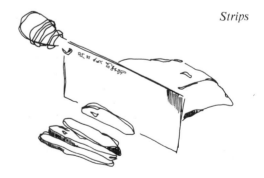

Strips

diversity of dishes, low in calories and cholesterol. Chinese culinary experts and nutritionists alike urge close observance of these five basic cookery methods.

STIR-FRY

The 'stir-fry' is the most notable of all Chinese cooking techniques. Indeed, the name, which so well evokes the action, is a recent addition to the English language, being the shortened form of the concept 'quickly stir and fry'. Stir-fry is somewhat similar to French sautéing, differing in that it calls for a higher heat and very little oil. (Butter is never used in authentic Chinese cooking.) It necessitates a constant and energetic stirring with a spatula in order to obtain uniform cooking. The stir-fry method is applied to both meat and vegetables.

The temperature of the oil is an extremely important factor in stir-frying. The oil must be sizzling hot, just at the smoking point before adding the first ingredient. If the pan is not hot enough, the food will absorb the oil and stick. Should this occur, sprinkle with a little sherry and stir vigorously.

Timing is also very important. Stir-frying is an extremely rapid process, the cooking in many cases being reduced to a matter of seconds. All ingredients must be prepared and placed within reach before the cooking is begun. Once the first ingredient is dropped in, it is impossible to let go of the pan.

Total cooking time will not exceed more than four to five minutes, and often less, for most stir-fried dishes. Therefore, it is necessary to programme the stir-fry cooking for the last moments before sitting down to the table.

Vegetables and meats are often stir-fried separately to prevent one or the other from over-cooking. A stir-fried vegetable is cooked to exactly the right point and its flavour at a maximum when its colour has intensified and it is crunchy-tender. Meat will be golden-brown, crispy on the outside and its juices sealed in.

BRAISING

Braising is a method common to European cooking and should cause no difficulty. Meats and vegetables are braised in a little liquid (usually soy sauce, sherry and water) over a medium flame. This usually takes a relatively short period of time and, while less demanding of attention than stir-frying, should also be planned as last-minute cooking.

DEEP-FRYING

Deep-frying is a very popular Chinese cooking technique. For successful results, the oil must be at just the right temperature. As a general rule, this will be when a piece of bread, thrown in, returns to the surface and browns in 45 to 60 seconds. A Chinese 'trick' is drop a piece of fresh ginger (or bread or potato) into the oil during the frying to keep it from spattering.

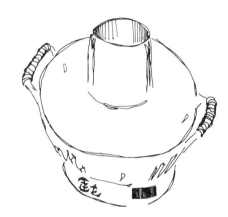

We frequently do a 'small deep-fry' to pre-cook ingredients, usually meat, sometimes vegetables or condiments. This type of deep-frying is done in small quantities of oil, from $\frac{1}{2}$ to 1 pint ($\frac{1}{4}$ to $\frac{1}{2}$ litre), heated to smoking point. The ingredient is dropped into the hot oil and quickly seared, sealing in its juices. Half-cooked, it is removed from the oil and drained on absorbent kitchen paper. Cooking will then be completed by the stir-fry method. Many Chinese recipes suggest this technique.

STEWING

The stewing and long simmering methods used for the tough pieces of meat are the same as in the west. If the stewing is done in soy sauce, it is called 'red cooked' and if in a clear stock 'white cooked'.

STEAMING

The technique of steaming is a familiar one. The food is cooked over boiling water in a container which permits the steam to circulate around the food without the water touching it. During the steaming, the water temperature must be maintained at the boiling point. The food is often steamed in unbreakable serving plates or bowls which are then placed directly on the table.

Each recipe in this book includes a guide

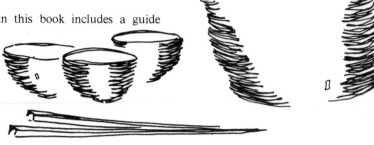

indicating the difficulties in preparation and cooking which may be encountered by the beginner. After several trials, however, I am sure that all of the recipes will be mastered with the greatest of ease and success.

INGREDIENTS

Chinese meals are based upon a concept quite different from that of western meals. Ours are not planned around one main dish such as roast beef or chicken, but rather, are composed of several 'main' dishes of vegetables, rice or noodles, all seasoned with small quantities of meat or fish. Each dish is contrasted with the others in flavour, colour and texture. The basic ingredients of the several dishes served at one meal may be the same although prepared in various ways. Or, on the other hand, the same sauce or cooking technique may be used for several of the basic ingredients. For example, a roast of beef would not be served strictly as roast beef in the Chinese household. It would be chopped, sliced, stir-fried, deep-fried, braised and so on. Its sauces and seasonings would vary greatly.

Consequently, any kind of vegetable or meat currently available on the market can be used to create a good Chinese meal. Never hesitate to replace one ingredient by another, depending upon personal preference and availability. I have tried to facilitate this concept, which is often new to western cooks, by making suggestions of appropriate alternatives and substitutes throughout the book.

The secondary ingredients, those which season the dish, are equally variable in Chinese cooking. Much as a French omelette may be made with herbs or onions or tomatoes or even jam, depending upon what is on hand, the secondary ingredients of numerous Chinese dishes may be chosen by personal preference and availability. Indeed, the flexibility of both primary and secondary ingredients cannot be stressed strongly enough. Add any bit of carrot or cabbage or spring onion which is lying in the bottom of the refrigerator to a stir-fried noodle or rice dish; it will only be the better for it.

Furthermore, one need not be too concerned, when 'cooking Chinese', about precise quantities of ingredients. Should a recipe of noodles or rice call for 6 oz (150 g) of shrimp or pork and you find yourself with only 4 oz (100 g) on hand, do not hesitate to go ahead with the dish. Simply increase the quantity of another ingredient, or perhaps add a bit more salt if the missing ingredient has a salty flavour. The art of Chinese cookery is one of precision techniques but not of precision quantities!

SEASONINGS

We say that newly married couples have need of seven things to begin their household: oil, soy sauce, vinegar, fuel, rice, sugar and tea. Notice that the majority of items on the list fall into the category of seasonings. Seasonings play an extremely important role in our cuisine, not only from the point of view of taste, but also for the effect that they have upon the appearance of the dish. Furthermore, it is the seasoning which creates the perfect harmony of all the elements of the meal.

The most well known of all Chinese seasonings is soy sauce. It is particularly used for the savour which it imparts to food. There are many varieties of soy sauce, which differ widely, from thick to thin, from light brown to almost black, and from very salty to barely salty. Chinese chefs like to mix the different soy sauces in order to obtain a certain perfect flavour and 'perfume'. But, for the most part, the soy sauces commonly available in the supermarkets and oriental groceries in the United Kingdom and Europe are of a medium blend which is appropriate to most Chinese recipes.

A seasoning of primary importance in our cookery is the spring onion, appreciated as much for its colour as for its taste. The white

called 'red and green caps'. It can be replaced in certain cases by tabasco sauce or Chinese hot pepper oil.

Another characteristic and very important Chinese seasoning is ginger. Ginger is a tubular root which can be bought fresh or in powdered form. The Chinese use only fresh ginger and many experts strongly denounce the substitution of the powdered variety. When I first tried the powdered ginger, I noticed a difference not only of taste and texture but primarily one of smell. For us, the smell of fresh ginger being sautéed in oil cannot be

bulb and about 6" (15 cm) of the green stem are used. Leek and chives are similar in odour and perfume but common yellow onions and shallots can also be used as substitutes.

A surprising seasoning, basic to numerous Chinese dishes, is the chilli pod, commonly

equalled. Nevertheless, the use of powdered ginger is valid in certain sauces and marinades which ordinarily call for a complicated procedure of extracting the juice from fresh ginger. Furthermore, the limited availability of fresh ginger in the United Kingdom and European markets often renders fastidious preference difficult for the person who wants to give Chinese cooking a try. So, I have tested and noted appropriate equivalents throughout the book. Here is the scale of equivalence which represents the minimum amount to be used. Should you prefer a more pronounced taste of ginger, you may slightly increase the quantities given but do take care not to cover the perfume and flavour of the other ingredients, for powdered ginger is very strong: 1 slice of fresh ginger about $1\frac{1}{2}$" (4 cm) across equals $\frac{1}{4}$ scant teaspoon powdered; 2 slices equal $\frac{1}{4}$ teaspoon powdered; 3 slices equal $\frac{1}{2}$ teaspoon powdered; 4 slices equal $\frac{3}{4}$ teaspoon powdered; 5 slices equal 1 teaspoon powdered.

Also ranking among the seasonings which play a primary role in our cuisine is one which few westerners consider a seasoning at all, cornflour. Dissolved in a little water, it thickens and binds sauces; added at the end of cooking, it gives a lustrous and translucent appearance to the food; in deep-frying, batters, it seals in natural juices; and as a seasoning, it enhances and enriches flavour.

Certain seasonings occupy a double function in Chinese cookery. They serve not only to heighten the savour and perfume of food but also to diminish disagreeable odours and flavours. For this latter usage, we readily employ garlic, ginger, radishes, turnips, walnuts and cooking wine. Wine is especially effective in eliminating the strong odour of cooking fish. As for garlic, ginger, radishes, turnips and walnuts, these are discarded in the middle or at the end of the cooking process when used as a mitigating agent.

COOKING FATS AND OILS

Oil is always used in Chinese cookery, and never butter or margarine, for several significant reasons. Oil can be heated to a much higher temperature than butter, thus permitting the flavours of different ingredients to blend subtly together. Cooking time is decreased, disagreeable odours eliminated and colour, texture and vitamin content retained. Solid blocks of shortening are not recommended for they conceal the natural flavour of the ingredients. On the other hand, chicken and duck fat, as well as lard, are much appreciated in certain dishes.

Any good vegetable oil, other than olive oil which is too strong for Chinese cooking, may be

used although peanut oil is the one preferred by the Chinese for it gives the best results and flavour. We also have a very special oil which is made from sesame seeds. Sesame oil is used as a seasoning rather than as a cooking oil. It is thick and amber coloured, very highly perfumed, and has a delicious, nutty taste. Intensive heat quickly destroys its delicate flavour so it should generally be added at the end of the cooking process. Indeed, its flavour is so different that there is no substitute for it. Only in its quality as an oil, can it be replaced by other oils. Although one can 'cook Chinese' without it, I encourage you to try sesame oil, not only for its unique savour but also for its rich iron and calcium content which make it a nutritious addition to the diet. It is available in oriental groceries and health food shops in the United Kingdom. A small bottle will last a long time for it is always used in small quantities. A few drops are sufficient to give an exquisite bouquet to any dish.

COOKING WINES AND ALCOHOLS

In the preparation and cooking of the majority of our dishes, we use rice wine in small quantities. This is a colourless or yellow wine which is very high in alcoholic content. There are many kinds of rice wine and you will find a certain selection in oriental and specialty liquor shops. There are, however, adequate substitutes for rice wine among the European alcohols. The most widely preferred is dry sherry. Other dry, white aperitif wines such as white vermouth and white port may also be used in Chinese cooking. Vodka, whisky and colourless spirits ('Eaux de Vie') are also perfectly acceptable alternatives. White dinner wines of the quality of Chablis are sometimes recommended for cooking use but I would suggest using the

stronger dry, white aperitif wines.

Chinese desserts are usually flavoured with almond essence. If this is not obtainable, kirsch may be used in its stead.

CHINESE DINNERS AND DRINKS

DINNER MENUS

Chinese banquets are renowned for their staggering parade of assorted delicacies. Even the simple peasant will have as many as six dishes for one meal, although these, depending upon his means, may be poor in quantity and quality. All Chinese meals, whether great banquets or humble suppers, are composed of rice or noodles and vegetables, seasoned with a little meat, fish or salted black beans. At home, we usually put these different dishes on the table at the same time. However, at elegant banquets, the great profusion of specialities are aesthetically and fastidiously disposed in front of the guests, according to taste, appearance, colour and perfume. In olden times, these sumptuous banquets would last all day and even continue into the next day and on to the next! One may yet be invited to large banquets at which 16 courses or more are served! This is a typical menu of a modern-day feast: a first course of four cold dishes such as spring rolls, ivory chicken, pork or shrimp balls and so forth; followed by eight 'main' dishes among which will figure duck, chicken, pigeon, fish, pork, two vegetables and two soups, accompanied by noodles or rice; and for dessert, two dishes, of which one will be a cake or sweet soup. (The sweet soup may already have been served between the main 'salty' dishes.)

Today we commonly give simple dinners for friends as is done in western cultures. However, these dinners will still include at least eight dishes, a large platter of artistically arranged cold meats for the first course, 'main' dishes of which four will consist of meat, fish and fowl as well as two others of vegetables accompanied by soup, rice or noodles; and, finally, one sweet dish.

It is very difficult to judge how many persons may be served by one Chinese dish. In our homes, at the arrival of unexpected guests, we add another dish to the menu rather than increase the amount of the one which is already being prepared. The recipes of this book indicate the number of persons who can be served as based upon quantities similar to those of restaurants. Should your party be more numerous than the number of persons served by the recipe, add one or more main dishes to your menu. However, should you hesitate to serve several main dishes at once, you may increase the quantity of any recipe without difficulty.

The preparation and even partial cooking of the majority of dishes may be undertaken well in advance of, or even the day before, your dinner. The approximate amount of time involved in both the preparation and the cooking are noted on each recipe and should be an additional help in selection and planning.

When deciding upon your dinner menu, be sure to take into consideration the cooking technique of each recipe. Choose only one stir-fried or deep-fried dish per meal. The others should involve different cooking methods so that you will be free at the very last minute to do the stir-fried or deep-fried dish. The selected dishes should be juxtaposed in flavour and colour. For example, a highly seasoned dish such as Stir-Fried Beef Szechwan should be contrasted with a lightly seasoned, delicate dish such as Chicken Kinghwa.

At the end of this chapter are a number of

menu suggestions to further assist you in preparing a perfect Chinese dinner.

DINNER DRINKS

As a general rule, Chinese never take cocktails before a meal nor liqueurs afterwards. On the other hand, the wine flows from the appearance of the first course onward. It is served warm in tiny cups, then disappears from the table along with the last delicacies, to be replaced by tea.

Certain Chinese wines are available in oriental and specialty liquor shops in the United Kingdom and Europe. Sau Hsin is a yellow wine of 14° to 15° alcoholic proof which comes from the province of Hanchow. It is called the 'daughter's wine' because the people of this region bottle it to celebrate the birth of a daughter, then keep it to be opened at her marriage. May Tai is made of wheat and millet, which comes from Kwi Chou where the water is reputed to be the best. This is the wine which is served at the great state banquets offered for visiting heads of state. A very strong wine is Kaoling, called 'white thunder'; it must be sipped very slowly. On the other hand Wu Chia Pi, made of herbs, is renowned for its tonic effects and therefore often drunk by older persons. In familiar terms it is called 'the medicinal wine'.

The Japanese rice wine, Saki, is equally appreciated at our tables.

We Chinese also love beer with which we wash down salty and spicy snacks. The most famous beer of China is Tsing-Tao, from the city of Tsing-Tao, which before World War II was controlled by the Germans who put their most outstanding technicians to work producing the regional beer.

Notwithstanding the availability of certain of our wines and spirits on the western market, many European wines and beers may suitably accompany our meals. Indeed, in some instances they may even be preferable to ours which are often too strong for the non-initiated. At the end of this chapter is a list of aperitifs, wines, beer and liqueurs which are appropriate to serve with Chinese food.

We Chinese drink tea all day long but never during the meal. Tea drinking was first developed in China and mentioned in certain manuscripts as early as the 4th century BC. Today, there are as many as 250 different varieties classified into three principal categories, according to their method of preparation: green, unfermented tea, such as 'Gun Powder', comes from the north of China; black, fermented tea, for example the 'Keemun' from the province of Anhwei, the many famous English and Indian teas such as Darjeeling as well as the smoked teas like the 'Lapsang Souchong' from the centre of China; and Oolong, mixtures of green and black teas from Taiwan and among which the most famous are Jasmin, Rose and Litchi teas.

We prefer to mix the black and green teas ourselves. In order to make a good cup of Chinese tea, we pour just-boiling water over the leaves, then cover the cup and let it steep three to five minutes. For the second cup, we pour more hot water over the same leaves because the second cup of tea made from the same leaves is even better than the first. In fact, some Chinese tea drinking experts go so far as to throw away the first cup of tea so as to immediately savour the second. We never put sugar or milk or lemon in our tea. But, inasmuch as the essence of tea drinking is the pleasure and relaxation it imparts, others should feel free to add whatever might increase their own enjoyment of this wonderful drink.

MENU IDEAS

FOR 2 TO 3 PERSONS

Egg Flower Soup II
Braised Spareribs I or II
Aubergine Salad
Stir-Fried Cabbage (see Stir-Fried Celery)
Steamed or Fried Rice
Lichees

Mushrooms Braised in Soy Sauce
Chicken of Three Colours
Steamed Rice with Peanuts
Stir-Fried Celery
Almond Biscuits

Egg Fu Yung with Scallops
Empress Chicken
Jade Rice
Pickled Aubergine
Chinese Sponge Cake

Soup of Two Flavours
Fish in Curry Sauce
Steamed Rice
Almond Tea Cream and Fortune Cookies

Asparagus Soup
Stir-Fried Fenszu or Stir-Fried Rice Noodles
Cantonese Salad
Almond Cream Jelly

Chicken Sesame Salad or Lion's Tooth Salad
Prawns with Almonds

Stir-Fried Rice with Curry
Stir-Fried Spinach with Ham
Fruit in Season

Chicken Livers with Five Spices
Soft-Fried Noodles with Pork
Cucumber Salad
Fortune Cookies

Szechwan Pork with Bean Curd
Steamed Chicken with Ginger or Chicken
    Sesame Salad
Mushrooms with Nuoc Mam
Almond Tea Cream

FOR 3 TO 4 PERSONS

Phoenix Tailed Shrimp
Pork Shoulder in Red Sauce
Steamed Rice
Szechuan Cucumbers
Almond Cream Pudding

Sour and Pungent Soup
Steamed Chicken with Ginger
Stir-Fried Liver with Green Peppers
Steamed Rice
Peanut Cream Pudding

Pickled Radishes
Chop Suey
Chinese Roast Chicken

Steamed Rice
Almond Cream Jelly

Chinese Grilled Beef
Steamed Rice
Salad of Three Colours or Gold and Silver
    Salad
Chinese Sponge Cake with Fruits in Season

Spring Roll or Egg Roll
Chicken with Little Flowers
Szechwan Noodles
Spinach Salad
Lichees

Jade Soup
Crystal Prawns
Steamed Rice with Peanuts
Red Cooked Pork
Almond Tea Cream

Chicken Soup with Cucumber
Chinese Roast Pork
White Cooked Sea Bass
Sweet and Sour Cabbage
Steamed Rice
Fruit in Season and Peanut Candy

Sour and Pungent Soup or Egg Flower Soup
Mixed Noodle Salad
Almond Cream Jelly

Scallop Soup
Chicken of Two Flavours
Steamed Fish
Steamed or Fried Rice
Fruit in Season
FOR 4 TO 6 ADD Stir Fried Beef with Pickles

Chinese Shrimp Soup
Kinghwa Chicken
Stir-fried Beef Szechwan

Steamed Rice
Almond Biscuits
FOR 4 TO 6 ADD Mixed Salad II; Golden
    Baked Fish

Floating Cloud Soup I or II
Chicken in Soy Sauce
Cucumber or Cabbage Salad
Sesame Pork or Parsley Pork
Steamed or Fried Rice
Fruit in Season
FOR 4 TO 6 ADD Stir-Fried Liver with
    Cashew Nuts

Watercress Soup
Barbecued Spareribs I or II
Chicken in Lemon Sauce
Steamed Aubergine
Steamed Rice
FOR 4 TO 6 ADD Stir-Fried Shrimp I or II or
    Drunken Shrimp; Chinese Sponge Cake

Egg Fu Yung with Oysters or Scallops
Roast Duck
Mixed Salad II
Eight Treasures Rice Pudding
FOR 4 TO 6 ADD instead of Mixed Salad II,
    Mixed Noodle Salad

Egg Flower Soup
Stir-Fried Kidneys with Vegetables
Ivory Chicken I or II
Steamed Rice
Fruit in Season
FOR 4 TO 6 ADD Red Cooked Beef or Beef of
    Four Flavours; Almond Biscuits

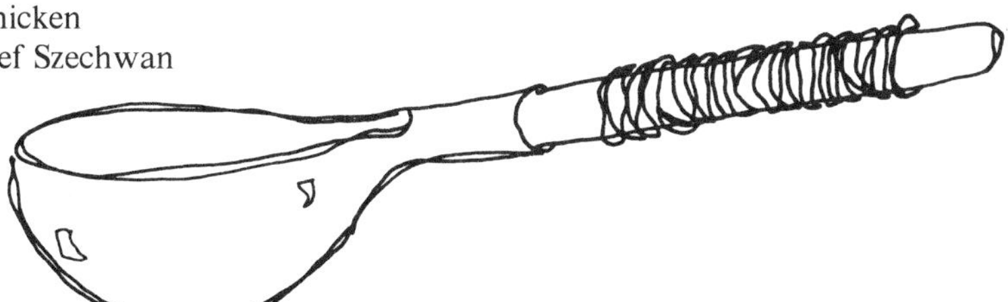

Spring Roll I
Mixed Salad I or II
Prawns (or Chicken) with Almonds
Sweet and Sour Pork
Steamed Rice
Fortune Cookies

FOR 4 TO 6 PERSONS

Hors d'oeuvre
Chinese Hot Pot
Steamed Rice
Lichees and Fortune Cookies

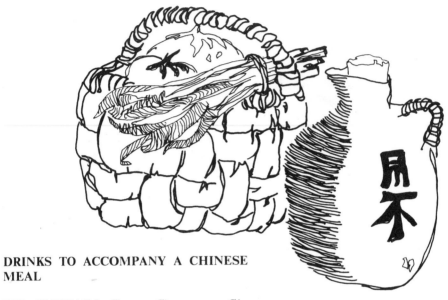

DRINKS TO ACCOMPANY A CHINESE MEAL

FOR COCKTAILS: Sherry; Champagne; Gin and Tonic; American Martinis; White Vermouth; White Port; Pisco; Pastis; Chablis; Pouilly Fuissé; Kir

WITH FISH, CHICKEN or PORK: Champagne; Chablis; Dry Moselle; Muscadet; Pouilly Fuissé; Wines of the Rhine, Rhone and Alsace; Rosé Wines; Beer

WITH DUCK: Champagne; Wines of Alsace; Riesling; Dry Moselle; Red Burgundy; Beaujolais; Rosé Wines

WITH DESSERTS: Tea; Cognac; Armagnac; Anisette; Iced Drambuie and Whisky

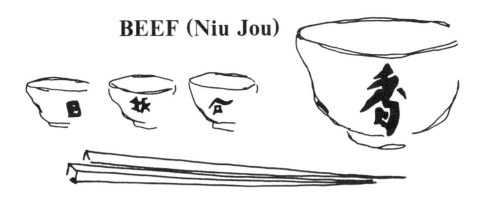

BEEF (Niu Jou)

Many Chinese refuse to eat beef, believing it to represent an obliging and hard-working animal – just the contrary of pigs and chickens! Indeed, bovine animals have always been considered part of the family, so much so that the consumption of beef was actually introduced into China by westerners.

BEEF OF FOUR FLAVOURS (Lu Jou)
fairly easy
preparation 5 minutes / marinade 4 hours
cooking 1 hour 45 minutes
serves 2 to 4

YOU NEED
$\frac{1}{2}$ lb (250g) stewing beef
$\frac{1}{2}$ lb (250g) liver
4 chicken thighs (or other part)
4 hard boiled eggs

SEASONING
$\frac{1}{2}$ tsp salt
1 star anise (optional)
1 good pinch powdered ginger
1 tsp five spice powder (or cinnamon)
1 piece rock candy (or 1 teaspoon brown sugar)
2 spring onions (or 1 leek)
1 tsp dry sherry
1 pint ($\frac{1}{2}$ litre) water
$\frac{1}{4}$ pint ($\frac{1}{8}$ litre) soy sauce

Hard boil the eggs, plunge into cold water and shell when cool. Cut the beef into bite size pieces. Cut the spring onions in half lengthwise. Rinse the liver under hot running water for several minutes. In a large saucepan, bring the seasoning ingredients to the boil. Add the pieces of beef and bring back to the boil. Lower the heat, cover and let simmer for 1 hour, stirring from time to time. Incorporate the chicken thighs, the shelled hard boiled eggs whole, and the whole piece of liver, adding water if needed. Simmer for a further 45 minutes. Turn off the heat and let the ingredients marinate for at least 4 hours or all night. Slice the liver thinly. Serve the dish hot or cold, sprinkled with sesame oil if desired.

TIPS & TRICKS
This versatile dish makes a delightful hot dinner, cold snack or speciality to carry along on a picnic. It can be kept up to two weeks if refrigerated; its taste becomes better and better as it marinates. Reserve the remainder of the sauce in a tightly closed jar under refrigeration. It can be re-used time and again, adding a little soy sauce, sugar and water as needed. If the sauce is boiled once a week it will keep for a very long time. Indeed, each Chinese family jealously conserves his sauce, called 'lou', as do many restaurants of which some advertise their 'lou' as being 100, or more, years old.

BEEF WITH CAULIFLOWER (Hau Yu Niu Jou)

fairly easy
preparation 15 minutes
cooking 7 minutes
serves 3 to 4

YOU NEED

¼ lb (250 g) rump steak
2 slices fresh ginger (or ⅓ tsp powdered)
3 spring onions (or leek)
1 lb cauliflower (or broccoli)
¼ pint (⅛ litre) oil for frying

MARINADE

1 good pinch salt
½ tsp sugar
½ tbsp cornflour
½ tbsp soy sauce
½ tbsp dry sherry

SEASONING

½ tbsp cornflour
½ tsp lemon juice
1 tsp soy sauce
2 tbsp nuoc mam (or Chinese fish sauce)
2 tbsp dry sherry

Prepare the marinade. Cut the steak across the grain in very thin strips. Mix with the marinade and set aside for 1 hour. Bring to the boil enough water to cover the cauliflower (or broccoli). Meanwhile, divide the cauliflower into equal-sized florets and wash. Plunge into the boiling water and cook until crunchy-tender, 3 to 4 minutes. Drain and immediately drop into cold water. Cut the spring onions (or leek) into matchstick-thin strips about 1½" (4 cm) long. Shred the fresh ginger. In a deep frying pan, heat the oil until almost smoking. Fry the steak strips 1 minute (until half-cooked). Drain on absorbent kitchen paper. Leave only 1 tbsp oil in the frying pan and reheat. Stir-fry the spring onion and ginger for 30 seconds. Add the steak, seasoning and cauliflower. Stir and cook for 30 seconds more. Remove from heat and serve immediately.

CHINESE GRILLED BEEF (K'au Jou)

easy
preparation 15 minutes / marinade 3 hours
cooking 2 minutes (see Tips & Tricks)
serves 3 to 4

YOU NEED

1 lb (500 g) beef fillet or rib or sirloin steak

MARINADE

2 tbsp sugar
1 pinch each salt and pepper
½ tsp powdered ginger
1 clove garlic
4 tbsp dry sherry
1 tbsp oil
½ tsp vinegar
1 spring onion (optional)
¼ pint (⅛ litre) water
¼ pint (⅛ litre) soy sauce

You also need a hibachi, electric roaster or oven grill. To facilitate slicing, place the fillet in the freezing compartment of the refrigerator until half-frozen, 15 to 60 minutes. Meanwhile, finely chop the garlic and spring onion. In a saucepan, combine the marinade ingredients. Bring to the boil, then remove from the heat and let cool. If using a hibachi, place the slices of fillet 3" to 4" (7 to 10 cm) from white hot coals. Under the oven grill or in the electric roaster, the fillet should be 3" to 4" (7 to 10 cm) from the source of the heat. Grill the fillet for 1 minute on each side, sprinkling continually with the marinade. Serve immediately.

TIPS & TRICKS

Pork or chicken may also be prepared by this recipe. Cooking time for chicken, cut in half, will be 25 minutes, skin side down, then 20 minutes on the other side. Rather than cutting in paper-thin slices, the steak may also be cooked whole, allowing 4 to 5 minutes each side. Reserve the remainder of the marinade for re-use. In a tightly closed jar, it will keep under refrigeration for 3 to 4 weeks.

JADE BEEF (Ts'ue Yü Niu Jou)

easy
preparation 10 minutes/marinade 30 minutes
cooking 7 minutes
serves 2

YOU NEED
¼ lb (250 g) rump steak
½ lb (250 g) fresh or tinned asparagus
3 tbsp oil

MARINADE
½–1 tsp curry (optional)

1 tbsp cornflour
1 tsp dry sherry
1 tbsp soy sauce
1 tbsp oil

SEASONING
½ tsp salt
1 tsp dry sherry
1 tbsp water

In 2 small bowls, prepare the marinade and seasoning. Cut the steak across the grain into very thin strips. Mix with the marinade and set aside for 30 minutes. Clean the asparagus, removing the hard ends. Cut on the diagonal into pieces 1" (2.5 cm) long. In a frying pan, heat 2 tbsp oil to the smoking point. Stir-fry the steak for 10 seconds. Remove from the pan and drain on absorbent kitchen paper. Add 1 tbsp oil to the pan and reheat. Stir-fry the asparagus for 30 seconds. Sprinkle with the seasoning and cook and stir until the colour of the asparagus intensifies, 4 to 5 minutes (tinned: 1 minute). Return the steak to the pan and stir-fry a further 30 seconds. Remove from the heat and serve immediately.

LITTLE BEEF BALLS (Chung Shih Han Pau)

very easy
preparation 10 minutes
cooking 5 minutes
makes 40 small meat balls
These meat balls can be served as hors d'oeuvre, a first course or main dish. Their taste is so delicate that it will please even those who ordinarily dislike any dish containing fish.

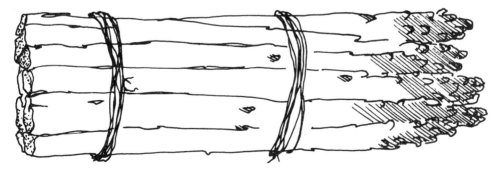

YOU NEED
$\frac{1}{2}$ lb (250 g) minced beef
$\frac{1}{2}$ lb (250 g) fish fillet
2 spring onions (or shallot or onion)
2 tbsp oil

SEASONING
1 pinch salt and pepper
$\frac{1}{2}$ tsp powdered ginger
1 egg
2 tbsp soy sauce
3 tbsp cornflour
1 tsp dry sherry

Mince the fish fillet, using an electric mixer or Mouli. Finely chop the spring onions (or shallots or onions). Mix together the minced beef, fish, spring onions and seasoning. Form bite-sized balls with this mixture. In a frying pan, heat 2 tbsp oil to the smoking point. Brown the meat balls on all sides, about 5 minutes. Serve hot or warm.

RED COOKED BEEF (Hung Shao Niu Jou)
easy
preparation 5 minutes
cooking 2 hours
serves 2 to 3

YOU NEED
1 lb (500 g) stewing beef
1 large carrot
1 spring onion (or leek)

SEASONING
1 tbsp sugar
2 slices fresh ginger (or $\frac{1}{3}$ tsp powdered)
1 tbsp dry sherry
$\frac{1}{4}$ pint ($\frac{1}{8}$ litre) soy sauce
1 pint ($\frac{1}{2}$ litre) water

Cut the beef into bite sized pieces and the carrot into pieces the same size, using the oblique cut. Cut the spring onion (or leek) into segments 3" (7 cm) long. In a large saucepan, combine the seasoning ingredients, then add the beef and spring onion. Bring to the boil and cook for 3 minutes. Skim and add the carrot. Lower heat and simmer until the meat is tender, about 2 hours, adding water from time to time if need be. Serve hot with steamed rice.

STIR-FRIED BEEF SZECHWAN (Ma La Niu Jou)
very easy
preparation 10 minutes
cooking 2 minutes
serves 2 to 3

YOU NEED
$\frac{1}{4}$ lb (250 g) rump steak
6–8 spring onions (or leek)
6–8 chilli pods

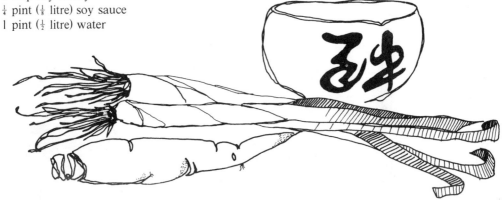

4–5 slices fresh ginger (or ¼ tsp powdered)
1 star anise (optional)
1 tbsp cornflour
3 tbsp oil

SEASONING
1 tbsp sugar
2 tbsp soy sauce
1 tbsp dry sherry

MARINADE
1 pinch each salt and pepper
1 tsp cornflour
1 tsp soy sauce
½ tsp vinegar
½ egg white

SEASONING
1 pinch each salt and pepper
1 tsp cornflour
1 tbsp water
1 tsp soy sauce
1 tsp dry sherry

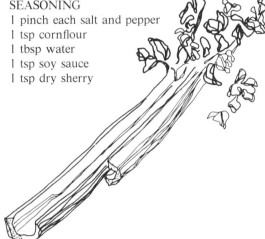

Prepare the seasoning and set aside. Cut the spring onions or leek in strips 1" (2.5 cm) long and the fresh ginger into matchstick-thin strips. Open and de-seed the chilli pods, then cut each into 4 pieces. Cut the steak against the grain into very thin strips and sprinkle with the cornflour. In a frying pan, heat 3 tbsp oil until almost smoking. Stir-fry the pieces of chilli pod until brown, about 30 seconds. Add the ginger and star anise, stir frying energetically for 5 seconds. Incorporate the steak, spring onions (or leek) and seasoning. Stir-fry for 3 minutes. Remove from heat and serve hot or cold.

TIPS & TRICKS
This recipe, originally from the province of Szechwan, is very highly seasoned and should be contrasted with a bland dish such as a steamed fish or delicately flavoured chicken.

STIR-FRIED BEEF WITH CELERY (Ch'in Ts'ai Niu Jou)
fairly easy
preparation 15 minutes / marinade 20 minutes
cooking 4 minutes
serves 2 to 3

YOU NEED
¼ lb (250 g) rump steak
½ head celery
2 slices fresh ginger (or ⅓ tsp powdered)
2 spring onions (or leek or onions)
1 pint (½ litre) oil for frying

In 2 small bowls, prepare the marinade and the seasoning. Cut the steak against the grain in very thin strips. Mix with the marinade and set aside for 20 minutes. Mince the garlic, fresh ginger and spring onions (or leek or onions). Bring to the boil enough water to cover the celery. Meanwhile, clean the celery and cut into thin strips about 1½" (4 cm) long. Plunge into the boiling water for 1 minute, then, drain. In a deep frying pan, heat the oil until almost smoking. Fry the strips of steak for 1 minute or until half-cooked. Drain on absorbent kitchen paper. Leave only 2 tbsp oil in the pan and reheat. Stir-fry the garlic, ginger and spring onion for 30 seconds. Add the celery and steak. Stir-fry for 1 minute. Pour in the seasoning and cook until thickened, about 30 seconds. Remove from the heat and serve immediately.

STIR-FRIED BEEF WITH ONIONS (Yeng Ts'ung Niu Jou)
easy
preparation 5 minutes
cooking 4 minutes
serves 2

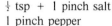

YOU NEED

½ lb (250 g) rump steak (or lean pork or chicken)
3–4 medium-sized onions (see Tips & Tricks)
½ tsp + 1 pinch salt
1 pinch pepper
1 tsp dry sherry
2 tbsp water
½ tbsp soy sauce
2 tbsp oil

STIR-FRIED BEEF WITH PICKLES (Suan Kua Niu Jou)

easy
preparation 10 minutes/marinade 15 minutes
cooking 2 minutes
serves 2

YOU NEED

½ lb (250 g) rump steak (or lean pork)
4–5 oz (120 g) dill pickles (or Chinese pickled
    mustard greens)
4–5 slices fresh ginger (or ¼ tsp powdered)
1–2 cloves garlic
2 spring onions (or onion)
1 tbsp cornflour
4 tbsp oil

MARINADE

1 tbsp soy sauce
1 tbsp dry sherry
1 tsp water

SEASONING

1 pinch salt
2 tbsp sugar
½ tbsp dry sherry

Cut the steak across the grain into very thin strips and mix with ½ tbsp soy sauce. Cut the onions in thin strips. In a frying pan, heat 1 tbsp oil until almost smoking. Stir-fry the onions, sprinkled with ½ tsp salt and 1 tsp sherry, for 30 seconds. Sprinkle with 2 tbsp cold water and cook until the onions become transparent, about 2 minutes. Remove from the pan. Add 1 tbsp oil to the pan and reheat to the smoking point. Stir-fry the strips of steak until they change colour, 1 to 2 minutes. Return the onions to the pan and season with a pinch each salt and pepper. Stir-fry for a further 30 seconds, then, remove from heat. Serve immediately.

TIPS & TRICKS

This is the basic Chinese recipe for stir-frying any tender meat with the vegetable of your choice: bean sprouts, cabbage, green peppers, courgettes, cucumbers, spinach, celery, string beans, etc.

Prepare the marinade in a medium sized bowl. Cut the meat across the grain in very thin strips. Mix with the marinade and set aside for 15 minutes. Cut in thin strips the pickles, spring onions (or onion), garlic and fresh ginger. In a frying pan, heat the oil until almost smoking. Sprinkle the strips of steak with cornflour. Stir-fry for 1 minute or until half-cooked. Drain on absorbent kitchen paper.

Reheat the remainder of the oil. Stir-fry the spring onion, garlic and ginger for 30 seconds. Add the pickles, seasoning and meat. Stir-fry energetically for 1 minute. Remove from the heat and serve immediately.

STIR-FRIED BEEF WITH THREE VEGETABLES (Kan Pien Niu Jou)

fairly easy
preparation 15 minutes/marinade 15 minutes
cooking 3 minutes
serves 2 to 3

YOU NEED

2/3 lb (300 g) rump steak
1 green pepper (or celery, spring onion or onion)
½ cucumber
1 carrot
½ chilli pod (optional)
1 tbsp dry sherry
½ pint (¼ litre) oil for frying

MARINADE

½ tsp sugar
½ tsp powdered ginger
1 tbsp water
2 tbsp soy sauce
1 tsp dry sherry

SEASONING A

1 pinch salt
1 tsp dry sherry
1 tbsp water

SEASONING B

½ tsp salt
½ tsp cornflour
2 tbsp water
1 tsp dry sherry

In 3 bowls, prepare the marinade and seasonings A and B. Cut the steak against the grain in very thin strips. Mix with the marinade and set aside for 15 minutes. Cut into matchstick-thin strips the green pepper (or celery, spring onion, onion), cucumber and carrot. Open and de-seed the chilli pod, then cut into matchstick-thin strips. In a deep frying pan, heat the oil until almost smoking. Drop in the strips of steak and fry for 30 seconds or until half-cooked. Drain on absorbent kitchen paper. Leave only 1 tbsp oil in the pan and reheat. Stir-fry the green pepper, cucumber, carrot and chilli pod for 10 seconds. Sprinkle with seasoning A and stir-fry for 1 minute, then, remove from the pan. Add 1 tbsp oil to the pan and re-heat. Stir-fry the steak for 30 seconds. Sprinkle with 1 tbsp dry sherry and stir. Add seasoning B and all the vegetables. Stir and cook until thickened, about 30 seconds. Remove from heat and serve immediately.

SPICED BEEF 'JERKY' (Niu Jou Kan)

rather difficult
preparation 5 minutes
cooking 2 hours 45 minutes
makes about 20 pieces

Beef jerky is a cured meat which is greatly enjoyed by the Chinese as a snack, usually accompanied by tea or beer. Indeed, it is not only popular among the Chinese but with the Americans as well for the first Chinese emigrants took with them their method for drying beef in the sun (today dried in the oven) which was soon adopted by the cowboys of the wild west. You will find jerky in Chinese shops

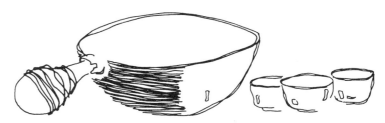

but you can also prepare it yourself by this recipe. It makes an unusual and savoury addition to any hors d'oeuvre tray.

YOU NEED

1 lb (500 g) topside or rump steak
½ tsp powdered ginger
2 spring onions (or leek)
2 star anise (optional)
3 pieces orange (or lemon or tangerine) peel
½ tbsp dry sherry

SEASONING

¼ pint (⅛ litre) soy sauce
1 tbsp sugar
2 tbsp dry sherry

Cut the spring onions (or leek) in 3" (7 cm) lengths. In a large saucepan, combine the star anise, orange peel, ginger, spring onions and sherry with enough water to cover the steak. Bring to the boil. Add the steak and simmer, uncovered, for 1 hour. Remove the steak, reserving ¼ pint (⅛ litre) of the cooking liquid, and allow to cool. Cut the steak into very thin, long strips. In a saucepan, combine the seasoning and the reserved cooking liquid. Bring to the boil and add the steak. Lower the heat and cook gently, uncovered, until all the liquid has been absorbed, about 1 hour. Pre-heat the oven to cool/warm (electricity 300°, gas regulo 3). Cover the bottom of a baking dish with foil. Place the strips of steak on the foil and dry in the oven for 15 minutes. Turn the strips over and let dry on the other side, 10 minutes. Remove from oven and let cool. Serve cold.

TIPS & TRICKS
Sometimes we add $\frac{1}{4}$ to $\frac{1}{2}$ tsp curry or tabasco to the seasoning.

CHICKEN (Chi)

We Chinese love chicken meat and cook it in a thousand different ways, many of which are known and appreciated the world over. The majority of our chicken recipes are surprisingly fast and easy to prepare due to the fact that the bird, including the bones, is first cut into bite-sized pieces. Several of the recipes of this chapter call for half a chicken, about 1 lb (500 g), since we often prepare two dishes of different flavours from one bird. You will enjoy doing so as well.

Many Chinese cooks remove the skin and fat of the chicken (unless it is to be roasted), then rub it with a little oil. This reduces the number of calories by one third and decreases the cholesterol without changing the taste and appearance.

Traditionally, the head is served on the dish with the rest of the chicken, thus symbolising the 'perfect whole'. The head is placed facing the guest of honour as a sign of respect.

BRAISED CHICKEN WITH HONEY (Mi Chien Chi)
very easy
preparation 10 minutes / marinade 30 minutes
cooking 10 to 12 minutes
serves 2

YOU NEED
½ chicken [about 1 lb (500 g)]
6 tbsp water
1 tbsp oil

MARINADE
¼ tsp salt
⅓ tsp powdered ginger
1½ tbsp honey
1 tbsp sherry
2 tbsp soy sauce

Prepare the marinade in a medium-sized bowl. With a cleaver, cut the chicken, including the bones, into small pieces. Mix with the marinade and set aside for 30 minutes. In a frying pan, heat the oil. Drain the chicken (reserving the marinade) and brown well on all sides 3 to 4 minutes. Sprinkle with the remaining marinade mixed with the water. Bring to the boil and cook over medium heat 10 to 12 minutes or until the liquid is reduced to a thick sauce and the chicken done. Serve hot or cold.

CHICKEN IN CURRY SAUCE (Shen Ch'au Chia Li Chi P'ien)
easy
preparation 15 minutes / marinade 5 minutes
cooking 3 minutes
serves 2

YOU NEED
2 chicken breasts (or turkey-breast steak)
4 oz (100 g) button mushrooms fresh or tinned
1 large onion (or bamboo shoots, cauliflower or
   radish)

3 spring onions (or leek)
2 tbsp green peas (or green pepper)
1 tbsp dry sherry
2 tbsp oil

MARINADE
1–2 tsp curry powder to taste
1 tsp cornflour
1 unbeaten egg white
1 tsp soy sauce
1 tsp dry sherry

SEASONING
½ tsp salt
½ tsp sugar
½ tsp monosodium glutamate (optional)
¼ pint (⅛ litre) chicken stock (1 stock cube)

THICKENING
1 tbsp cornflour dissolved in
1 tbsp water

Prepare the marinade in a medium-sized bowl. Cut the breasts in strips about ½" (1 cm) wide. Mix with the marinade and set aside for 5 minutes. Cut the onion (or other chosen vegetable), spring onions (or leek) and mushrooms into thin strips. If it is to be used dice the green pepper. In 2 small bowls, prepare the seasoning and the thickening. In a frying pan, heat the oil until almost smoking. Stir-fry the spring onions for 10 seconds. Add the meat and stir-fry for 1 minute. Add the onion and mushrooms, then, sprinkle with 1 tablespoon sherry. Stir-fry 1 minute. Incorporate the seasoning and green peas (or pepper), then bring to the boil. Pour in the thickening and boil for 30 seconds or until thickened. Remove from the heat and serve at once accompanied by steamed rice.

CHICKEN IN LEMON SAUCE (Ning Mong Chi)
easy
preparation 15 minutes
cooking 8 minutes
serves 2 to 3

YOU NEED
2–3 chicken breasts (or turkey-breast steaks)
2 pints (1 litre) oil for frying

FRITTER BATTER
2 tbsp cornflour
1 tsp salt
1 pinch pepper
1 egg

SAUCE
2 tsp sugar
4 tbsp dry sherry
1 tbsp soy sauce
3 tbsp lemon juice
½ pint (¼ litre) water

THICKENING
2 tbsp cornflour dissolved in
2 tbsp water

Cut the breasts in even, bite-sized pieces, about 1" × 1" (2.5 cm × 2.5 cm). Combine the batter ingredients and beat for 1 minute with a fork. Add the pieces of meat and set aside for 10 minutes. Prepare the thickening and set aside. In a deep, heavy pan, heat the oil until almost smoking. Drop in the pieces of meat and fry until brown, about 4 minutes. Drain on absorbent kitchen paper. In a saucepan, bring to the boil the sauce ingredients. Add the thickening and boil for 30 seconds or until thickened. Add the meat and cook for 2 minutes more. Remove from heat and serve accompanied by steamed rice.

CHICKEN IN RED SAUCE (Ku Yu Chi)

fairly easy
preparation 5 minutes
cooking 25 minutes/marinade 25 minutes
serves 2

YOU NEED
½ chicken, about 1 lb (500 g)

SAUCE
1 pinch salt
½ tsp powdered ginger
2 oz sugar
1 star anise (optional)
1 tbsp soy sauce
4 tbsp sherry
2 tbsp sesame oil
¼ pint (⅛ litre) water

You also need a steamer.

Bring to the boil the water in the steamer. Steam the chicken for 20 minutes (or until half-done) then remove. In a large, heavy saucepan with a tight-fitting lid, bring to the boil the sauce ingredients. Plunge the chicken into the boiling sauce and cook rapidly for 3 minutes. Cover the saucepan tightly, then, remove it from the heat. Set aside for 15 minutes without lifting the lid. Remove the chicken from the sauce. Bring the sauce back to the boil. Plunge the chicken once again into the sauce and boil for 2 minutes. Cover again, tightly, the saucepan and remove from the heat. Set aside for 10 minutes. Remove the chicken and cut into bite-sized pieces. Arrange the pieces of chicken on a serving dish and cover with the sauce. Serve hot or cold.

TIPS & TRICKS
Removing the chicken from the sauce during the re-heating, then plunging it back in when boiling, permits a maximum absorption of the seasoning with a minimum amount of cooking.

CHICKEN IN SESAME OIL (Ma Yiu Chi)

very easy
preparation 5 minutes
cooking 10 to 13 minutes
serves 2

YOU NEED
½ chicken (or about 1 lb (500 g) lean pork)

3 tbsp sesame oil
2 good-sized pieces of fresh ginger
½ tsp salt
1 tbsp dry sherry
½ pint (¼ litre) water

With a cleaver, cut the chicken (or pork) into bite-sized pieces, including the bones. Peel the ginger and shred. In a frying pan, heat the sesame oil until almost smoking. Stir-fry the ginger for 1 minute. Add the chicken (or pork) and salt. Sprinkle with 1 tbsp sherry and, stirring, brown the chicken (or pork) on all

sides, about 4 minutes. Pour in the water and bring to the boil. Cook rapidly 5 to 8 minutes or until the meat is done and the sauce reduced. Remove from the heat and serve at once.

TIPS & TRICKS
This is a dish traditionally served to renew strength and vigour. Serve with steamed rice which may be generously seasoned by the sauce.

CHICKEN KINGHWA (Chin Hua Chi)

fairly easy
preparation 15 minutes/marinade 30 minutes
cooking 23 to 24 minutes
serves 2 to 3

Kinghwa, a region near Shanghai, produces the ham which is considered the finest of all of China, whence the name of this recipe.

YOU NEED

2 chicken breasts (or turkey-breast steak or duck)
⅓ lb (150 g) ham
½ lb (250 g) fresh spinach (or mustard greens or broccoli)
2 slices fresh ginger (or ⅓ teaspoon powdered)
½ tbsp dry sherry
1 tbsp water
¼ tsp salt
1 tbsp oil

MARINADE

¼ tsp salt
1 tbsp dry sherry
¼ tsp sesame oil (optional)

SEASONING

1 tsp cornflour
½ tsp salt
½ tbsp dry sherry
1 tsp sesame oil (optional)
¼ pint (⅛ litre) chicken broth (or water)

You also need a steamer.

Place the meat on an unbreakable plate which will fit into the steamer. Rub with the marinade ingredients. Marinate for 30 minutes. Prepare the seasoning and set aside. Clean the spinach (or other greens) and cut the leaves diagonally into 2 or 3 pieces. Cut the ham into bite-sized pieces, about 1" × 2" (2.5 cm × 5 cm). Peel the fresh ginger and mince finely. Bring to the boil the water in the steamer. Steam the chicken for 20 minutes then remove from the steamer. Cut into bite-sized pieces. In a deep frying pan, heat the oil. Stir-fry the fresh ginger for 30 seconds (powdered: 10 seconds). Add the greens and sprinkle with salt, sherry and water. Stir-fry for 2 minutes. Remove from the pan. Pour the seasoning into the same pan and bring to the boil. Incorporate the ham, greens and meat. Cook, stirring for 30 seconds, then remove from the heat. Serve hot accompanied by steamed rice.

CHICKEN OF RARE FLAVOURS (Kuan Wei Chi)

fairly easy
preparation 15 minutes

cooking 43 minutes
serves 2

YOU NEED

½ chicken (or turkey leg)
2 tbsp sesame seeds
2 tbsp water
¼ tsp salt
¼ tsp dry sherry

SAUCE

2 slices fresh ginger (or ¼ tsp powdered)
2 spring onions (or shallot)
1 chilli pod
2 cloves garlic
1 tsp sugar
2 tsp vinegar
¼ tsp pepper
¼ tsp tabasco (or Chinese hot pepper oil)
¼ tbsp sesame oil
¼ tsp monosodium glutamate (optional)
1½ tbsp soy sauce

You also need a steamer.

Bring to the boil the water in the steamer. Place the chicken (or turkey) on an unbreakable plate which will fit into the steamer, then rub with the sherry and salt. Steam for 35 minutes (45 minutes for the turkey) or until done. Meanwhile, open and de-seed the chilli pod. Mince finely the garlic, spring onion (or shallot) and fresh ginger. Combine all the ingredients of the sauce and mix well. Heat a small, unoiled frying pan. Roast the sesame seeds, shaking the pan or stirring, 2 to 3 minutes. Crush the seeds by passing them through a blender, or by using a mortar and pestle or a rolling pin (put the seeds into a plastic bag). Mix the resulting powder with the water. Add to the sauce and mix well. Cut the chicken (or turkey) into small pieces. Arrange the pieces on a serving dish and cover with the sauce. Serve warm or cold.

CHICKEN OF THREE COLOURS (San Se Chi P'ien)

fairly easy
preparation 15 minutes / marinade 10 minutes
cooking 3 minutes
serves 2 to 3

YOU NEED

2 chicken breasts (or turkey-breast steak)
8 oz (250 g) pineapple in chunks, tinned, drained
1 small cucumber
1 tbsp dry sherry
¼ pint (⅛ litre) oil for frying

MARINADE

¼ tsp powdered ginger
1 tbsp cornflour
1 tbsp dry sherry

SEASONING A

½ tsp salt
½ tsp dry sherry
1 tsp water

SEASONING B

¼ pint (⅛ litre) pineapple juice
1½ tbsp sugar
1 tbsp cornflour
1 tbsp soy sauce
2 tbsp vinegar
1 tbsp water
½ tsp monosodium glutamate (optional)

In 3 bowls, prepare the marinade and the seasonings A and B. Cut the breasts in even, bite-sized pieces (about 1" × 1" (2.5 cm × 2.5 cm)). Mix with the marinade and set aside for 10 minutes. Peel the cucumber, open lengthwise and de-seed. Cut into slices, then plunge into cold water. In a frying pan, heat the oil until smoking. Stir-fry the chicken (or turkey) pieces for 1 minute. Drain on absorbent kitchen paper. Pour all but ½ tbsp oil from the pan and re-heat. Drain the cucumber and stir-fry for 30 seconds. Sprinkle with seasoning A and stir-fry 2 minutes. Remove from the pan. Add ½ tbsp oil to the pan and re-heat. Drop in the chicken (or turkey) and sprinkle with 1 tbsp sherry. Stir-fry for 10 seconds. Add the pineapple and seasoning B. Bring to the boil, then incorporate the cucumber. Let boil 30 seconds (or until thickened) and remove from the heat. Serve at once.

CHICKEN OF TWO FLAVOURS (Cha Tsu Chi)

easy
preparation 10 minutes / marinade 1 hour
cooking 10 minutes
serves 2 to 3

YOU NEED

½ chicken, about 1 lb (500 g)
2 tbsp lemon juice
1 pint (½ litre) oil for frying

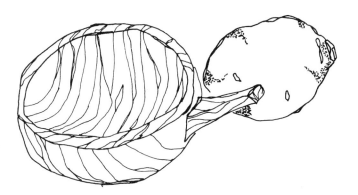

MARINADE

2 slices fresh ginger (or ⅓ tsp powdered)
2 spring onions (or leek)
3 tbsp dry sherry
2 tbsp soy sauce

CONDIMENT (roast salt)

2 tsp salt
½ tsp peppercorns (see Tips & Tricks)
1 pinch monosodium glutamate (optional)

Shred the spring onions and fresh ginger. Combine the marinade ingredients in a medium-sized bowl. With a cleaver, cut the chicken, including the bones, into bite-sized pieces. Mix with the marinade and set aside for 1 hour. Meanwhile, heat a small, unoiled frying pan. Toast the salt and peppercorns, shaking the pan or stirring, 4 to 5 minutes. Remove from the heat and, with a mortar and pestle, crush to a fine powder. Pass the powder through a sieve and incorporate the monosodium glutamate. Transfer to a small bowl or individual salt dishes and set aside. In a deep frying pan, heat the oil until almost smoking. Drain the chicken and plunge into the hot oil. Fry 4 to 5 minutes or until done. Drain on absorbent kitchen paper. Arrange the pieces of chicken on a serving dish and sprinkle with the lemon juice. Serve accompanied by the roasted salt in which each guest may dip the pieces of chicken.

TIPS & TRICKS

If you do not have a mortar and pestle, you may use powdered pepper. In this case, do not roast the pepper but incorporate it at the same time as the monosodium glutamate.

CHICKEN WITH CABBAGE (Lu Pai Ts'ai Chi)

easy
preparation 15 minutes / marinade 15 minutes
cooking 35 minutes
serves 2 to 3

YOU NEED

½ chicken, about 1 lb (500 g)
1 lb (500 g) cabbage (or Chinese cabbage or spinach)
2 slices fresh ginger (optional)
2 spring onions (or leek)
2 pints (1 litre) water
1 pint (½ litre) oil for frying
½ tsp salt

MARINADE

2 tbsp soy sauce
1 tsp sugar
1 tbsp dry sherry

THICKENING

1 tbsp cornflour dissolved in
1 tbsp water

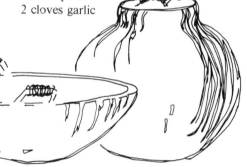

In 2 bowls, prepare the marinade and the thickening. With a cleaver, cut the chicken, including the bones, into small pieces. Mix with the marinade and set aside for 15 minutes. Discard the outer leaves and thick stalks of the cabbage (or wash spinach). Cut into several large pieces. In a deep frying pan, heat the oil until almost smoking. Fry the uncut spring onions (or leek) and the whole ginger slices for 30 seconds, then, drain on absorbent kitchen paper. Drain the chicken (reserving the marinade) and plunge into the hot oil. Fry until golden brown, 3 to 4 minutes. Drain on absorbent paper. Place the cabbage, chicken, ginger slices and spring onion in a heavy saucepan and cover with the water. Add ½ tsp

salt to the marinade, mix well and incorporate in the chicken and cabbage. Bring to the boil. Lower the heat and simmer, uncovered, for 30 minutes. Discard the spring onions and ginger slices. Place the chicken and cabbage in a deep serving dish, leaving the soup in the saucepan. Bring the soup back to the boil, then pour in the thickening. Boil rapidly for 1 minute or until slightly thickened. Pour over the chicken and serve hot accompanied by steamed rice.

CHICKEN WITH GREEN PEPPER (La Tsu Chi)

fairly easy
preparation 15 minutes / marinade 10 minutes
cooking 6 to 7 minutes
serves 2 to 3

YOU NEED

½ chicken, about 1 lb (500 g)
2 spring onions
3 chilli pods
2 cloves garlic
2 tbsp cornflour
1 tbsp dry sherry
1 pint (½ litre) oil for frying

MARINADE

1 unbeaten egg white
1 tbsp soy sauce
1 tbsp dry sherry

SEASONING

1 tsp cornflour
2 tbsp soy sauce
1 tbsp vinegar
2 tsp sugar
½ tsp salt

Prepare the marinade in a medium-sized bowl. With a cleaver, cut the chicken, including the bones, into small pieces. Mix with the marinade and set aside for 10 minutes. Open and de-seed the green peppers, then cut each into 6 long strips. De-seed the chilli pods and mince finely. Finely mince the garlic. Prepare the seasoning and set aside. In a deep frying pan, heat the oil until almost smoking. Roll the pieces of chicken in the cornflour, then plunge them into the hot oil. Fry until golden brown, 3 to 4 minutes. Drain on absorbent kitchen paper. Plunge the green pepper into the hot oil. Fry until golden brown, about 10 seconds, then drain on absorbent paper. In another pan, heat 1 tbsp of the oil until almost smoking. Stir-fry the chilli pods and garlic 30 seconds. Add the chicken and stir-fry for 1 minute. Sprinkle with the sherry and stir. Pour in the seasoning and bring to the boil. Add the green pepper and cook rapidly 30 seconds, while stirring. Remove from the heat and serve at once.

CHICKEN WITH LITTLE FLOWERS (Ts'ai Hua Chi Chiu)

easy

preparation 15 minutes/marinade 10 minutes
cooking 7 to 8 minutes
serves 2 to 3

YOU NEED

2 chicken breasts (or turkey-breast steak)
1 small cauliflower
2 spring onions (or leek)
2 slices fresh ginger (or $\frac{1}{3}$ tsp powdered)
5 dried Chinese mushrooms
1 tbsp dry sherry
$\frac{1}{4}$ pint ($\frac{1}{8}$ litre) oil for frying

MARINADE

$\frac{1}{4}$ tsp salt
1 tbsp cornflour
1 unbeaten egg white
1 tbsp dry sherry

SEASONING

$\frac{1}{2}$ tsp salt
1 pinch pepper
1 tbsp cornflour
1 tsp monosodium glutamate (optional)

1 tbsp soy sauce
$\frac{1}{2}$ pint ($\frac{1}{4}$ litre) water (or mushroom soaking water)

Rinse the dried mushrooms and soak in warm water 10 minutes or until soft. Drain (reserving the water), remove the tough stalks and cut each into 4 pieces. Prepare the marinade in a medium-sized bowl. Cut the breasts into strips and mix with the marinade. Marinate for 10 minutes. Separate the cauliflower into small, even florets, then wash and drain. Cut the spring onions (or leek) into 1" (2.5 cm) lengths. Peel the fresh ginger and shred. Prepare the seasoning and set aside. Bring to the boil a large saucepan of water. Drop the cauliflower florets into the boiling water and cook rapidly 3 to 4 minutes or until crunchy-tender, then drain. In a deep frying pan, heat the oil until almost smoking. Stir-fry the meat 1 minute (half-cooked). Remove from the pan and drain on absorbent kitchen paper. Leave only 1 tbsp oil in the pan and re-heat. Stir-fry the spring onions (or leek) and ginger for 30 seconds. Add the meat and mushrooms, then sprinkle with the sherry. Stir-fry for 30 seconds. Incorporate the cauliflower and seasoning, bringing to the boil. Cook rapidly for 1 minute, stirring all the while. Remove from the heat and serve at once.

CHICKEN WITH LOTUS SEEDS (Lien Tze Yia Keng)

easy

preparation 10 minutes
cooking 6 minutes
serves 2 to 3

For elegant banquets and important occasions, we prepare this recipe with duck.

YOU NEED

2 chicken breasts (or turkey-breast steak or duck)
3 oz (75 g) tinned lotus seeds (or blanched almonds)
2 slices fresh ginger (optional)
1 carrot
2 dried Chinese mushrooms
1 tbsp dry sherry

1 tsp sugar
1 tbsp oil

MARINADE
¼ tsp salt
¼ tsp pepper
1 tsp cornflour
1 tbsp dry sherry

SEASONING
1 tsp salt
1 generous pinch pepper
1 tsp soy sauce
1 tsp sesame oil
½ pint (¼ litre) water (or mushroom soaking water)

THICKENING
2 tbsp cornflour dissolved in
2 tbsp water

Rinse the dried mushrooms and soak in warm water for 10 minutes or until soft. Drain (reserving the water), remove the tough stalks and cut each into 4 pieces. In 3 bowls, prepare the seasoning, thickening and marinade. Dice the breasts, about ¼" × ¼" (6 mm × 6 mm), and mix with the marinade. Dice the carrot into similar sized pieces. Shred the ginger. In a frying pan, heat the oil until almost smoking. Stir-fry for 30 seconds the ginger, mushrooms and sugar. Add the meat and stir-fry for 1 minute. Incorporate the carrot, lotus seeds and seasoning. Bring to the boil and cook rapidly for 3 minutes. Pour in the thickening and cook 1 minute (or until thickened). Remove from heat and serve.

CHICKEN WITH PEANUTS (Kong Bau Chi Ting)
easy
preparation 12 minutes/marinade 1 hour
cooking 4 to 5 minutes
serves 2 to 3

YOU NEED
2 chicken breasts, or about ½ lb (250 g) lean pork
2 oz (50 g) peanuts
8 chilli pods
1 spring onion (or leek)
2 slices fresh ginger (or ½ tsp powdered)
1 tbsp dry sherry
¼ pint (⅛ litre) oil for frying

MARINADE
1½ tbsp cornflour
1 tbsp soy sauce
½ tsp dry sherry

SEASONING
¼ tsp salt
1 tsp cornflour
1 tsp sugar
1 tbsp soy sauce
½ tbsp vinegar
½ tsp dry sherry
1 tsp sesame oil (optional)

Prepare the marinade in a medium-sized bowl. Cut the chicken breasts (or pork) into even, bite-sized pieces, about 1" × 1" (2.5 cm × 2.5 cm). Mix with the marinade and set aside for 1 hour. Meanwhile, prepare the seasoning and set aside. Finely mince the spring onion (or leek) and fresh ginger. Open the chilli pods, de-seed and cut each into 4 pieces. In a deep frying pan, heat the oil until almost smoking. Brown the chilli pods for 20 seconds, then drain on absorbent kitchen paper. Fry the pieces of chicken (or pork) for 1 minute (or until half-cooked). Drain on absorbent kitchen paper. Leave only 1 tbsp oil in the pan and re-heat. Stir-fry the spring onion,

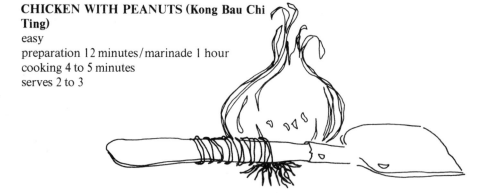

ginger, chilli pods and meat for 1 minute. Sprinkle with 1 tbsp sherry and continue to stir-fry 1 minute. Add the seasoning and the peanuts. Stir and cook for 30 seconds until thickened. Remove from heat and serve at once.

TIPS & TRICKS
If you have a green pepper on hand, cut it into even, bite-sized pieces and add to the ingredients being stir-fried at the same time as the sherry.

CHINESE ROAST CHICKEN (Kau Chi)
easy
preparation 15 minutes
cooking 1 hour
serves 3 to 4

YOU NEED
1 chicken (or pheasant)
3 spring onions (or shallot)
2 cloves garlic
3 slices fresh ginger (or ½ tsp powdered)
1 tbsp salt

MARINADE
4 tbsp soy sauce
4 tbsp honey
1 tbsp dry sherry
½ tsp powdered ginger

Pre-heat your oven to medium/hot (electricity 375°, gas regulo 5–6). In a small saucepan, combine the marinade ingredients. Bring to the boil over moderate heat and boil for 1 minute, stirring constantly. Remove from the heat and allow to cool. Cover the bottom of a baking dish with aluminium foil. Place the bird on the foil and sprinkle the salt inside it. Stuff with the spring onion (or shallot), ginger and crushed garlic, then close the opening with a small skewer or sew with heavy thread. Brush with the marinade. Roast for 1 hour or until done, basting from time to time with the marinade. Remove and cut into small pieces. Arrange on a serving dish and sprinkle with the cooking juices. Serve hot or cold.

COLD SZECHWAN CHICKEN (Liang Pan Pa La Chi)
very easy
preparation 5 minutes

cooking 15 minutes
serves 2 to 3

YOU NEED
½ chicken, about 1 lb (500 g)
1 tsp salt

SAUCE
1 pinch salt
1 spring onion (or chives)
1 tsp tabasco to taste (or Chinese hot pepper oil)
½ tbsp sesame oil
2 tbsp soy sauce
2–3 slices fresh ginger (or ½ tsp powdered)

Bring to the boil enough water to cover the chicken. Plunge in the chicken, season with salt and bring back to the boil. Skim and simmer gently for 15 minutes or until done. Drain the chicken (reserving the water to use as a soup base) and allow to cool. Finely mince the spring onion (or chives) and fresh ginger. Combine with all other ingredients of the sauce and mix well. Cut the chicken into bite-sized pieces and arrange on a serving dish. Cover with the sauce and serve cold.

EMPRESS CHICKEN I (Kue Fei Chi)
fairly easy
preparation 15 minutes
cooking 35 minutes
serves 2 to 3

Empress Chicken owes its name to the young and epicurean Empress of the Tang dynasty who preferred this dish to all others.

YOU NEED
½ chicken, about 1 lb (500 g)
2 dried Chinese mushrooms
1 small carrot
4 oz (100 g) bamboo shoots
1 spring onion (or leek)
2 slices fresh ginger
1 tbsp soy sauce
2 pints (1 litre) oil for frying

SEASONING
1 pinch each salt and pepper
1 tsp sugar
2 tbsp soy sauce
1 tbsp dry sherry

½ tbsp sesame oil (optional)
¼ pint (⅛ litre) water (or mushroom soaking water)

THICKENING
1 tbsp cornflour dissolved in
¼ pint (⅛ litre) water

Wash the dried mushrooms and soak in warm water for 10 minutes or until soft. Drain (reserving the water), remove the hard stalks and cut each into 4 pieces. Rub the chicken with 1 tbsp soy sauce and set aside. Cut the carrot and bamboo shoots diagonally into thin slices and the spring onion (or leek) into 2" (5 cm) lengths. Peel and finely mince the fresh ginger. In 2 small bowls, prepare the seasoning and the thickening. In a deep frying pan, heat the oil until almost smoking. Reduce the heat and brown the chicken (uncut), 4 to 5 minutes. Drain on absorbent kitchen paper. In another pan, heat 1 tbsp oil until almost smoking. Stir-fry the spring onion (or leek), mushrooms and ginger for 20 seconds. Pour in the seasoning and bring to the boil. Add the chicken, lower the heat, cover and simmer for 25 minutes. Incorporate the carrot and bamboo shoot. Simmer for 5 minutes more. Remove the chicken from the pan and place it on a serving dish. Bring the sauce back to the boil and pour in the thickening. Boil rapidly for 1 minute (or until thickened). Pour the sauce over the chicken and serve hot.

EMPRESS CHICKEN II (Kuei Fei Chi)
easy
preparation 15 minutes
cooking 36 to 40 minutes
serves 2 to 3

This modern version omits the deep frying.

YOU NEED
½ chicken (or chicken thighs and wings)
4 oz (100 g) bamboo shoots
2 dried Chinese mushrooms (or button mushrooms)
1 small carrot
1 spring onion (or leek)
2 slices fresh ginger (or ⅓ tsp powdered)

1 tbsp soy sauce
2 tbsp oil
¼ pint (⅛ litre) water (or mushroom soaking water)

SEASONING A
1 tbsp dry sherry
1 tbsp soy sauce

SEASONING B
½ tsp salt
½ tsp sugar
1 pinch pepper
1 tsp sesame oil (optional)

THICKENING
1 tbsp cornflour dissolved in
¼ pint (⅛ litre) water

Wash the dried mushrooms and soak in warm water 10 minutes, or until soft. Drain (reserving the water), remove the hard stalks and cut each into 4 pieces. With a cleaver, cut the chicken

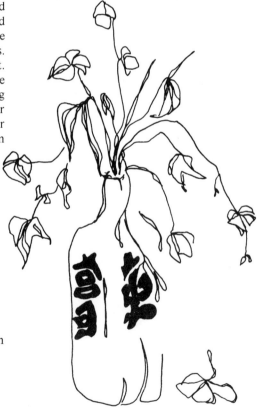

into 5 or 6 pieces. Rub with 1 tbsp soy sauce and set aside. In 2 bowls, prepare the seasoning A and the thickening. Cut the carrot and bamboo shoots diagonally into thin slices and the spring onion (or leek) into 2" (5 cm) lengths. Peel and finely mince the fresh ginger. In a deep frying pan, heat the oil until almost smoking. Stir-fry the ginger, spring onion (or leek) and chicken for 2 minutes. Sprinkle with seasoning A and stir and cook for 1 minute. Pour in the water (or the mushroom soaking water). Lower the heat, cover and simmer for 20 minutes. Incorporate the mushrooms, bamboo shoots, carrot and seasoning B. Simmer another 15 minutes or until the chicken is done. Pour in the thickening and boil for 1 minute or until thickened. Remove from the heat and serve.

IVORY CHICKEN I (Pai Ch'ieh Chi)

very easy
preparation 10 minutes
cooking 35 minutes
serves 3 to 4

YOU NEED
1 chicken
1 spring onion (or leek)
4 slices fresh ginger (or 1 tsp powdered)
2 tbsp sesame oil (or other)
2 tbsp dry sherry
2 tbsp salt

GINGER SAUCE
$\frac{1}{4}$ tsp pepper
$\frac{1}{2}$ tsp salt
1 slice fresh chopped ginger (or $\frac{1}{4}$ tsp powdered)
2 tbsp sesame oil (or other)
1 tsp soy sauce

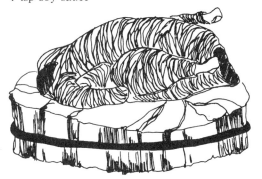

SESAME SAUCE
1 pinch salt
1 dash tabasco (or Chinese hot pepper oil)
1 tbsp sesame oil
1 tsp soy sauce

Bring to the boil enough water to cover the chicken. Rub the chicken with the sherry and salt, then plunge it into the boiling water. Add the spring onion (or leek), cut in half, and the ginger. Cover and simmer for 35 minutes or until done. Drain the chicken, reserving the water for a soup base. Rub the chicken with 2 tbsp sesame oil. Cut into small pieces and arrange prettily on a serving dish. Prepare one, or both, of the sauces. Serve the chicken hot or cold, accompanied by the sauce for dipping.

IVORY CHICKEN II (Pai Chieh Chi)

easy
preparation 10 minutes
cooking 40 minutes
serves 3 to 4

YOU NEED
1 chicken (or turkey leg)
1 spring onion (or onion)
5 slices fresh ginger (or 1 tsp powdered)
1 tbsp salt
5 tbsp dry sherry

GINGER SAUCE
$\frac{1}{4}$ tsp pepper
$\frac{1}{2}$ tsp salt
1 slice fresh chopped ginger (or $\frac{1}{4}$ tsp powdered)
2 tbsp sesame oil (or other)
1 tsp soy sauce

SESAME SAUCE
1 pinch salt
1 dash tabasco (or Chinese hot pepper oil)
1 tbsp sesame oil
1 tsp soy sauce

You also need a steamer.

Bring to the boil the water in the steamer. Rub the chicken with the sherry and the salt. Put the whole spring onion and the ginger inside the cavity. Steam for 40 to 45 minutes or until done. Remove the chicken from the steamer and allow to cool. Cut the chicken into small pieces and arrange prettily on a serving dish. Prepare one, or both, of the sauces. Serve cold, accompanied by the sauce for dipping.

MANDARIN CHICKEN (Kan Peng Chi)

easy
preparation 15 minutes/marinade 30 minutes
cooking 6 minutes
serves 2 to 3

YOU NEED
½ chicken, about 1 lb (500 g)
3 slices fresh ginger (or ½ tsp powdered)
2 cloves garlic
2 spring onions (or leek)
1 tbsp vinegar
2 tbsp cornflour
2 tbsp flour
1 pint (½ litre) oil for frying

MARINADE
2 tbsp soy sauce
2 tbsp dry sherry

SEASONING
1 tbsp sugar
3 tbsp water
1 tsp soy sauce
1 tbsp dry sherry

Prepare the marinade in a medium-sized bowl. With a cleaver, cut the chicken, including the bones, into small pieces. Mix with the marinade and set aside for 30 minutes. Meanwhile, prepare the seasoning in a small bowl and set aside. Finely mince the spring onions (or leek), garlic and fresh ginger. Combine the flour and cornflour in a shallow dish. In a deep frying pan, heat the oil until almost smoking. Roll the chicken pieces in the flour/cornflour mixture, then plunge into the hot oil. Brown well, 3 to 4 minutes. Drain on absorbent kitchen paper. In another pan, heat 1 tbsp of the oil until almost smoking. Stir-fry for 30 seconds: the spring onions (or leek), garlic and ginger. Add the chicken and seasoning and stir-fry for 1 minute. Sprinkle with the vinegar, stir and remove from the heat. Serve hot.

STEAMED CHICKEN WITH GINGER (Ts'ung Yu Chi)

easy
preparation 15 minutes
cooking 36 minutes
serves 2 to 3

YOU NEED
½ chicken (or turkey leg)
5 spring onions (or chives)
4 slices fresh ginger (or 1 tsp powdered)
1 cucumber

MARINADE
1 tsp salt
2 tbsp dry sherry
1 tsp sesame oil

SEASONING
1 tsp salt
1 tbsp dry sherry
1 tsp sesame oil

THICKENING
2 tsp cornflour dissolved in
2 tbsp water

You also need a steamer.

Bring to the boil the water in the steamer. Wash and dry the chicken (or turkey), then remove skin and fat. Place it on a shallow, unbreakable dish which will fit into the steamer. Steam for 35 minutes (50–60 minutes for the turkey) or until done. Meanwhile, shred the fresh ginger and spring onions (or chives), then plunge them into cold water and set aside. Peel the cucumber, cut open lengthwise and de-seed. Cut into bite-sized pieces, about 1" × 1" (2.5 cm × 2.5 cm) and arrange on a serving dish. Remove the chicken from the steamer, carefully reserving the cooking juices. Cut into bite-sized pieces, and place on top of the cucumber. Drain the ginger and spring onions (or chives), then sprinkle over the chicken and cucumber. Pour the cooking juices which have been reserved, into a small saucepan. (If there is less than ¼ pint (⅛ litre), add water to make up the difference.) Add the seasoning ingredients and bring to the boil. Incorporate the thickening and cook for 30 seconds or until thickened. Pour this sauce over the chicken. Serve warm or cold.

SMOKED CHICKEN (Hsün Chi)

rather difficult
preparation 5 minutes/marinade 1 hour
cooking 1 hour 20 minutes
serves 3 to 4

YOU NEED
1 chicken (see Tips & Tricks)
2 tbsp salt
4 tbsp dry sherry
½ tsp powdered ginger
½ pint (¼ litre) soy sauce
3 pints (1½ litres) water

SEASONING
2 tbsp black tea
4 tbsp dry sherry
3 oz (75 g) brown sugar

You also need a steamer.

Rub the chicken with the salt and set aside for 1 hour. In a large saucepan, bring to the boil the water, soy sauce and ginger. Boil rapidly for 10 minutes. Plunge in the chicken, reduce the heat and simmer for 30 minutes, turning the chicken from time to time. Drain the chicken. Cover the bottom of the steamer, as well as the inside of the lid, with aluminium foil. Place all the seasoning ingredients on the foil in the bottom of the steamer. Put the chicken into the steamer basket. (Do not use a plate.) Cook (smoke) over medium/low heat for 20 minutes. Open the steamer, add the sherry to the seasoning and turn the chicken over. Close tightly and cook for 20 minutes more. Remove the chicken and cut it into bite-sized pieces. Serve hot or cold.

TIPS & TRICKS

Duck, turkey, pork or beef can all be smoked in the same way. For these, season the boiling water with an additional teaspoon of powdered ginger.

STIR-FRIED SZECHWAN CHICKEN (Ma La Chi)

very easy
preparation 10 minutes/marinade 30 minutes
cooking 13 to 14 minutes
serves 2

This dish is very highly seasoned, as are all those which bear the name of the province of Szechwan.

YOU NEED
2 chicken breasts (or turkey-breast steak)
1 tsp tabasco (or Chinese hot pepper oil)
4 tbsp water
3 tbsp sesame oil (or other, 1½ tbsp)

MARINADE
⅓ tsp powdered ginger
1 tsp sugar
1 pinch salt
1 tbsp dry sherry
2 tbsp soy sauce
1 spring onion (or shallot)

Finely mince the spring onion (or shallot). Combine all marinade ingredients in a medium-sized bowl. Cut the breasts into even, bite-sized pieces. Mix with the marinade and set aside for 30 minutes. In a frying pan, heat the sesame oil over a medium flame. Drain the chicken (or turkey) pieces, reserving the marinade, and stir-fry for 3 minutes. Mix the water with the remaining marinade and add to the chicken. Simmer for 8 minutes over medium/low heat. Add the tabasco and cook and stir for 2 minutes or until done. Serve hot accompanied by steamed rice.

SWEET AND SOUR CHICKEN (T'ien Suan Chi)

easy
preparation 15 minutes/marinade 2 hours
cooking 25 minutes
serves 2 to 3

YOU NEED
¼ chicken (or about 1 lb (500 g) lean pork)

MARINADE
1 generous pinch salt
4 tbsp honey
2 tbsp dry sherry
3 tbsp ketchup
1 tbsp oil
½ tbsp vinegar (or lemon juice)
2 tbsp soy sauce
¼ tsp powdered ginger

In a small saucepan, bring to the boil the marinade ingredients. Lower the heat and simmer for 10 minutes, stirring frequently. Remove from the heat and set aside to cool. Meanwhile, with a cleaver, cut the chicken (or pork), including the bones, into even, bite-sized pieces. Mix with the marinade and set aside for 2 hours, turning the pieces from time to time. Turn on the oven grill and pre-heat the oven to very hot (electricity 500°, gas regulo 8–9). Cover the bottom of a baking dish with aluminium foil. Put the pieces of meat on the foil and baste with the marinade. Place the dish on the grill rack the furthest away from the source of heat. Grill for 15 minutes, basting often. (Watch carefully that it does not burn.) Turn over the pieces of meat and grill on the other side, 10 minutes or until done, basting frequently. Serve hot.

TIPS & TRICKS

In the summer, Sweet and Sour Chicken may be cooked on an outside grill or hibachi.

EGGS (Tan)

In China, the colour red is the symbol of luck and the egg a symbol of fertility. For this reason, at the birth of a baby boy, the father offers his friends, instead of a cigar or a drink, red hard boiled eggs.

The Chinese prepare eggs in countless ways, each more exotic than the other. The most renowned of all are the 'Thousand Year Eggs'. In reality, these eggs are aged only 60 days or so by being buried in lime, whence their antiquated appearance and taste reminiscent of cheese. Thousand Year Eggs may be bought from oriental grocers and need only be peeled and washed before eating. Serve with Marble Tea Eggs as an unusual tea or cocktail titbit.

All these egg dishes make very good hors d'oeuvres.

CHICKEN EGG FU YUNG (Kuo Tieh Chi Pein)
easy
preparation 15 minutes / marinade 10 minutes
cooking 6 to 7 minutes
serves 2 to 3

YOU NEED
2 chicken breasts (or turkey-breast steak)
3 eggs
2 spring onions (or leek)
1½ tbsp flour
3 tbsp oil

MARINADE
1 pinch pepper
1 tsp salt
1 tsp dry sherry

Cut each chicken (or turkey) breast into 5 or 6 pieces. Mix with the marinade ingredients and set aside for 10 minutes. Finely chop the spring onion (or leek). Beat the eggs. In a frying pan, heat 2 tbsp oil. Meanwhile, drain the chicken pieces (or turkey), pouring the remaining marinade into the beaten egg. Roll the pieces in the flour, then dip into the egg. Brown the pieces on all sides, 3 to 4 minutes. Add the spring onion (or leek) and stir and fry for 1 minute more. Remove the meat and spring onion or leek from the pan and let cool, about 10 minutes. Add the cooled chicken (or turkey) and spring onion (or leek) to the beaten egg. In the frying pan, heat 1 tbsp oil. Pour 1 very full tbsp of the egg/chicken mixture into the pan to form a small omelette. Brown on both sides, about 2 minutes, then remove from the pan. Repeat until all the egg/chicken mixture is used, making several small omelettes at a time. Serve hot or warm.

OYSTER EGG FU YUNG (Chien Hau)
easy
preparation 15 minutes
cooking 2 minutes per omelette
serves 2 to 3

YOU NEED

4 oz (100 g) frozen oysters or about 12 large fresh

4 oz (100 g) bean sprouts

2 eggs

2 spring onions (or chives)

½ tsp soy sauce

2 tbsp oyster juice (or water)

1 tbsp flour

1 tbsp cornflour

1 pinch salt and pepper

¼ tsp baking powder

1 tbsp oil

Wash and drain the bean sprouts. Coarsely chop the spring onions (or chives). Beat the eggs for 1 minute. Add the spring onion (or chives), oysters, oyster juice (or water) and soy sauce, mixing well. Sift together flour, cornflour, baking powder, salt and pepper, then, combine with the egg/oyster mixture. Add the bean sprouts and stir until well mixed. In a frying pan, heat ½ tbsp oil. Pour in 1 generous tbsp of the egg/oyster mixture, forming a small omelette. Brown on both sides, about 2 minutes, and remove from the pan. Repeat the process, making several small omelettes at a time, until all the egg/oyster mixture is used. If needed, add ½ tbsp oil to pan. Serve hot or warm.

SCALLOP EGG FU YUNG (Fu Yung Kan Pei)

easy

preparation 20 minutes

cooking 5 minutes

serves 2 to 3

YOU NEED

4 oz (100 g) scallops (or crab or shrimp)

2 eggs

2 spring onions (or leek)

1 medium-sized onion

1 carrot

1 tbsp water

½ tsp sugar

½ tbsp dry sherry

2 tbsp oil

SEASONING

¼ tsp dry sherry

¼ tsp salt

¼ tsp soy sauce

1 pinch pepper

¼ tsp sesame oil (optional)

Cut or tear the scallops (or crab or shrimp) into shreds. Cut the spring onions (or leek) and carrot in fine shreds about 2" (5 cm) long. Shred the

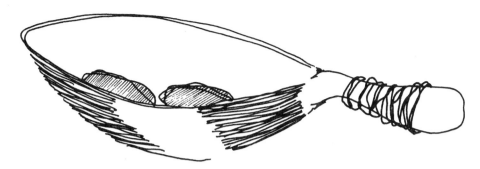

onion. Beat the eggs with the dry sherry and water. Prepare the seasoning and set aside. In a frying pan, heat 1 tbsp oil. Stir-fry the spring onion (or leek) sprinkled with sugar, 30 seconds. Add the carrot, onion, scallops (or other shellfish) and seasoning. Stir-fry for 2 minutes. Remove from the pan and let cool, about 10 minutes, then mix with the beaten egg. In the frying pan, heat 1 tbsp oil. Pour 1 generous tbsp of the egg/scallop mixture into the pan, forming a small omelette. Brown on both sides, about 2 minutes, then remove from pan. Repeat the process, making several small omelettes at a time, until all the egg/scallop mixture is used. Serve hot or warm.

MARBLE TEA EGGS (Ch'a Yeh Tan)

very easy
preparation 5 minutes
cooking 1 hour 10 minutes
serves 2 to 4

In China, marble eggs are sold by street vendors to be eaten as snacks. Served for tea, cocktails or on picnics, they are simply delightful, both in taste and appearance.

YOU NEED
4–8 eggs
1¼ pints (¾ litre) water
1½ tbsp salt
2 tbsp black tea
3 tbsp soy sauce
2 tsp five spice powder (or allspice)

Hard boil the number of eggs desired for 10 minutes, then plunge into cold water. With the back of a spoon, gently crack each egg over the entire surface of its shell but do not peel. Place the cracked eggs in a saucepan. Add all other ingredients and bring to the boil. Reduce the heat, cover and simmer for 1 hour. Turn off the heat and let marinate several hours or all night. Shell and serve cold. The eggs may be shelled and served immediately after cooling; however, the delicate 'smoky' tea flavour will be less distinct.

PEKING MARBLE TEA EGGS (Ch'a Yeh Tan)

very easy
preparation 5 minutes
cooking 1 hour 10 minutes
serves 2 to 4

YOU NEED
4–8 eggs
1¼ pints (¾ litre) water
5 tbsp brown sugar (or rock candy)
2 tbsp black tea

Hard boil the number of eggs desired for 10 minutes, then plunge into cold water. With the

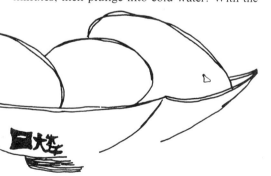

back of a spoon, gently crack each egg over the entire surface of its shell, but do not peel. Put the cracked eggs into a saucepan. Add all other ingredients and bring to the boil. Lower heat, cover and simmer for 1 hour. Turn off the heat and let marinate several hours or all night. Shell the eggs and serve cold. The eggs may be shelled and served upon cooling, but their delicate flavour will be less distinct.

PORK STUFFED EGGS (Ts'ue P'i Ch'üan Tan)

rather difficult
preparation 20 minutes
cooking 16 minutes
makes 8 stuffed eggs

YOU NEED

6 eggs
4 oz (100 g) minced pork (or beef)
4—6 tbsp breadcrumbs (or crushed unsweetened cereal)
1 small onion
1 tbsp flour
$\frac{1}{2}$ tsp salt
1 good pinch pepper
4 tbsp water
2 pints (1 litre) oil for deep frying

Hard boil 4 eggs for 10 minutes, then plunge into cold water. Shell and cut each egg in half lengthwise. Gently remove the yolks taking care not to break the whites. Sprinkle the white halves with the flour. Beat 1 raw egg with 4 tbsp water. Mince the onion. Mix together: hard boiled yolks, 1 raw egg, minced pork (or beef), onion, salt and pepper. Fill each white half with a portion (about 2 tbsp) of the pork mixture, heaping it to re-form a rounded, whole egg. Dip

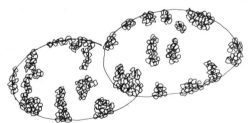

the stuffed eggs into the beaten egg, then roll in the breadcrumbs. In a deep pan, heat the oil at a medium/low temperature. (When a piece of bread, thrown in, returns to the surface and browns in 1 minute, the oil will be at the right temperature.) Slip the eggs, stuffing side down, into the oil and fry for 3 minutes. Increase the heat to medium/high and let the eggs fry for another 3 minutes. Drain on absorbent kitchen paper. Serve hot or cold.

SPRING OMELETTE ROLL WITH PORK (Tan Chuan)

rather difficult
preparation 20 minutes
cooking 25 minutes
serves 3 to 4

This dish is very popular and frequently served in China. It makes a sensational first course for any meal.

YOU NEED

4 oz (100 g) minced pork
4 oz (100 g) shelled shrimp (or fish fillet)
5 eggs
4 tsp oil
$\frac{1}{2}$ tsp dry sherry
$\frac{1}{4}$ tsp soy sauce

SEASONING

2 tsp soy sauce
$\frac{1}{2}$ tsp salt
1 tbsp cornflour
1 tbsp dry sherry

You also need a steamer.

Finely chop the shrimp (or fish fillet). Mix together: 1 egg, shrimp (or fish fillet), minced pork and seasoning. Beat 4 eggs with a scant $\frac{1}{4}$

tsp soy sauce and the sherry. In an omelette or frying pan, heat 1 tsp oil over a medium/hot flame. Pour in 3 tbsp beaten egg, spreading thinly to make a very fine omelette. Cook until set, about 30 seconds, then remove to a plate. Repeat the process, preparing 4 omelettes and using all but 1 small tsp of beaten raw egg which you will set aside. Spread an equal quantity of the pork/shrimp (or fish) mixture on each omelette. Roll very tightly and seal the edges with the remainder of the beaten egg.

Place the omelette rolls on a plate which will fit into the steamer. Bring the water in the steamer to a fast boil. Steam the omelettes for 20 minutes. Remove and let cool slightly, then, cut each omelette diagonally into slices about $\frac{1}{2}$" (1.25 cm) thick. Serve warm or cold.

TIPS & TRICKS
Instead of combining two flavours, 8 oz (250 g) of minced pork may be used, omitting the shrimp, or 8 oz (250 g) of fish, omitting the pork.

FISH AND SHELLFISH
(Yü Chi Hai Shien)

Much symbolism surrounds the fish in Chinese cookery, partly due to the fact that the word for fish, 'Yü', is pronounced in the same manner as the word for 'abundance'. For this reason, a fish course is always included on the menu of New Year's celebrations, symbolizing the hope that the coming year will bring great abundance. Likewise, a fish is invariably pictured on Chinese New Year's greeting cards. Furthermore, the fish, if at all possible, is served whole to symbolize 'wholeness – without blemish', and even garnished to appear as though it were still swimming in its natural environment.

Added to the symbolism are certain superstitions concerning the eating of fish. For example, if one is in the company of a Chinese fisherman or sailor, it is considered extremely bad taste to turn the fish over, for the fish represents a boat, and a boat overturned, sinks....

Nearly all the recipes of this chapter may be prepared with any fresh fish available on the market.

CRISPY FISH WITH GARLIC SAUCE I (Ta Suan Yü)
very easy
preparation 5 minutes/marinade 5 minutes
cooking 4 to 6 minutes
serves 3 to 4

YOU NEED
1 whole fish, 1½–2 lb (800 g) (see Tips & Tricks)
1 pinch powdered ginger
½ tsp dry sherry
1 pint (½ litre) oil for frying

SAUCE
1–2 cloves garlic
2 tbsp sugar (optional)
2 tbsp soy sauce

Wash the fish and pat dry, then, sprinkle with the sherry. Rub with a generous pinch of powdered ginger and set aside for 5 minutes. Finely mince the garlic. Combine all sauce ingredients, mix well, and set aside. In a deep frying pan, heat the oil until almost smoking. Plunge the whole fish into the hot oil and fry 4 to 6 minutes or until done. Drain on absorbent kitchen paper, then place on a serving platter. Pour the sauce over the fish and serve at once.

TIPS & TRICKS
Any whole fish, large or small, may be chosen for this recipe: whiting, sea bream, smelt, etc.

CRISPY FISH WITH GARLIC SAUCE II (Ta Suan Yü)
very easy
preparation 5 minutes / marinade 5 minutes
cooking 4 to 6 minutes
serves 3 to 4

This variation, adapted to modern ovens, eliminates the deep frying.

YOU NEED
1 whole fish, 1½–2 lb (600 g)
1 good pinch powdered ginger
½ tsp dry sherry
1 tbsp oil

SAUCE
1–2 cloves garlic
2 tbsp soy sauce
2 tbsp sugar (optional)

Preheat your oven at electricity 350°, gas regulo 4. Wash the fish and pat dry, then sprinkle with the sherry. Rub with a generous pinch of powdered ginger and set aside for 5 minutes. Mince the garlic finely. Combine all sauce ingredients, mix well and set aside. Cover the bottom of a baking dish with aluminium foil. Place the fish on the foil and brush it with 1 tablespoon oil. Bake for 20 minutes or until done. Transfer the fish to a serving dish and pour the sauce over it. Serve immediately.

CRYSTAL PRAWNS (Swei Chin Ming Shia)
easy
preparation 20 minutes
cooking 4 minutes
serves 3 to 4

YOU NEED
8–10 shelled Dublin Bay prawns (or scampi)
3 oz (80 g) ham

10 large fresh mushrooms
1 small cucumber
1 tsp dry sherry
½ tsp salt
½ tsp monosodium glutamate (optional)
¼ pint (⅛ litre) water
1 pint (½ litre) oil for frying

MARINADE
½ tsp salt
1 tbsp cornflour
1 unbeaten egg white
½ tsp dry sherry

THICKENING
1 tbsp cornflour dissolved in
2 tbsp water

Prepare the marinade. Cut each prawn (or scampi) into 2 or 3 pieces. Mix with the marinade and set aside. Clean the mushrooms and cut each into 3 or 4 pieces. Cut the ham in thin strips. Peel the cucumber and cut open lengthwise. De-seed, then slice thinly. In a deep frying pan, heat the oil until almost smoking. Drop in the pieces of prawn and fry for 10 seconds. Drain on absorbent kitchen paper. Leave only ½ tbsp oil in the pan and reheat. Add sherry, water, salt and monosodium glutamate. Bring to the boil. Incorporate the ham, cucumber and mushrooms. Bring back to the boil, then, pour in the thickening. Cook until thickened, about 1 minute. Add the pieces of prawn and stir. Remove from heat and serve at once.

DRUNKEN SHRIMP (Tsue Hsia)

very easy
preparation 15 minutes/marinade 2 hours
cooking 4 minutes
serves 2 to 3

YOU NEED

½ lb (250 g) unshelled shrimp
1 spring onion (or leek)
2 slices fresh ginger (or ⅓ tsp powdered)
2 tbsp oil

MARINADE

1 good pinch salt
1 tsp sugar
½ tbsp soy sauce
3 tbsp dry sherry

Prepare the marinade. Remove the legs of the shrimp and take out the veins if desired, slitting along the back of the shell with scissors or a sharp knife, but do not shell. Wash and pat dry, then mix with the marinade. Place in the refrigerator for 2 hours. Meantime, shred the spring onion (or leek) and fresh ginger. In a frying pan, heat the oil until almost smoking. Stir-fry the spring onion (or leek) and ginger for 10 seconds. Add the shrimp and stir-fry 3 minutes or until their colour intensifies and becomes pinkish. Remove from the heat and serve.

FISH IN CURRY SAUCE (Chia Li Yü)

fairly easy
preparation 20 minutes/marinade 10 minutes
cooking 10 minutes (see Tips & Tricks)
serves 2 to 3

YOU NEED

1 whole fish (or fillet), 1 lb (500 g)
3 oz (80 g) pork (or ham or bacon)
1 medium onion (see Tips & Tricks)
1 carrot
1 green pepper (or string beans)
2 cabbage leaves
2 spring onions (or leek)
1 chilli pod
1 tbsp flour
1 pint (½ litre) oil for frying

MARINADE

1 tsp salt
1 tbsp dry sherry

SEASONING A

½–1 tbsp curry to taste
1 tsp salt
1 tbsp dry sherry

SEASONING B

1 pinch salt
1 tsp sugar
1 tsp soy sauce
1 tbsp dry sherry

THICKENING

1 tbsp cornflour dissolved in a scant
½ pint (¼ litre) water

Rub the fish with the marinade ingredients and set aside for 10 minutes. Cut into shreds the onion, carrot, green pepper (or string beans), cabbage, spring onions (or leek) and pork (or ham or bacon). Open the chilli pod, de-seed and cut into shreds. In 3 bowls, prepare seasonings A and B and the thickening. Sprinkle the fish with the flour. In a deep frying pan, heat the oil until almost smoking. Fry the fish 3 to 4 minutes or until golden brown. Drain on absorbent kitchen paper. Leave only 1 tbsp oil in the pan and reheat. Stir-fry the spring onions (or leek), onion and chilli pod for 10 seconds. Add the seasoning A and stir-fry for 1 minute. Incorporate the pork (or ham or bacon) and continue to stir-fry, 1 minute. Add carrot, cabbage and green pepper (or string beans) and stir-fry for 30 seconds. Sprinkle with seasoning B, then add the fish, and cook for 2 minutes. Pour in the thickening and boil until thickened, about 1 minute. Remove from heat and serve at once accompanied by steamed rice.

TIPS & TRICKS
Any one of the vegetables may be omitted and replaced by a larger quantity of one of the others. If you prefer not to deep fry the fish, brush it with 1 tbsp oil and bake in a pre-heated moderate oven (electricity 350°, gas regulo 4) for 20 minutes or until done.

FILLET OF FISH WITH MUSHROOMS
(Yü Pien Shwang Tong)
fairly easy
preparation 15 minutes
cooking 2 minutes
serves 2 to 3

YOU NEED
½ lb (250 g) fish fillet
5 dried Chinese mushrooms (or fresh button)
1 carrot (or bamboo shoots or celery)
1 spring onion (or leek)
2 slices fresh ginger (optional)
1 pint (½ litre) oil for frying

MARINADE
1 good pinch each salt and pepper
1 tsp cornflour
1 unbeaten egg white
1 tbsp soy sauce
1 tbsp dry sherry

SEASONING
½ tsp cornflour
1 tbsp water (or mushroom soaking water)
1 tsp soy sauce
1 tbsp dry sherry

Wash the dried mushrooms and soak in warm water 10 minutes or until soft. Drain (reserving the soaking water), remove the hard stalks and cut each into 4 pieces. Prepare the marinade. Cut the fish fillet into even-sized pieces about 1½" (4 cm) square. Mix with the marinade and set aside. Cut the spring onion (or leek) in half lengthwise. Thinly slice the carrot (or bamboo shoots or celery) on the diagonal. In a deep frying pan, heat the oil until a piece of bread, thrown in, returns to the surface and browns in 60 seconds. Plunge in the pieces of fish and fry for 30 seconds. Drain on absorbent kitchen paper. Leave only 1 tbsp oil in the pan and re-heat until almost smoking. Stir-fry for 1 minute the mushrooms, spring onion (or leek) and ginger (the slices of fresh ginger should be whole). Remove the fresh ginger and spring onion (or leek) and discard. Incorporate the fish, carrot (or bamboo shoots or celery) and seasoning. Bring to the boil and cook until thickened about 30 seconds. Remove from heat and serve immediately.

FISH WITH SPRING ONIONS (Ts'ung Chien Yü)
very easy
preparation 5 minutes / marinade 5 minutes
cooking 15 minutes
serves 2 to 3

YOU NEED
1 whole fish (or fillet) about 1½ lb (800 g)
2 spring onions (or leek)
1 tbsp soy sauce

1 tbsp water
2 tbsp oil

MARINADE
1 generous pinch powdered ginger
½ tsp salt

Wash the fish, pat dry, and rub with the marinade ingredients. Marinate for 5 minutes. Cut the spring onions (or leek) in 2 or 3 sections. In a frying pan large enough to hold the fish, heat 1 tbsp oil until almost smoking. Brown the fish well on one side, 3 to 4 minutes, then turn carefully over and brown on the other side, another 3 to 4 minutes. Remove from the pan. Add 1 tbsp oil to the pan and reheat. Stir-fry the spring onion (or leek) for 30 seconds. Return the fish to the pan and sprinkle with the soy sauce and water. Cook for 5 to 6 minutes or until done. Remove from heat and serve immediately.

GOLDEN BAKED FISH (Kau Yü)
very easy
preparation 10 minutes
cooking 25 minutes
serves 3 to 4

YOU NEED
1 whole fish (or fillet), 1½–2 lb (800 g)
4 oz (100 g) pork (or bacon)
1 spring onion (or leek)
1 slice fresh ginger (or 1 pinch powdered)
1 tbsp oil (optional)

SEASONING
1 tsp salt
2 tbsp soy sauce
4 tbsp dry sherry
1 tsp vinegar

Pre-heat your oven to electricity 350°, gas regulo 4. Cover the bottom of a baking dish with aluminium foil. Cut in shreds the pork (or bacon), spring onions (or leek) and fresh ginger. Combine the seasoning ingredients. Make deep, diagonal slashes on each side of the fish. (Slash the fillet in a criss-cross pattern.) Place the fish in the baking dish and top with the ginger, spring onions (or leek) and pork (bacon). Sprinkle with the seasoning. Bake the fish for 20 minutes. Sprinkle with the oil (optional) and bake for another 5 minutes. Remove from the oven and serve hot or cold.

PHOENIX TAIL PRAWNS (San Se Kan Pei)
fairly easy
preparation 30 minutes
cooking 6 minutes
serves 2 to 3

YOU NEED
10 oz (300 g) unshelled prawns
1 tbsp flour
1 pint (½ litre) oil for frying

FRITTER BATTER
2 eggs
½ tsp sugar
1 good pinch baking powder
4 tbsp flour
1 tsp soy sauce
2 tbsp water
1 tbsp lard (or oil)

SAUCE

2 tbsp ketchup
2 tbsp soy sauce
1 dash tabasco to taste
1 tsp sesame oil (optional)

Prepare the sauce in a small serving bowl and set aside. Prepare the fritter batter. Shell the prawns without touching the tail which should remain intact. Take out any veins and sprinkle the flour. In a deep frying pan, heat the oil for frying to a medium temperature, 350°. Holding 2 prawns together by their tails, dip them first into the fritter batter, then, drop them into the hot oil. Fry for 5 minutes. Increase the heat to the highest temperature (385°–390°) and fry for 30 seconds more. Serve hot accompanied by the sauce for dipping.

PRAWNS SZECHWAN (Kan Ch'au Hsia Jen)

easy
preparation 15 minutes/marinade 1 hour
cooking 3 to 4 minutes
serves 3 to 4

YOU NEED

¼ lb (350 g) unshelled prawns
2 slices fresh ginger (or ⅓ tsp powdered)
2 spring onions (or leek)
1 tbsp dry sherry
1½ tbsp cornflour
1 pint (½ litre) oil for frying

MARINADE

1 good pinch salt
1 unbeaten egg white
1 tsp dry sherry
¼ tbsp lard (or oil)
½ tsp sesame oil (optional)

SEASONING

¼ tsp salt
¼ tsp sugar
2 tsp cornflour
4 tbsp water
3 tbsp ketchup
½ tsp tabasco
1 tsp sesame oil (optional)

Prepare the marinade. Shell the prawns and remove veins, then mix with the marinade. Place in the refrigerator for 1 hour (or in the freezer for 15 minutes). Finely chop the spring onions (or leek) and fresh ginger. Prepare the seasoning and set aside. In a deep frying pan, heat the oil until almost smoking. Sprinkle the prawns with 1½ tbsp cornflour. Plunge into the hot oil and fry for 30 seconds or until their colour begins to intensify (half-cooked). Drain on absorbent kitchen paper. Leave only 1 tbsp oil in the pan and reheat. Stir-fry the ginger and spring onions (or leek) for 30 seconds. Add the prawns and the seasoning. Bring to the boil and cook for 1 minute. Remove from heat and serve at once.

PRAWNS WITH ALMONDS (Ch'in Chiao Hsia Jen)

fairly easy
preparation 15 minutes/marinade 1 hour
cooking 5 minutes
serves 2 to 3

This is one of the most famous of all Cantonese dishes.

YOU NEED

½ lb (250 g) shelled prawns (or chicken breast)
2 oz (50 g) blanched almonds (or cashews or peanuts)
1 small green pepper (or mange-tout or green peas)
1 slice fresh ginger (or 1 good pinch powdered)
4 spring onions (or leek)
1 chilli pod
1 tbsp cornflour

1 tbsp dry sherry
1 pint ($\frac{1}{2}$ litre) oil for frying

MARINADE
$\frac{1}{2}$ tsp salt (optional for the prawns)
1 pinch pepper
1 unbeaten egg white
1 tbsp lard (or oil)
$\frac{1}{2}$ tsp sesame oil (optional)

SEASONING
1 tsp cornflour
$\frac{1}{2}$ tsp water
$\frac{1}{2}$ tsp soy sauce
$\frac{1}{2}$ tsp sesame oil (optional)

Prepare the marinade. Wash and dry the prawns (or cut the chicken into even, bite-sized pieces) then mix with the marinade. Place in the refrigerator for 1 hour (or the freezer 15 minutes). Open the chilli pod and green pepper, de-seed and cut into even-sized pieces, about 1" × 1" (2.5 cm × 2.5 cm). Mince the spring onion (or leek) and fresh ginger. Prepare the seasoning and set aside. In a deep frying pan, heat the oil until almost smoking. Drop the pieces of green pepper (or mange-tout or green peas) into the hot oil for 5 seconds. Drain on absorbent kitchen paper. Sprinkle the prawns with 1 tbsp cornflour. Fry for 10 seconds (half cooked), then drain on absorbent paper. Leave only 1 tbsp oil in the pan and reheat. Stir-fry the spring onion (or leek), ginger and chilli pod for 1 minute. Add the shrimp and sprinkle with 1 tbsp sherry. Stir-fry for 2 minutes. Incorporate the green pepper (or mange-tout or green peas), almonds and seasoning. Cook while stirring, 1 minute, then remove from heat. Serve hot.

SCALLOPS WITH CUCUMBER SAUCE (San Se Kan Pei)
very easy
preparation 15 minutes
cooking 10 minutes
serves 2 to 3

YOU NEED
$\frac{1}{2}$ lb (250 g) scallops (or abalone)
4 oz (100 g) lean pork (or ham)
1 small cucumber
1 carrot

1 stick celery
1 tsp salt
1 good pinch pepper
$\frac{1}{2}$ tsp monosodium glutamate (optional)
1 tbsp dry sherry
$\frac{1}{2}$ pint ($\frac{1}{4}$ litre) water

MARINADE
1 tsp cornflour
1 tsp soy sauce

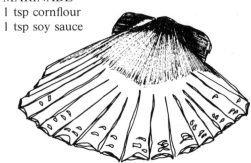

THICKENING
1 tbsp cornflour dissolved in
1 tbsp water

In 2 bowls, prepare the marinade and thickening. Cut the pork (or ham) against the grain in very thin strips. Mix with the marinade and set aside. Peel the cucumber and cut it open lengthwise. De-seed, then, cut it into thin strips about 1" (2.5 cm) long. Cut the celery and carrot into strips the same size as the cucumber. Tear each scallop (or the abalone) into 2 or 3 pieces. Bring water to the boil. Drop in the pork (or ham) and cucumber. Reduce the heat and simmer, uncovered, for 5 minutes. Incorporate sherry, salt, pepper, scallops, celery, carrot and monosodium glutamate. Bring back to the boil and cook rapidly for 3 minutes. Pour in the thickening and boil until thickened, about 30 seconds. Remove from heat and serve at once, accompanied by steamed rice.

SMELT FRITTERS (Cha Hsiao Yü)
easy
preparation 15 minutes / marinade 10 minutes
cooking 1 minute per fritter
serves 4

YOU NEED
1 lb (500 g) smelt (or sand eels, gudgeon or other small fish)

2 pints (1 litre) oil for frying

FRITTER BATTER
4 oz (100 g) flour
2 tsp baking powder
½ tsp salt
½ tbsp sugar
¼ pt (⅛ litre) water

SAUCE
2 spring onions (or chives)
3 tbsp soy sauce
1 tsp vinegar
¼ tsp tabasco
½ tsp sesame oil (optional)

Mince the spring onion (or chives). Combine all sauce ingredients, mix well and set aside. Clean, wash and dry the smelt. Prepare the fritter batter. In a deep pan, heat the oil until almost smoking. Add the fish to the fritter batter, then, plunge by small spoonfuls into the hot oil. Fry for 1 minute or until golden brown. Drain on absorbent kitchen paper. Serve hot accompanied by the sauce for dipping.

SMOKED FISH (Hsün Yü)
rather difficult
preparation 5 minutes/marinade 30 minutes
cooking 50 minutes
serves 2 to 3

YOU NEED
1 whole fish (or fillet or squid) about 1½ lb (800 g)
6 tbsp dry sherry

MARINADE
2 tsp salt
½ tsp sugar

2 tbsp dry sherry
4 tbsp soy sauce

SEASONING
2 tbsp black tea
6 tbsp brown sugar
4 tbsp dry sherry

You also need a steamer, or heavy saucepan with steaming basket.

Prepare the marinade and pour over the fish. Marinate for 30 minutes. Cover the bottom of the steamer with aluminium foil. If using a heavy saucepan, also cover with foil the inside of the lid. Remove the fish from the marinade and place in the steamer basket. Do not use a plate. Cook (smoke) the fish over medium/low heat for 20 minutes. Open the steamer, add 6 tbsp sherry and close again. Cook for another 30 minutes over medium/low heat. Remove from steamer and serve hot or cold.

SPICY BRAISED FISH (Hsiang Ts'ue Yü)
very easy
preparation 20 minutes
cooking 1 hour
serves 2 to 3

YOU NEED
1 lb (500 g) sardines (or herring or other small fish)
1 medium-sized onion
1 clove garlic
1 slice fresh ginger (or 1 good pinch powdered)
2 pieces tangerine (or lemon) peel
1 tbsp sugar
3 tbsp soy sauce
3 tbsp dry sherry
3 tbsp vinegar
½ tsp salt
¼ pint (¼ litre) water

Cut the onion in half, then slice thinly. Crush the garlic. After cleaning, place the sardines (or other fish) in a heavy saucepan. Pour in the water and add all other ingredients. Leave the slice of fresh ginger whole. Bring to the boil, then, reduce the heat and simmer, uncovered, for 1 hour or until the liquid is completely absorbed. Discard the fresh ginger slice and tangerine (or lemon) peel. Serve hot or cold.

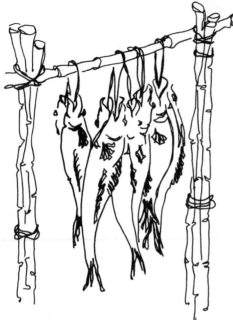

TIPS & TRICKS

In China, tangerine peel is dried and used as a favourite condiment. It is believed that the older the peel, the better. In fact, the price of the peel is based upon its age. Thus, a dried tangerine peel 40 or 50 years old will cost more than its weight in gold!

SQUID OF FIVE FLAVOURS (Wu Wei Wu Tsei)

fairly difficult
preparation 20 minutes
cooking 2 minutes
serves 2 to 3

YOU NEED

1 lb (500 g) squid
2 green peppers
2 spring onions (or leek)
2 chilli pods
1 slice fresh ginger (or 1 good pinch powdered)
1 pint (½ litre) oil for frying

FRITTER BATTER

1 egg yolk
½ tsp salt
2 tbsp cornflour

SEASONING

1 good pinch salt
1 tbsp sugar
1 tbsp dry sherry
2 tbsp soy sauce
3 tbsp ketchup
3 tbsp vinegar
½ tsp monosodium glutamate (optional)
1 tsp sesame oil (optional)

With a quick jerk, separate the tentacles of the squid from the body (hood). Open the body lengthwise and remove the transparent shell. Cut the tentacles from the head, discarding the latter. Wash the body and tentacles under cold, running water, removing the dark membrane which covers them. Cut the tentacles in 1" (2.5 cm) pieces and the body into even, bite-sized pieces. Prepare the fritter batter and add the piece of squid. Cut the green peppers into even, bite-sized pieces. Open and de-seed the chilli pods, then, mince finely. Mince the fresh ginger and spring onions (or leek). Combine the seasoning, ginger, chilli pods and spring onions (or leek). In a deep frying pan, heat the frying oil until almost smoking. Drop in the pieces of green pepper and fry for 10 seconds. Drain on absorbent kitchen paper. Plunge the pieces of squid into the oil and fry for 1 minute. Drain on absorbent kitchen paper. Heat another very lightly oiled frying pan. Pour in the seasoning and bring to the boil. Add the squid and green peppers. Stir, remove from heat and serve at once.

STEAMED FISH (La Chiao Cheng Yü)

easy
preparation 15 minutes/marinade 10 minutes
cooking 20 minutes
serves 3 to 4

YOU NEED

1 whole fish (or fillet) 1½–2 lb (800 g)
3 oz (80 g) ham (or bacon)
1 chilli pod
2 slices fresh ginger (or ⅓ tsp powdered)
1–2 cloves garlic

MARINADE

1 good pinch powdered ginger

½ tsp salt
1 tbsp dry sherry

SEASONING
½ tsp salt
4 tbsp soy sauce
1 tbsp dry sherry
1 tsp monosodium glutamate (optional)

You also need a steamer.

Wash the fish and pat dry, then rub with the marinade ingredients. Marinate for 10 minutes. Meanwhile, cut the ham (or bacon) in thin strips. Mince the garlic. Shred the fresh ginger. Open and de-seed the chilli pod, then cut in shred-like strips. Prepare the seasoning. Put the steamer water to heat. Oil an unbreakable plate which will fit into the steamer. Place the fish on the plate and top with the garlic, ginger, ham

and chilli pods. Sprinkle with the seasoning. Steam the fish for 20 minutes or until done. Serve immediately.

STIR-FRIED DUBLIN BAY PRAWNS (Hong Shau Ta Hsia)
fairly easy
preparation 20 minutes
cooking 3 minutes
serves 3 to 4

YOU NEED
8–10 Dublin Bay prawns (or scampi)
2 chilli pods
2 spring onions (or leek)
1 slice fresh ginger (or 1 good pinch powdered)
1 tbsp dry sherry

2 tbsp cornflour
1 pint (½ litre) oil for frying

MARINADE
½ tsp salt
1 tsp powdered ginger
2 tbsp dry sherry

SEASONING
1 tbsp cornflour
1 tsp salt
2 tbsp sugar
6 tbsp water
4 tbsp ketchup
1 tbsp soy sauce
1 tsp sesame oil (optional)

Remove the legs of the prawns and, with a sharp knife, take out veins but do not shell. Wash and pat dry, then mix the prawns with the marinade ingredients. Marinate for 15 minutes. Meanwhile, open and de-seed the chilli pods. Mince finely the chilli pods, spring onions (or leek) and fresh ginger. Combine the seasoning, chilli pods, spring onions (or leek) and ginger. In a deep frying pan, heat the oil until almost smoking. Sprinkle the prawns with 2 tbsp cornflour. Plunge into the hot oil and fry for 1 minute, or until half-done. Drain on absorbent kitchen paper. Leave only ½ tbsp oil in the pan and reheat. Add the prawns and sprinkle with the sherry. Stir-fry for 2 minutes. Pour in the seasoning and cook until thickened, about 30 seconds. Remove from heat and serve at once.

STIR-FRIED FISH WITH VEGETABLES (Sheng Ch'au Yü Pien)
fairly easy
preparation 10 to 12 minutes / marinade 5
    minutes
cooking 3 to 4 minutes
serves 2

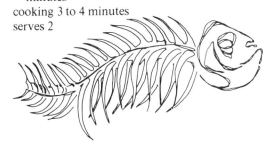

YOU NEED

½ lb (250 g) fillet of fish
1–2 cloves garlic
1 stick celery
1 green pepper
1 small onion
2 slices fresh ginger (or ⅓ tsp powdered)
1 pint (½ litre) oil for frying

MARINADE

1 tbsp cornflour
1 generous pinch powdered ginger
1 unbeaten egg white
1 pinch salt
½ tsp dry sherry

SEASONING

1 tsp salt
1 good pinch pepper
½ tbsp soy sauce
1 tbsp dry sherry

THICKENING

2 tbsp cornflour dissolved in
½ pint (¼ litre) water

Prepare the marinade. Cut the fish fillet into thin strips. Mix with the marinade and set aside for 5 minutes. Cut the green pepper into even-sized pieces about 1" × 1" (2.5 cm × 2.5 cm). Cut into thin strips the garlic, fresh ginger, onion and celery. In 2 bowls, prepare the seasoning and the thickening. In a deep frying pan, heat the oil until almost smoking. Drop the strips of fish into the hot oil and fry for 20 seconds. Drain on absorbent kitchen paper. Fry the celery and green onion for 2 seconds. Drain, then place on a serving plate. Leave only 1 tbsp oil in the pan and re-heat. Stir-fry the onion, ginger and garlic for 30 seconds. Add the seasoning and fish. Stir-fry for 1 minute. Incorporate the thickening and cook until thickened, about 1 minute. Pour over the celery and green onion. Serve hot.

STIR-FRIED SHRIMP I (Ch'au Hsia)

very easy
preparation 15 minutes / marinade 10 minutes
cooking 4 minutes
serves 2 to 3

YOU NEED

½ lb (250 g) unshelled shrimp
1 clove garlic
1 spring onion (or leek)
1 pinch each salt and pepper
1 tbsp dry sherry
1½ tbsp oil

MARINADE

½ tsp salt
1 tsp dry sherry

Prepare the marinade. Remove the legs of the shrimp and take out veins if desired, but do not shell. Wash and pat dry, then, mix with the marinade. Set aside for 10 minutes. Mince the garlic and spring onion (or leek). In a frying pan, heat the oil until almost smoking. Stir-fry the garlic and spring onion for 1 minute. Add the shrimp and sprinkle with the sherry. Season with the salt and pepper and continue to stir-fry for 3 minutes, or until the colour of the shrimp intensifies and becomes pinkish. Remove from heat and serve.

STIR-FRIED SHRIMP II (Hsien Su Hsia)

easy
preparation 10 minutes / marinade 10 minutes
cooking 5 to 6 minutes
serves 2 to 3

YOU NEED

½ lb (250 g) unshelled shrimp
1 clove garlic

1 tbsp flour
½ tsp salt
1 pinch pepper
1 tbsp dry sherry
¼ pint (⅛ litre) oil for frying

MARINADE
½ tsp salt
1 tsp dry sherry

Remove the legs of the shrimp and take out veins if desired but do not shell. Wash and pat dry, then, mix with the ingredients of the marinade. Marinate for 10 minutes. Mince the garlic. In a deep frying pan, heat the oil until almost smoking. Drop in the shrimp and fry for 30 seconds. Remove from the pan and sprinkle with the flour. Return the shrimp to the hot oil and fry for another 2 minutes. Drain on absorbent kitchen paper. Leave only 1 tbsp oil in the pan and reheat. Stir-fry the garlic for 30 seconds. Add the shrimp and sprinkle with the sherry. Season with ½ tsp salt and a pinch of pepper. Stir-fry for 1 minute more. Remove from heat and serve.

STIR-FRIED SQUID (Sheng Ch'au Wu Tseu)
very easy
preparation 10 to 15 minutes
cooking 3 minutes
serves 2 to 3

YOU NEED
1 lb (500 g) squid
5 spring onions (or leek)
1 tbsp dry sherry
1 tsp salt
1 tsp oil

With a sharp jerk, separate the tentacles of the squid from the body (hood). Open the body lengthwise and remove the transparent shell. Cut the tentacles from the head, discarding the latter. Wash under cold, running water, removing the dark membrane which covers the body and tentacles. Cut the tentacle into 1" (2.5 cm) lengths and the body into even, bite-sized pieces. In a frying pan, heat the oil until almost smoking. Stir-fry the spring onions (or leek) for 30 seconds. Add the squid and sprinkle with the sherry. Season with the salt. Stir-fry for 3 to 4 minutes or until done. Remove from heat and serve at once.

SWEET AND SOUR FISH I (Tang Tsu Yü)
easy
preparation 15 minutes
cooking 7 to 8 minutes (see Tips & Tricks)
serves 3 to 4

YOU NEED
1 whole fish, 1½–2 lb (800 g)
1 onion
1 slice fresh ginger (or 1 pinch powdered)
1 clove garlic
1 chilli pod
2 tbsp cornflour
3 oz (80 g) sugar
1 pint (½ litre) oil for frying

MARINADE
2 tbsp soy sauce
1 tbsp dry sherry

SEASONING
¼ tbsp cornflour
6 tbsp vinegar
1 tsp oil
1½ tbsp soy sauce
¼ pint (⅛ litre) water

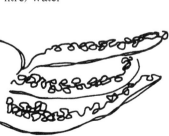

Combine the marinade ingredients. Wash the fish and pat dry, then, make 3 or 4 deep diagonal slashes on each side. Rub well with the marinade and set aside for 15 minutes. Meanwhile, mince finely the onion, fresh ginger and garlic. Open and de-seed the chilli pod, then mince finely. Prepare the seasoning and set aside. In a deep frying pan, heat the oil until almost smoking. Sprinkle the fish with the cornflour. Plunge into the hot oil and fry for 4 to 6 minutes or until golden brown and done. Drain, place on a serving plate and keep warm. In a small frying pan, heat 1 tbsp oil until almost smoking. Stir-fry the onion, garlic, chilli pod, ginger and sugar for 1 minute. Add the seasoning and bring to the boil. Incorporate 1 tsp oil, stir and remove from the heat. Pour the sauce over the fish and serve immediately.

TIPS & TRICKS

If you do not wish to deep fry the fish, you may brush it with 1 tbsp oil, then, bake it in a pre-heated moderate oven (electricity 350°, gas regulo 4) for 20 minutes or until done.

SWEET AND SOUR FISH II (Ts'ue Pi Ch'üan Yü)

easy
preparation 15 minutes / marinade 5 minutes
cooking 8 to 9 minutes
serves 3 to 4

YOU NEED

1 whole fish, 1½–2 lb (800 g)
2 chilli pods
1 green pepper
1 spring onion (or leek)
1 slice fresh ginger (or 1 good pinch powdered)
1 tbsp dry sherry
1 egg yolk
1 tbsp cornflour
1 pint (½ litre) oil for frying

MARINADE

1 tsp salt
½ tbsp dry sherry

SEASONING

2 tbsp sugar
1 tsp cornflour
4 tbsp water
½ tbsp soy sauce
3 tbsp ketchup
½ tsp sesame oil (optional)

Wash the fish and pat dry. Rub with the marinade ingredients, then, set aside for 5 minutes. De-seed the chilli pods and green pepper. Mince finely the chilli pods, green pepper, spring onion (or leek) and fresh ginger. Beat the egg yolk and brush it over the fish,

then, roll the fish in the cornflour, pressing down so that the cornflour adheres well. In a deep frying pan, heat the oil until almost smoking. Slip the fish gently into the hot oil and fry 4 to 6 minutes or until golden brown and thoroughly cooked. Drain, then place on a serving dish and keep warm. In a small frying pan, heat 1 tsp oil until almost smoking. Pour in 1 tbsp sherry. Add the spring onion (or leek), ginger, chilli pods, and seasoning. Bring to the boil and incorporate the green pepper. Stir, then pour over the fish. Serve immediately.

WHITE COOKED SEA BASS (Pai Shue Yü)
very easy
preparation 5 minutes
cooking 10 minutes
serves 3 to 4

YOU NEED
1½–2 lb (800 g) sea bass
4 spring onions (or leek)
2 slices fresh ginger (or ⅓ tsp powdered)
2 tbsp soy sauce
1 tbsp oil

Wash and dry the fish. Cut the spring onions (or leek) into shred-like 1" (2.5 cm) lengths. Shred the fresh ginger. In a large saucepan, bring to the boil enough water to cover the fish. Plunge the fish into the boiling water and bring back to the boil. Cover the saucepan, turn off the heat and let stand, 8 to 10 minutes or until the fish is done. Drain the fish, reserving the water for a soup base. Place on a serving platter, sprinkle with the soy sauce and keep warm while preparing the garnish. In a small frying pan, heat the oil until almost smoking. Stir-fry the spring onions (or leek) and ginger 20 seconds, then, pour over the fish. Serve immediately.

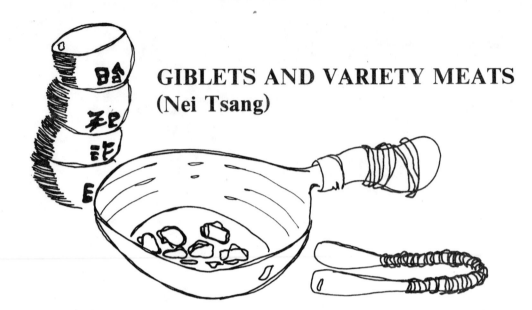

GIBLETS AND VARIETY MEATS
(Nei Tsang)

Giblets, liver and kidneys are considered extremely delicate morsels by the Chinese. Indeed, in the olden days, they were the food of the rich for their price was very dear. Even those who do not ordinarily care for such meats will be won over by the delicious ways in which we prepare them. With the exception of the stir-fried dishes, the recipes in this chapter make splendid hors d'oeuvre and first courses.

CHICKEN LIVERS IN SOY SAUCE (Hung Shao Chi Kan)
very easy
preparation 5 minutes
cooking 10 minutes
serves 2

YOU NEED
¼ lb (100 g) chicken (or lamb or calves') liver

SEASONING
1 tbsp sugar
1 tbsp dry sherry
3 tbsp soy sauce

Rinse the livers under hot running water for several minutes to prevent scum from forming during the cooking. Cut each liver into 2 or 3 pieces. Combine the seasoning ingredients in a small saucepan. Bring to the boil and add the livers. Cook rapidly, uncovered, 8 to 10 minutes or until all the liquid has been absorbed. Remove from heat and serve hot or cold.

CHICKEN LIVERS VINAIGRETTE (Liang Pan Chi Kan)
very easy
preparation 5 minutes
cooking 10 minutes
serves 2

YOU NEED
¼ lb (100 g) chicken livers
1 tsp salt
½ tbsp dry sherry
¼ pint (½ litre) water

SAUCE
½ tsp salt
1 tbsp dry sherry
1 tbsp water
½ tsp sugar

1 tbsp vinegar
1 dash tabasco to taste

Rinse the livers under hot running water for several minutes to prevent formation of scum during the cooking. Cut each liver into 2 or 3 pieces. Bring the water to the boil. Add 1 tsp salt, ½ tbsp sherry and the livers. Bring back to the boil, lower the heat and simmer for 8 to 10 minutes or until done. Drain and place the livers in a serving dish. While the livers are cooking, in a small saucepan bring the sauce ingredients to the boil. Stir until the sugar is dissolved, then remove from heat. Pour the sauce over the livers. Serve warm or cold.

CHICKEN LIVERS WITH FIVE SPICES (Jou Kuei Chi Kan)
easy
preparation 5 minutes/marinade 30 minutes
cooking 15 minutes
serves 2

YOU NEED
¼ lb (100 g) chicken (or lamb or calves') liver

MARINADE
½ tsp five-spice powder (or all-spice)
1 tbsp soy sauce
½ tbsp dry sherry
½ tsp monosodium glutamate (optional)

You also need a steamer.

Prepare the marinade in a heat-resistant bowl which will fit into the steamer. Rinse the livers under hot running water for several minutes. Cut each chicken liver into 2 or 3 pieces (or the lamb or calves' liver into bite-sized pieces). Mix with the marinade and set aside for 30 minutes. Bring the steamer water to the boil. Place the bowl containing the livers into the steamer and cover. Steam for 15 minutes or until done. Serve hot or cold.

RED COOKED GIBLETS (Lu Cheng Kan)
very easy
preparation 4 minutes
cooking 15 to 20 minutes
serves 2 to 3

YOU NEED
½ lb (250 g) giblets (see Tips & Tricks)
¼ pint (⅛ litre) water

SEASONING
1½ tbsp sugar
1 star anise (optional)
3 tbsp dry sherry
6 tbsp soy sauce

Rinse the giblets under hot running water for several minutes to prevent scum from forming during the cooking. Cut each giblet into 2 or 3 pieces. Combine the seasoning ingredients in a saucepan and bring to the boil. Add the giblets and water. Bring back to the boil, lower the heat and simmer for 15 to 20 minutes or until the giblets are done. Serve hot or cold.

TIPS & TRICKS

Any piece of meat or chicken may be prepared by this recipe: steaks, chops, spareribs, chicken thighs, wings and so on. It is such a versatile dish that it can be served as a first course, as one of several main dishes for a large dinner, or carried along on a picnic.

SALTED CHICKEN LIVERS (Yen Shue Chi Kan)

easy
preparation 5 minutes
cooking 15 minutes
serves 2

YOU NEED

¼ lb (100 g) chicken (or lamb or calves') livers
1 tbsp dry sherry
1 tsp salt
1 good pinch pepper

You also need a steamer.

Bring the steamer water to the boil. Meanwhile, rinse the livers under hot running water. Cut each liver into 2 or 3 pieces (or the lamb or calves' liver into bite-sized pieces). In a heat-resistant bowl which will fit into the steamer, combine the pieces of liver with the other ingredients. Place the bowl in the steamer and cover. Steam for 15 minutes or until done to taste. Serve hot or cold.

SALTED LIVER (Yen Shue Kan)

very easy
preparation 2 minutes
cooking 45 minutes
makes about 20 pieces

This liver makes a surprisingly tasty and unusual hors d'oeuvre.

YOU NEED

1 lb (500 g) liver
½ pint (¼ litre) water
5 tbsp salt
5 peppercorns
2 tbsp dry sherry

Bring to the boil enough water to cover the liver. Drop in the liver and cook rapidly for 15 minutes. Drain, discarding the water. In a saucepan, bring to the boil the water, salt, peppercorns and sherry. Add the liver and simmer, uncovered, for 30 minutes. Remove from heat and allow to cool. Cut the liver in thin slices and serve cold.

SALTED TONGUE (Yen Niu She)

rather difficult
preparation 15 minutes / marinade 12 hours
cooking 1 hour 45 minutes
serves 3 to 4

YOU NEED

1 small tongue (or chicken) about 2 lb (1 kg)
2 tbsp dry sherry
½ tsp peppercorns
5 tbsp salt

You also need a steamer.

Place the tongue (or chicken) in a large saucepan and cover it with cold water. Bring to the boil and cook for 1 hour (15 minutes for the chicken). Drain and allow to cool. Meanwhile, heat a small, unoiled frying pan. Pour in the salt and peppercorns. Stirring, cook until roasted, 4 to 5 minutes. Remove from heat and allow to cool. Remove the tough, outer skin from the tongue. Cut the tongue in half lengthwise. Rub with sherry, then with the roasted salt and peppercorns. Put the tongue (or chicken) in the refrigerator to marinate overnight. The next day, bring the steamer water to the boil. If desired, rinse the tongue (or chicken) before final cooking to reduce the saltiness. Steam for 45 minutes (30 minutes for the chicken) or until tender. Cut into thin slices and serve hot or cold.

STIR - FRIED KIDNEYS WITH VEG-ETABLES (Shih Chin Yau Hua)

difficult
preparation 20 minutes / marinade 10 minutes
cooking 7 minutes
serves 2 to 3

YOU NEED

½ lb (250 g) pork kidneys
⅓ lb (150 g) lean pork
¼ lb (100 g) button mushrooms (fresh or tinned)
1 green pepper
1 carrot
2 spring onions (or leak or onion)
2 slices fresh ginger (optional)
1 chilli pod
1 tbsp dry sherry
1 tsp sugar
¼ pint (⅛ litre) oil

MARINADE

1 tsp cornflour
1 tsp dry sherry
1 tsp soy sauce
1 good pinch monosodium glutamate (optional)

SEASONING

½ tsp salt
½ tbsp dry sherry
1 tbsp water

THICKENING

1½ tbsp cornflour
2 tbsp vinegar (or oyster sauce)
1 tbsp soy sauce
1 tsp sesame oil (optional)
¼ pint (⅛ litre) water

Cut the kidneys lengthwise into halves and rinse well under cold, running water; then, remove white membrane and fat. Slash the interior of each kidney-half in criss-cross diamond patterns. Cut the halves into bite-sized pieces. Cover with cold water to soak for 10 minutes. Drain and pat dry on absorbent kitchen paper. In 3 bowls, prepare the marinade, seasoning and thickening. Cut the pork into thin strips, mix with the marinade and set aside. Open and de-seed the chilli pod, then, cut into 4 pieces. Cut the green pepper into bite-sized pieces and the spring onions (leek or onion) into strips 1" (2.5 cm) long. Mince the fresh ginger. Cut the carrot and mushrooms into thin slices. In a frying pan, heat 5 tbsp oil until almost smoking. Fry the pork strips 1 minute or until half done. Drain on absorbent kitchen paper. Stir-fry the carrot for 30 seconds, then drain. Fry the pieces of kidney until half done, about 3 minutes. Drain well, discarding the oil. In a frying pan, heat 1 tsp.oil until almost smoking. Stir-fry the spring onion (or leek or onion) for 10 seconds. Sprinkle with the seasoning and stir-fry for 1 minute more. Remove from the pan. Add 2 tbsp oil to the

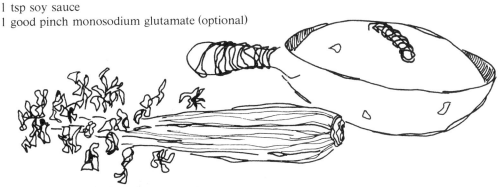

frying pan and reheat. Stir-fry for 30 seconds the ginger, spring onion (or leek or onion) and chilli pod sprinkled with 1 tsp sugar. Add the pork, carrot, green pepper and mushrooms. Sprinkle with 1 tbsp sherry and stir-fry for 10 seconds. Incorporate the kidney and thickening and cook until thickened, about 30 seconds. Remove from heat and serve immediately.

STIR-FRIED LIVER WITH CASHEW NUTS (Yiau Kuo Chi Kan)

easy
preparation 15 minutes/marinade 5 minutes
cooking 3 to 4 minutes
serves 2 to 3

YOU NEED
¼ lb (250 g) liver (or chicken livers)
2 oz (60 g) cashew nuts (or roast peanuts)
1 stick celery (or water chestnuts, bamboo shoots or string beans)
1 carrot
2 cloves garlic
2 tbsp oil

MARINADE
1 good pinch pepper
1 good pinch powdered ginger
1 tsp dry sherry

SEASONING
1 good pinch salt
1 tsp cornflour
½ tbsp soy sauce
2 tbsp water

In 2 small bowls, prepare the marinade and seasoning. Cut the liver into thin strips and mix with the marinade. Marinate for 5 minutes. Meanwhile, cut the celery (or water chestnuts, bamboo shoots or string beans) and carrot into small pieces the size of the nuts. Crush the garlic. In a frying pan, heat the oil to smoking point. Brown the garlic, then discard. Stir-fry the strips of liver 1 to 2 minutes or until half-cooked. Add the carrots and celery (or water chestnuts, bamboo shoots or string beans), stir and cook for 30 seconds. Pour in the seasoning and stir-fry until thickened, about 30 seconds. Remove the pan from the heat and add the cashew nuts. Stir once again and serve immediately.

STIR-FRIED LIVER WITH PEPPERS (Cha Chu Kan)

fairly easy
preparation 15 minutes/marinade 10 minutes
cooking 2 minutes
serves 2 to 3

YOU NEED
¼ lb (250 g) liver (or squid)
2 green peppers
1 medium-sized onion
1 chilli pod
2 tbsp cornflour
1 pint (½ litre) oil for frying

MARINADE
¼ tsp salt
1 tbsp dry sherry

SEASONING
1 clove garlic
1 spring onion (optional)
1 slice fresh ginger (or 1 good pinch powdered)
½ tbsp sugar
1 tsp dry sherry
1 tsp soy sauce

3 tbsp vinegar
1 tsp sesame oil (optional)
1 good pinch pepper

Cut the liver or squid in strips and mix with the marinade ingredients. Marinate for 10 minutes. Cut the onion in thin strips. De-seed the green peppers and cut in strips. Open and de-seed the chilli pod, then, cut in 4 pieces. Finely chop the garlic, spring onion and fresh ginger. Combine the seasoning ingredients in a small saucepan. Bring to the boil and stir until the sugar is dissolved, then, remove from heat and set aside. In a deep frying pan, heat the oil until almost smoking. Sprinkle the strips of liver (or squid) with the cornflour. Let stand for 30 seconds, then, plunge into the hot oil and fry for 1 minute. Drain on absorbent kitchen paper, then mix with the seasoning and let stand for 5 minutes. Meanwhile in the same hot oil, fry for 10 seconds each: the onion, green peppers and chilli pod. Drain on absorbent kitchen paper. Place the onion in a serving dish, then, top with the liver (or squid) and seasoning. Garnish with the green pepper and chilli pod. Serve at once.

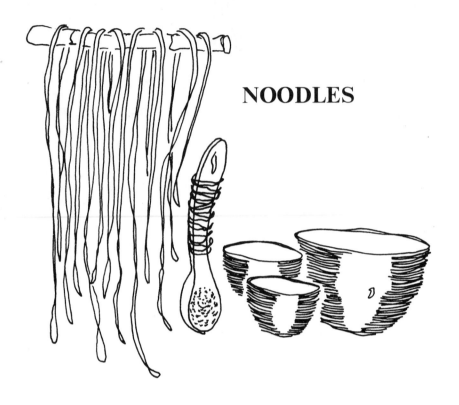

NOODLES

An infinite variety of Chinese noodles exist, many of which can be found in oriental shops in the United Kingdom. The most exotic of these is *fenszu*, commonly called transparent or cellophane noodles. *Fenszu* are made from the mung bean and starch. A second very special variety of noodle is made from rice. Rice noodles come in many different widths and lengths. They must never be used to replace *fenszu* even though appearance and cooking procedure are similar. In fact, neither *fenszu* nor rice noodles can be substituted by any other noodle, either Chinese or western. You will find recipes appropriate to each kind in the following pages.

Contrary to those made of mung and rice, the Chinese egg noodles, best known of all, can be replaced by spaghetti. In fact, it is believed that the western egg noodles are the descendants of this Chinese variety, thanks to the travels of Marco Polo. Spaghetti actually lends itself very well to Chinese cooking and we expatriate Chinese use it as an alternative when we cannot procure our own. As to the cooking of egg noodles, we often add a small quantity of oil to the boiling water to prevent the noodles from sticking and the water from boiling over.

In certain regions of China, as well as in many overseas Chinese restaurants, soft-fried noodles (Ch'au Mein) are served on 'nests' of crisp rice noodles. To prepare this 'nest', we simply 'crisp' the dry, uncooked rice noodles in very hot, deep-frying oil.

Noodle soups and salads also appear in this chapter because, to the Chinese way of thinking, noodles are always noodles, whether they be deep-fried, stir-fried, presented in salads, or served in soup.

BEEF NOODLE SOUP (Niu Jou Mein T'ang)

easy
preparation 15 minutes
cooking 1 hour
serves 3 to 4

In China, this soup is often sold by street soup vendors.

YOU NEED

4 oz (100 g) Chinese egg noodles (or spaghetti)
1 lb (500 g) stewing beef (see Tips & Tricks)
2–3 chilli pods
4–6 cloves garlic
1 spring onion (or leek)
2 pints (1 litre) water
1 tbsp oil

SEASONING

1 tsp sugar
$\frac{1}{2}$ tsp salt
1 tbsp soy sauce
3 tbsp dry sherry

Cut the meat into bite-sized pieces. Shred the fresh ginger and spring onion (or leek). Crush the garlic. Open the chilli pods, de-seed and cut each into 4 pieces. Prepare the seasoning and set aside. In a heavy saucepan, heat 1 tbsp oil until almost smoking. Stir-fry for 1 minute: the garlic, ginger, spring onion (or leek) and chilli pods. Add the pieces of beef and brown well, about 2 minutes. Pour in the seasoning, then the water and bring to the boil. Reduce the heat, skim and cover. Simmer for 1 hour or until the meat is very tender. Meanwhile, bring to the boil a large saucepan of salted water. Add 1 tbsp oil and drop in the noodles (or spaghetti), separating them with a fork. Cook at a fast boil for 5 minutes (10 minutes for the spaghetti) or until barely tender. Drain and place in a soup bowl. Pour the soup over the noodles and serve at once.

TIPS AND TRICKS

This recipe may be prepared with any cut of beef requiring long cooking such as shank, ribs, etc. Sometimes we add a small chopped tomato at the same time as the seasoning or, just before serving, we sprinkle the soup with sesame oil.

CHICKEN AND NOODLES (Hung Shao Chi Mein)

easy
preparation 15 minutes/marinade 1 hour
cooking 36 to 40 minutes
serves 2 to 3

YOU NEED

4 oz (100 g) Chinese egg noodles (or spaghetti)
$\frac{1}{2}$ chicken, about 1 lb (500 g)
1 tsp honey
2 sticks celery
1 pint ($\frac{1}{2}$ litre) water
2 tbsp oil

MARINADE

$\frac{1}{4}$ tsp powdered ginger
$\frac{1}{2}$ tsp sugar
1 spring onion (optional)
1 tbsp dry sherry
4 tbsp soy sauce

Cut the spring onion in half and, in a large bowl, combine the marinade ingredients. With a cleaver, cut the chicken, including the bones, into small pieces. Mix with the marinade and set aside for 1 hour. In the meantime, cut the celery on the diagonal into matchstick-thin strips. In a large, heavy saucepan, heat 1 tbsp oil over a medium flame. Add the honey and stir for 5 seconds. Drain the chicken (reserving the marinade) and brown on all sides, about 3 minutes. Pour in the marinade and bring to the boil. Add the water and bring once again to the boil. Lower the heat and simmer for 30 minutes. Cover the pan with a tight-fitting lid, remove it from the heat and set aside. Bring to the boil a large saucepan of water lightly salted for the noodles. Add 1 tbsp oil and drop in the noodles (or spaghetti). Boil rapidly for 3 minutes (6 minutes for the spaghetti) or until half-cooked, then drain. Add the noodles to the chicken and re-heat over a medium flame. Simmer until the noodles are completely cooked, about 2 minutes (5 minutes for the spaghetti). Discard the spring onion. Add the celery and cook for 1 minute more. Remove from heat and serve at once.

CHICKEN NOODLE SOUP (Suan Ts'ai Chi Mein)

very easy
preparation 5 minutes
cooking 18 to 21 minutes
serves 2
This soup represents a simple and typical Chinese family meal.

YOU NEED
4 oz (100 g) Chinese egg noodles (or spaghetti)
½ lb (250 g) sauerkraut (or Chinese pickled mustard greens)
2 chicken thighs (or other chicken parts)
1 tsp salt
1 tbsp oil
1 spring onion (or chives)
1½ pints (¾ litre) water

SEASONING
1 tsp soy sauce
1 tbsp dry sherry
½ tsp monosodium glutamate (optional)

In a large saucepan, bring the water to boil. Add 1 tsp salt, then plunge the chicken into the boiling water. Skim and cook rapidly for 15 minutes. Meanwhile, bring to the boil a large saucepan of salted water. Add 1 tbsp oil and drop in the noodles (or spaghetti), separating them with a fork. Boil rapidly for 3 minutes (6 minutes for the spaghetti) or until half-cooked, then drain. Chop finely the spring onion (or chives). Rinse and drain the sauerkraut (or mustard greens). Add the noodles (or spaghetti), sauerkraut (or mustard greens) and seasoning to the soup. Boil 3 minutes (6 minutes for the spaghetti). Garnish with the spring onion (or chives), and serve hot.

CHRYSANTHEMUM FLOWERS (Tsa Chiu Hwa)

difficult
preparation 10 minutes
cooking 1 minute per 'flower'
serves 3 to 4

YOU NEED
2 oz (50 g) *fenszu* (transparent noodles)
4 oz (100 g) shelled shrimp (or minced beef)
6–8 water chestnuts (optional)
2 oz (50 g) lard
½ tsp salt
1 unbeaten egg white
1 pinch pepper
½ tbsp cornflour
2 pints (1 litre) oil for frying

CONDIMENT (optional)
1 large carrot
½ tsp tabasco (or hot pepper oil)
Prepare the condiment by passing the carrot

through a blender or Mouli or by crushing it with the flat side of a cleaver. Combine the carrot and tabasco and set aside.

With scissors, cut the dry *fenszu* into pieces about 1" (2.5 cm) long. To prevent the *fenszu* from scattering about while being cut, put it inside a paper bag. Finely chop the shrimp and crush the water chestnuts. Mix the shrimp (or mince), water chestnuts, egg white, salt, pepper, cornflour and lard. Form small, flat patties about 1½" (3 cm) in diamater with equal portions of the mixture. Press the patties into the cut *fenszu*, covering well. In a deep pan, heat the oil until a piece of *fenszu*, dropped in, returns immediately to the surface and puffs up. Slide the patties into the hot oil and fry for 1 minute. Drain on absorbent kitchen paper. Garnish the centre of each patty (flower) with condiment. Serve hot.

FISH NOODLE SOUP (Hwang Yü Mein)
easy
preparation 15 minutes/marinade 10 minutes
cooking 12 to 18 minutes
serves 2

YOU NEED
4 oz (100 g) Chinese egg noodles (or spaghetti)
3 oz (80 g) shelled shrimp (or 1 oz (25 g) dried shrimp)
1 small fish fillet, about 4 oz (100 g)
1 carrot (optional)
1 stick celery (or water chestnuts)
2 spring onions (or leek)
2 slices fresh ginger (or ¼ tsp powdered)
2 tbsp oil

MARINADE A (shrimp)
¼ tsp salt
1 tsp dry sherry

MARINADE B (fish fillet)
½ tsp salt
1 tsp dry sherry
1 good pinch powdered ginger

SEASONING
½ tsp salt
½ tsp sugar
1 tbsp soy sauce
1 tsp dry sherry
1 pint (½ litre) water

If you are using dried shrimp, wash them, then soak in warm water for 15 minutes or until soft. Bring to the boil a large saucepan of salted water. Add 1 tbsp oil and the noodles, separating them with a fork. Cook at a fast boil for 3 minutes (6 minutes for the spaghetti) or until half-cooked. Drain and set aside. In 2 bowls, prepare the marinades A and B. Mix the shrimp with marinade A and set aside for 10 minutes. Cut the fish fillet into bite-sized pieces about ½" × 1" (1.25 cm × 2.5 cm). Mix with marinade B and set aside. Cut into matchstick-thin strips the spring onion (or leek), fresh ginger, celery (or water chestnuts) and carrot. Prepare the seasoning and set aside. In a heavy saucepan, heat 1 tbsp oil until almost smoking. Stir-fry the spring onion (or leek) and ginger for 30 seconds. Add the fish fillet and stir-fry for 2 minutes. Toss in the shrimp and continue to stir-fry for 1 minute. Pour in the seasoning and bring to the boil. Incorporate the noodles (or spaghetti), carrot and celery (or water chestnuts). Bring back to the boil and cook rapidly until the noodles (or spaghetti) are tender, about 3 minutes (6 minutes for the spaghetti). Remove from heat and serve at once.

HARD FRIED NOODLES CALLED CHOW MEIN (Kwang Chou Ch'au Mein)
difficult
preparation 40 minutes
cooking 16 to 20 minutes
serves 3 to 4

YOU NEED
½ lb (250 g) Chinese egg noodles (or spaghetti)
4 oz (100 g) raw or cooked pork
4 oz (100 g) spinach (or mustard greens or endive)
3 oz (80 g) shelled shrimp
3 oz (80 g) chicken (or giblets)
1 carrot
2 dried Chinese mushrooms (optional)
2 spring onions (or leek)
1 tbsp dry sherry
5 tbsp oil

MARINADE A (shrimp)
1 pinch salt
1 tsp cornflour
½ unbeaten egg white

MARINADE B (raw pork)
1 tsp cornflour
1 tsp soy sauce
½ unbeaten egg white

SEASONING A
1 tbsp soy sauce
1 tbsp sesame oil (or other)

SEASONING B
1 tbsp cornflour
1 tsp soy sauce
1 tsp sesame oil (optional)
½ pint (¼ litre) chicken stock (1 stock cube)

Wash the dried mushrooms and soak in warm water for 10 minutes. Drain, remove the hard stalks and cut each mushroom into 4 pieces. Bring to the boil a large saucepan of salted water. Add 1 tbsp oil and the noodles (or spaghetti). Cook rapidly for 4 minutes (8 minutes for the spaghetti), half-cooked. Meanwhile, prepare seasoning A in a large bowl. Drain the noodles, rinse and mix with seasoning A. Prepare marinade A, add the shrimp and set aside for 5 minutes. Cut the pork against the grain into thin strips. If the pork is raw, mix with marinade B and set aside for 5 minutes. Cut into matchstick-thin strips the chicken (or giblets), carrot and spring onion (or leek). Clean the spinach (or mustard green or endive) and cut diagonally into 2 or 3 strips. Prepare the seasoning B. In a frying pan, heat 2 tbsp oil until almost smoking, then reduce the heat to medium/low. Add the noodles (or spaghetti) and brown on both sides, about 10 minutes. In a deep, heavy pan, heat 2 tbsp oil until almost smoking. Stir-fry the spring onion (or leek) and mushrooms for 20 seconds. Add the pork and stir-fry for 1 minute. Sprinkle with the dry sherry and stir. Incorporate the shrimp, chicken, carrot and seasoning B. Bring to the boil, drop in the spinach (or mustard greens or endive) and cook for 1 minute. Place the noodles (or spaghetti) in a serving dish, add the vegetables and meat and serve at once.

MIXED NOODLE SALAD (Liang Mein)
fairly easy
preparation 30 minutes
cooking 7 to 12 minutes
serves 4

This exotic dish is a complete meal in itself.

YOU NEED
6 oz (200 g) Chinese egg noodles (or spaghetti)
4 oz (100 g) cooked chicken (or turkey)
4 oz (100 g) ham (or cooked pork or beef)
4 oz (100 g) shelled cooked shrimp (optional)
¼ tsp dry sherry
1 egg
1 pinch salt
1½ tbsp oil

CHOICE OF THREE
4 oz (100 g) bean sprouts
4 oz (100 g) green peas
4 oz (100 g) bamboo shoots
½ head cabbage (or Chinese cabbage)
2 sticks celery (or 4 oz water chestnuts)
1 small cucumber
1 carrot
1 green pepper
1 leek

DRESSING
1 from the dressings given in the next recipe

Prepare the chosen dressing and pour half of it into a large salad bowl. Bring to the boil a large saucepan of salted water. Add 1 tbsp oil and drop in the noodles (or spaghetti). Cook at a fast boil for 5 minutes (10 minutes for the spaghetti) until barely tender. Drain, rinse and mix the noodles (or spaghetti) with the sauce in the salad bowl. Cover and set aside. Cut the 3 chosen vegetables into matchstick-thin strips. Pass through boiling water for 1 minute the leek, bamboo shoots, green pepper, bean sprouts, green peas; then plunge into cold water. Beat the egg with a pinch of salt and the sherry. In a small frying pan, heat ½ tbsp oil until almost smoking. Pour in the beaten egg, rolling the pan to make a thin omelette. Brown quickly on both sides, then remove from the pan. Roll the omelette tightly and cut crosswise into thin strips. Cut into matchstick-thin strips the chicken (or turkey) and the ham (or pork or beef). Cut the shrimp into halves lengthwise. Drain the vegetables which have been plunged in cold water. Arrange on top of the noodles: the chicken (or turkey), ham (or pork or beef), shrimp and vegetables. Garnish with the strips of omelette and chill in the refrigerator. Before serving, pour the remainder of the dressing over the salad and toss.

DRESSINGS FOR MIXED NOODLE SALAD (Liang Pan Ju)

Red Oil Dressing (Hung Yu Ju)

YOU NEED

4 tbsp soy sauce
1 tbsp sugar
2 spring onions (or shallot or chives)
2 slices fresh ginger (or $\frac{1}{3}$ tsp powdered)
1$\frac{1}{2}$ tbsp sesame oil (or other)
1$\frac{1}{2}$ tbsp vinegar (or lemon juice)
1–2 tsp tabasco (or hot pepper oil)

Finely chop the spring onion (or shallot or chives) and fresh ginger.
Combine all ingredients and mix well.

Ginger Vinegar Dressing (Ch'aing Tsu Ju)

YOU NEED

1$\frac{1}{2}$ tbsp vinegar (or lemon juice)
5 slices fresh ginger (or 1 tsp powdered)
4 tbsp soy sauce
1 tbsp sugar

Peel and finely chop the fresh ginger.
Combine all ingredients and mix well.

Soy Vinegar (Chia Ch'ang Ju)

YOU NEED

1 pinch salt to taste
$\frac{1}{2}$ tbsp sugar
1 tbsp vinegar (or lemon juice)
1 tsp tabasco (or hot pepper oil)

Combine all ingredients and blend well.

Sesame Dressing (Pang Pang Ju)

YOU NEED

1 pinch salt
1 tbsp sugar
4 tbsp sesame paste (or peanut butter)
4 tbsp soy sauce
1 tbsp vinegar (or lemon juice)
3 tbsp sesame oil
2 spring onions (or shallot or chives)
2 slices fresh ginger (or $\frac{1}{3}$ tsp powdered)

Mince the spring onion (or shallot or chives) and fresh ginger.
Mix well all the ingredients. This dressing, although thick, is absorbed very well.

NOODLE SOUP OF LONG LIFE (Taiwan Lu Mein)

fairly easy
preparation 20 minutes
cooking 12 to 19 minutes
serves 2 to 3

For the Chinese, noodles symbolize long life. Thus, for birthday gatherings, marriage celebrations and feast days, they are served at the lunch which precedes the long evening banquet. The guests are expected to eat great quantities of the noodles, thereby demonstrating their sincere hope that the person honoured may live a long and happy life. Here is my family's recipe for such occasions.

YOU NEED

4 oz (100 g) Chinese egg noodles (or spaghetti)
4 oz (100 g) pork (or ham)
3 oz (80 g) shelled shrimp (or 1 oz (20 g) dried shrimp)
2 dried Chinese mushrooms
3 black fungus called cloud ears (optional)
1 egg
$\frac{1}{2}$ cucumber (or bamboo shoots or radish)
1 spring onion (or leek)
$\frac{1}{2}$ tsp dried minced shallot (or onion)
1 clove garlic (optional)
1 tbsp sherry
2 tbsp oil

SEASONING
1 tbsp soy sauce
½ tsp salt
1½ pints (¾ litre) chicken stock (2 stock cubes)

THICKENING
1 tbsp cornflour dissolved in
1 tbsp water

Wash the dried mushrooms, cloud ears and dried shrimp. Cover each with warm water to soak for 10 minutes or until soft. Drain, remove the hard stalks of the mushrooms and cut the mushrooms and cloud ears into 4 pieces. Bring to the boil a large saucepan of salted water. Add 1 tbsp oil and drop in the noodles (or spaghetti). Boil rapidly for 5 minutes (12 minutes for the spaghetti), until barely tender. Drain, place in a large soup dish and cover to keep warm. Cut the pork (or ham) into ½" (1.5 cm) cubes. Peel the cucumber, de-seed and cut into ½" (1.5 cm) cubes. Mince the spring onion and garlic. Beat the egg. In 2 bowls, prepare the seasoning and thickening and set aside. In a large, heavy saucepan, heat 1 tbsp oil. Sauté the dried minced onion for 10 seconds. Add the dried Chinese mushrooms and pork (or ham), stir-frying for 2 minutes. Incorporate the shrimp and sprinkle with sherry. Stir-fry for 1 minute. Add the cucumber and seasoning, then bring to the boil. Boil until the cucumber becomes transparent, about 2 minutes. Incorporate the thickening and cook for 1 minute (until thickened). Pour in the beaten egg in a slow, steady stream and cook 20 seconds. Add the spring onion (or leek) and cloud ears. Cook 1 minute more, then, remove from the heat. Pour the soup over the noodles and garnish with the minced garlic. Serve hot.

NOODLE SOUP WITH DEEP FRIED PORK (P'ai Ku T'ang Mein)
rather difficult
preparation 10 minutes/marinade 30 minutes
cooking 12 to 16 minutes
serves 2

YOU NEED
4 oz (100 g) Chinese egg noodles (or spaghetti)
2 pork chops (or chicken thighs or legs)
2 oz (60 g) dill pickles
1 egg yolk
1 tbsp cornflour
1 tbsp flour
1½ pint (¼ litre) chicken stock (1 stock cube)
1 pint (½ litre) oil for frying

MARINADE
½ tsp salt
1 pinch of pepper
½ tbsp dry sherry
½ tbsp soy sauce
½ tbsp vinegar
½ tsp sesame oil (optional)

SEASONING
½ tsp salt
1 tsp soy sauce
½ tbsp dry sherry
1 dash tabasco (optional)
1 tsp sesame oil (optional)

Combine the marinade ingredients and rub into the pork chops. Marinate for 30 minutes. Meanwhile, cut the pickles into long, thin strips. Mix the cornflour and flour in a shallow dish. Beat the egg yolk. Bring to the boil a large saucepan of salted water. Add 1 tbsp oil and the noodles (or spaghetti), separating them with a fork. Cook at a fast boil for 5 minutes (12 minutes for the spaghetti) or until just tender. Drain, then place the noodles (or spaghetti) in a soup dish. Cover and keep warm. In a deep pan, heat the oil over a medium/hot flame or until a piece of bread, thrown in, returns to the surface and browns in 60 seconds. Dip the pork chops (or chicken) into the egg, then roll them in the flour/cornflour mixture. Plunge into the hot oil and fry for 2 minutes. Increase the heat to high and fry for 1 minute more. Drain on absorbent kitchen paper, then place on top of the noodles. Bring to the boil the chicken stock. Add the pickles and the seasoning ingredients. Boil for 2 minutes, then pour the soup over the noodles. Serve hot.

PLAIN FRIED NOODLES (Suh Ch'au Mein)
very easy
preparation 5 minutes
cooking 14 to 20 minutes
serves 3 to 4

YOU NEED

¼ lb (250 g) Chinese egg noodles (or spaghetti)
1 spring onion (or chives or celery)
2 tbsp oil

SEASONING

1 pinch pepper
1 tbsp sesame oil (or other)
2 tbsp soy sauce
1 pinch monosodium glutamate (optional)

Bring to the boil a large saucepan of lightly salted water. Add the oil and drop in the noodles (or spaghetti). Boil rapidly for 4 minutes (10 minutes for the spaghetti) or until just barely tender. Meanwhile, mix the seasoning in a large bowl. Drain the noodles (or spaghetti), rinse and combine with the seasoning. Finely chop the spring onion. In a pan, heat 1 tbsp oil until almost smoking, then lower the heat to medium/low. Drop in the noodles (or spaghetti) and brown well, stirring frequently, 10 to 12 minutes. Garnish with the chopped spring onion and serve hot.

SOFT FRIED NOODLES WITH PORK (Shin Chin Ch'au Mein)

fairly difficult
preparation 20 minutes/marinade 10 minutes
cooking 12 to 15 minutes
serves 3 to 4

YOU NEED

6 oz (200 g) Chinese egg noodles (or spaghetti)
½ lb (250 g) raw or cooked pork (or chicken)
¼ head cabbage (or see Tips & Tricks)
1 carrot
2 sticks celery
3 spring onions (or leek)
2 eggs
1 pinch salt
½ tsp dry sherry
4 tbsp oil

MARINADE (for raw pork)

¼ tsp salt
½ tsp soy sauce
½ tsp dry sherry

SEASONING

½ tsp salt
½ tsp pepper
1 tbsp dry sherry
2 tbsp soy sauce

Bring to the boil a large saucepan of salted water. Add 1 tbsp oil and drop in the noodles (or spaghetti). Cook at a fast boil 3 minutes (6 minutes for the spaghetti) or until half-cooked, then drain. Cut the pork (or chicken) into matchstick-strips; if raw, mix the marinade and set aside for 10 minutes. Cut into matchstick-thin strips the spring onion (or leek), carrot, cabbage and celery. Prepare the seasoning and set aside. Beat the eggs with a pinch of salt and the sherry. In a small frying pan, heat ½ tbsp oil until almost smoking. Pour in half of the beaten egg, rolling the pan to make a thin omelette. Brown on both sides and remove from the pan. Add ½ tbsp oil to the pan and re-heat. Repeat the same procedure with the remainder of the beaten egg. Roll the omelette tightly and cut crosswise into thin strips. In a deep frying pan, heat 2 tbsp oil until almost smoking. Stir-fry the spring onion (or leek) for 10 seconds. Add the pork (or chicken) and stir-fry for 1 minute. Incorporate the seasoning, cabbage and carrot, stir and cook for 30 seconds. Pour in the chicken stock and bring to the boil. Add the noodles (or spaghetti) and cook rapidly until all liquid has been absorbed, about 5 minutes. Add celery and strips of omelette. Remove from heat and serve at once.

TIPS & TRICKS

Almost any vegetable may replace those indicated above: mushrooms, green peppers, onions, celeriac, water chestnuts, bamboo shoots and so on. This is a dish in which you can use whatever you have on hand.

SOFT FRIED NOODLES WITH SHRIMP (Hsiah Jen Ch'au Mein)

fairly easy
preparation 15 minutes
cooking 10 to 15 minutes
serves 3 to 4

YOU NEED

6 oz (200 g) Chinese egg noodles (or spaghetti)
4 oz (100 g) shelled shrimp, fresh or frozen
4 oz (100 g) pork
1 medium onion (or spring onion or leek)
½ pint (¼ litre) oil for frying

MARINADE A (shrimp)

1 tsp cornflour
1 pinch salt
1 tsp dry sherry

MARINADE B (pork)

1 tsp cornflour
1 tsp soy sauce

SEASONING

1 good pinch each salt and pepper to taste
½ tsp sugar
1 tbsp soy sauce
1 tsp sesame oil (optional)

THICKENING (optional)

½ tbsp cornflour dissolved in
½ tbsp water

Bring to the boil a large saucepan of salted water. Add 1 tbsp oil and drop in the noodles (or spaghetti). Boil rapidly 3 minutes (6 minutes for the spaghetti) or until half-cooked, then drain. Mix the shrimp with the marinade A and set aside. Cut the pork against the grain into thin strips. Mix with the marinade B and set aside. Cut the onion into thin strips. In 2 bowls, prepare the seasoning and the thickening. In a deep frying pan, heat the oil until almost smoking. Plunge in the shrimp and fry for 1 minute. Drain on absorbent kitchen paper. Fry the pork for 1 minute, then drain. Leave only 2 tbsp oil in the pan and re-heat. Sauté the onion (spring onion or leek) until soft, 1 to 2 minutes. Add the seasoning, pork and noodles (or spaghetti). Reduce the heat and simmer, while stirring, until all liquid is absorbed, 3 to 4 minutes. Add the shrimp and cook, continuing to stir, for 1 minute more. Pour in the thickening, stir and remove from heat. Serve hot.

SPRING NOODLE SOUP (Yang Chu Mein)

easy
preparation 5 minutes
cooking 45 minutes
serves 2 to 3

The name of this soup in Chinese means 'spring sun' for, after eating it, one feels as happy and as warm as a sunny, spring day.

YOU NEED

4 oz (100 g) Chinese egg noodles (or spaghetti)
½ lb (250 g) bean sprouts (optional)
2–3 spring onions (or chives)
1 small loin or spring pork roast (or pork bones), about 1 lb (500 g)
½ tsp salt
1 tbsp oil
3 pints (1½ litres) water

SEASONING

½ tsp salt
1 tsp sesame oil
1 dash tabasco (optional)
½ tsp monosodium glutamate (optional)
1½ tsp soy sauce

Place the pork in a large saucepan, cover with the water and add the salt. Bring to the boil, lower the heat and simmer for 45 minutes or longer. Meanwhile, bring to the boil another large saucepan of salted water. Add 1 tbsp oil and drop in the noodles (or spaghetti), separating them with a fork. Cook at a fast boil for 5 minutes (10 minutes for the spaghetti) or until barely tender. Drain, rinse and place in a deep serving dish. Cover to keep warm. Bring to the boil enough water to cover the bean sprouts. Pass the sprouts through the boiling water for 30 seconds. Drain and add to the noodles (or spaghetti). Finely chop the spring onion (or chives). Remove the pork from the broth and cut into thin slices. Arrange the slices on top of the noodles (or spaghetti). Garnish with the spring onion (or chives). Add the seasoning to the broth, stir and bring back to the boil. Pour the broth over the noodles and serve hot.

STIR-FRIED FENSZU WITH LAMB (Yang Jou Fen Szu)
rather difficult
preparation 10 minutes
cooking 35 to 40 minutes
serves 2 to 3

YOU NEED

4 oz (100 g) *fenszu* (transparent noodles)
⅗ lb (300 g) de-boned lamb
1½ pints (¾ litre) water
2 turnips (optional)
2 spring onions (or leek)
2 tbsp dry sherry
3 cloves garlic
2 slices ginger (or ⅓ teaspoon powdered)
1 pinch pepper
1 tbsp oil

SEASONING A

1 tbsp soy sauce
1 tbsp dry sherry
1 tsp rock candy (or brown sugar)
¼ pint (⅛ litre) water

SEASONING B

1 tsp salt
1 tsp dry sherry

Soak the *fenszu* in warm water 1 to 2 minutes. Drain and, with scissors, cut it into 3 or 4 lengths. Peel the turnips and cut them into 3 or 4 pieces. Shred the fresh ginger and spring onion (or leek). Crush the garlic. Cut the lamb into even, bite-sized pieces. In a large saucepan, bring 1 pint water to the boil. Drop the turnips into the boiling water and cook rapidly for 5 minutes. Add the lamb and the sherry. Boil for 2 minutes. Drain and rinse the lamb under cold running water. (Discard the turnips.) In a large

saucepan, bring to the boil seasoning A. Add the ginger, spring onion (or leek) and lamb. Cook until the sauce has been completely absorbed and the lamb dry, 25 to 30 minutes. Remove from heat. In a deep frying pan, heat 1 tbsp oil until almost smoking. Brown the garlic for 30 seconds. Pour in ½ pint (¼ litre) water and bring to the boil. Incorporate the lamb, seasoning B and the *fenszu*. Bring back to the boil and cook rapidly for 2 minutes. Add a pinch of pepper and remove from heat. Serve very hot.

STIR-FRIED RICE NOODLES (Ch'au Mi Fen)
easy
preparation 15 minutes
cooking 16 minutes
serves 3 to 4

YOU NEED
⅓ lb (150 g) rice noodles
⅓ lb (150 g) bean sprouts (or cabbage)
4 oz (100 g) lean pork (or beef, chicken or ham)
4 oz (100 g) shelled shrimp (optional)
1 medium-sized onion
1 carrot
1 green pepper (or celery)
2 eggs
1 pinch salt
1 tbsp + ½ tsp dry sherry
6 tbsp oil

SEASONING
½ tsp salt
1 pinch pepper
3 tbsp soy sauce
1 pint (½ litre) water

Bring to the boil a large saucepan of water to pour over the noodles. Place the noodles in a drainer, being careful not to break them. Pour the boiling water over the noodles and drain. Prepare the seasoning and set aside. Cut into matchstick-thin strips the pork (or beef, chicken or ham), onion, green pepper (or celery) and carrot. Beat the eggs with a pinch of salt and ½ tsp sherry. In a frying pan, heat ½ tbsp oil until almost smoking. Pour in half of the beaten egg, rolling the pan to make a thin omelette. Brown quickly on both sides, then, remove from the pan. Add ½ tbsp oil to the pan and re-heat. Repeat the same procedure with the remainder of the beaten egg. Roll each omelette tightly and cut crosswise into thin strips. In a deep frying pan, heat 4 tbsp oil until almost smoking. Stir-fry the onion for 1 minute. Add the pork (or beef, chicken or ham) and shrimp. Sprinkle with 1 tbsp sherry and stir-fry for 1 minute. Pour in the seasoning and bring to the boil. Incorporate the noodles and reduce the heat to medium/low. Simmer until the liquid is completely absorbed, about 10 minutes. Add the carrot,

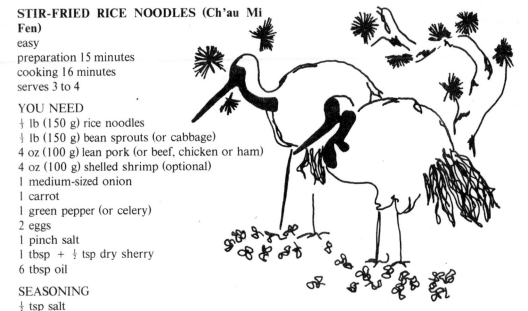

bean sprouts (or cabbage) and green pepper (or celery) as well as 1 tbsp oil. Stir, add the strips of omelette and serve at once.

SZECHWAN NOODLES (Sau Ch'uan Tan Mein)
very easy
preparation 4 minutes
cooking 14 minutes
serves 3 to 4

YOU NEED
6 oz (200 g) Chinese egg noodles (or spaghetti)
½ lb (250 g) bean sprouts (or see Tips & Tricks)
1 tbsp oil

SEASONING

1 spring onion (or leek or shallot)
1 tbsp sesame paste (or peanut butter)
6 tbsp chicken stock (1 stock cube)
2 tbsp soy sauce
2 tsp vinegar
$\frac{1}{2}$ tsp tabasco (or hot pepper oil)
1 tbsp sesame oil

Bring to the boil a large saucepan of salted water for the noodles (or spaghetti). Add 1 tbsp oil and drop in the noodles (or spaghetti). Boil rapidly for 6 minutes (12 minutes for the spaghetti) or until they are just cooked and barely tender ('al dente'). Drain, rinse and place the noodles in a large serving bowl. Cover to keep warm. In a saucepan, bring to the boil enough water to cover the bean sprouts. Pass the sprouts through the boiling water for 30 seconds. Drain and add to the noodles. Finely chop the spring onion (or leek or shallot). In a small saucepan, bring to the boil the chicken stock. Add the other seasoning ingredients. Bring back to the boil, stirring constantly, then remove from heat. Pour the seasoning over the noodles (or spaghetti) and bean sprouts. Toss and serve hot or warm.

TIPS & TRICKS

The bean sprouts may be replaced by green pepper, fennel, celery, celeriac, etc. Cut the chosen vegetables into matchstick-thin strips before passing it through boiling water for 1 minute.

PORK (Chu Jou)

We believe that the pig's mission in life is simply to be eaten. Pork is the favourite meat of the Chinese. In fact, legend has it that a poor sidewalk vendor became a millionaire by just selling pork chops!

The texture and taste of pork contrasts and blends delectably with many other ingredients and a very small quantity of pork, combined with vegetables, noodles or rice can create a delicious Chinese meal. The majority of our pork dishes are prepared using lean pork. Highly recommended are any of the shoulder, hind or loin parts from which the meat may be cut, using the bones for soup.

Pork may be adapted to any method of Chinese cooking, but whatever the method, pork should always be tested to make sure it is thoroughly cooked.

BARBECUED SPARERIBS I (Kau P'ai Ku)
easy
preparation 10 minutes / marinade 2 hours
cooking 50 to 60 minutes
serves 3 to 4

YOU NEED
2 lb (1 kg) spareribs (or pork chops or loin)

MARINADE
2 slices fresh ginger (or ⅓ tsp powdered)
1 spring onion (or shallot or onion)
1 tbsp sugar
5 tbsp soy sauce
2 tbsp dry sherry

Pre-heat your oven to a moderate temperature (electricity 350°, gas regulo 4). Prepare the marinade, cutting the spring onion in half and leaving the ginger slices whole. Cut the ribs apart, slicing between the bones with a sharp knife. Mix with the marinade and set aside for 2 hours, turning from time to time. Cover the bottom of a baking pan with aluminium foil. Place the ribs on the foil and brush with the marinade. Bake the ribs, basting every 10 minutes or so with the marinade, for 50 to 60 minutes or until done. Serve hot.

BARBECUED SPARERIBS II (Chiu P'ai Ku)
easy
preparation 10 minutes / marinade 30 minutes
cooking 50 minutes
serves 3 to 4

YOU NEED
2 lb (1 kg) spareribs (or pork chops or loin)

MARINADE
1 clove garlic
½ tsp salt
2 tbsp sugar
½ tsp five-spice powder (or all-spice)
2 tbsp soy sauce

1 tbsp dry sherry
2 tbsp hoisen sauce (or ketchup)

Crush the garlic and combine all marinade ingredients. Cut apart the ribs, slicing between the bones with a sharp knife. Mix with the marinade and set aside for 30 minutes. Pre-heat your oven to a moderate temperature (electricity 350°, gas regulo 4). Cover the bottom of a baking pan with aluminium foil. Place the ribs on the foil and brush with the marinade. Bake for 50 to 60 minutes or until done, basting every 10 minutes or so with the marinade. Serve hot.

BRAISED SPARERIBS I (Mong P'ai Ku)

very easy
preparation 5 minutes
cooking 2 to 2½ hours
serves 3 to 4

YOU NEED
2 lb (1 kg) spareribs
1 tbsp sugar
2 tbsp dry sherry
3 tbsp soy sauce
1 pint (½ litre) water

Cut the ribs apart, slicing between them with a sharp knife. Place in a large, heavy saucepan and cover with the water. Bring to the boil, then lower the heat. Simmer, without covering, until the water is reduced to approximately ¼ pint (⅛ litre) 1 to 1¼ hours. Add the soy sauce, sugar and sherry. Continue to simmer until all liquid is absorbed, 45 to 50 minutes. Remove from heat and serve.

BRAISED SPARERIBS II (Mong P'ai Ku)

very easy
preparation 5 minutes
cooking 2 to 2½ hours
serves 3 to 4

YOU NEED
2 lb (1 kg) spareribs
1 tbsp soy sauce
1 tbsp dry sherry
2 tbsp hoisen sauce (or 1 tbsp each ketchup, soy sauce, and honey or sugar)
1 pint (½ litre) water

Cut the ribs apart, slicing between the bones with a sharp knife. Put the ribs into a large, heavy saucepan and cover with the water. Bring to the boil over medium heat. Lower the heat and simmer, uncovered, until the water is reduced to approximately ¼ pint (⅛ litre), 1 to 1¼ hours. Add the soy sauce, hoisen sauce and sherry. Continue to simmer until the liquid is completely absorbed, 45 to 60 minutes. Remove from heat and serve.

CHINESE ROAST PORK (Ch'a Shao Jou)

very easy
preparation 5 minutes/marinade 2 hours
cooking 40 minutes
serves 2 to 3

This is the same roast pork, coloured red, that you will see hung in the windows of the Hong Kong grocers and in Chinese neighbourhoods the world over.

YOU NEED
1 pork fillet, ⅘–1 lb (400–500 g)

MARINADE
½ tsp salt
2 tbsp sugar
1 tbsp soy sauce
2 tbsp dry sherry
4–6 drops red food colouring (optional)

Prepare the marinade. Cut the pork into several big slices about 2" (5 cm) thick. Mix with the marinade and set aside for 2 hours. From time to time, prick the meat with a fork so that the marinade will penetrate deeply. Pre-heat your oven to medium/hot (electricity 375°, gas regulo 5–6). Drain the pork (reserving the marinade, see Tips & Tricks) and place it in an ovenproof dish. Bake for 40 minutes or until done. Remove from the oven and serve hot or cold.

TIPS & TRICKS
The remaining marinade may be used to season stir-fried rice or noodles.

87

MARINATED PIGS' FEET (Pai Yun Chu Shou)

easy

preparation 5 minutes/marinade 12 hours (see
Tips & Tricks)

cooking 1½ hours

serves 2 to 3

The Chinese like to personalize the pig, the bear
and so on, calling the dishes prepared from
certain parts of these animals by poetic rather
than real names. In the case of this recipe, the
pigs' feet become 'hands' and the marinade,
'clouds', giving it the charming name of 'Cloudy
Pigs' Hands'.

YOU NEED

2–3 pigs' feet

MARINADE

4 oz (100 g) sugar

½ tbsp salt

¼ pint (⅛ litre) vinegar

Bring to the boil a large saucepan of water.
Plunge in the pigs' feet. Boil for 5 minutes, then
drain, discarding the water. Bring to the boil
enough water to cover the pigs' feet. Plunge in
the pigs' feet and bring back to the boil. Reduce
the heat, cover and simmer for 1½ hours or until
the pigs' feet are tender but firm. Drain
(reserving the cooking liquor to make a jelly if so
desired; see Tips & Tricks). Plunge the feet into
ice-cold water for 1 hour. Add ice cubes from
time to time to keep the water very cold.
Meantime, bring to the boil the marinade
ingredients. Boil for 1 minute or until the sugar
is dissolved. Remove from the heat and allow to
cool. Drain the pigs' feet and mix with the
marinade. Place in the refrigerator overnight
(see Tips and Tricks). Serve cold.

TIPS & TRICKS

If you do not have time to marinate the pigs' feet
overnight, add them to the marinade while it is
boiling and cook rapidly for 20 minutes.
Remove from the heat, allow to cool and serve.
Make a jelly from the cooking liquor, adding a
little minced celery, ham and parsley as well as
salt to taste. Serve the jelly with the pigs' feet.

PARSLEY PORK (Kau Li Jou)

easy

preparation 10 minutes/marinade 10 minutes

cooking 4 minutes

serves 2 to 3

YOU NEED

½ lb (250 g) lean pork

3 tbsp flour

1 bunch Chinese or common parsley (or celery
leaves)

1 pint (½ litre) oil for frying

MARINADE

½ tsp salt

1 good pinch pepper

1 tsp cornflour

½ tsp sesame oil (optional)

FRITTER BATTER

½ tsp salt

3 tbsp flour

1 egg

1 tbsp water

Prepare the marinade. Cut the pork against the
grain into slices ½" (1 cm) thick. Mix with the
marinade and set aside for 10 minutes.
Meanwhile, finely mince the parsley. Prepare
the batter and add the parsley, mixing well. In a
deep frying pan, heat the oil until almost
smoking. Roll the pork slices in the flour, then
dip into the batter. Plunge into the hot oil and
fry 3 to 4 minutes or until done. Drain on
absorbent kitchen paper. Serve immediately
accompanied by Chinese mustard, or prepared
mustard.

PORK FRITTERS (Pao Jou)

easy

preparation 10 minutes/marinade 5 minutes

cooking 4 minutes per fritter

serves 2 to 3

YOU NEED
½ lb (250 g) lean pork (or fish fillet)
2 pints (1 litre) oil for frying

MARINADE
½ tsp soy sauce
½ tsp dry sherry
¼ tsp sesame oil (optional)

FRITTER BATTER
2½ tbsp flour
1 tsp sugar
1 pinch pepper
½ tsp salt
1 egg
1 tbsp water
½ tbsp lard (or oil)

Prepare the marinade. Cut the pork into even, bite-sized pieces. Mix with the marinade and set aside for 5 minutes. Prepare the fritter batter. In a deep frying pan, heat the oil to medium/hot (375°). When a piece of bread, thrown in, returns to the surface and browns in 45 seconds, the oil will be at the right temperature. Dip the pork pieces into the batter, then plunge into the hot oil. Fry for 3 minutes. Increase the heat to its highest temperature and fry another 30 seconds. Drain on absorbent kitchen paper. Serve hot.

PORK SHOULDER IN RED SAUCE (Hong Shau T'i Pang)
easy
preparation 5 minutes/marinade 2 to 3 hours
cooking 2 hours 30 minutes
serves 4

YOU NEED
1 pork shoulder (or knuckle), about 2 lb (1 kg)
1 tbsp sugar

MARINADE
1 tsp salt
2 cloves garlic
2 tbsp soy sauce

SEASONING
1 good pinch powdered ginger
1 star anise (optional)
1 tbsp dry sherry
½ pint (¼ litre) water

Pre-heat your oven to a moderate temperature (electricity 350°, gas regulo 4). Mince finely the garlic and combine all marinade ingredients. Rub the marinade into the shoulder. Marinate for 2 to 3 hours, turning the shoulder over from time to time. Place the shoulder in an ovenproof dish with a lid or which can be covered with aluminium foil. Add the seasoning. Bake, covered, for 30 minutes. Sprinkle the shoulder with the sugar and reduce the oven temperature to warm/cool (electricity 300°, gas regulo 1–2). Bake, covered, for 2 hours more until tender, turning from time to time. Remove from the oven and slice thinly. Arrange the slices on a serving dish and cover with the sauce. Serve hot or cold.

TIPS & TRICKS
In China, this dish is most frequently cooked on top of the stove. Boil the shoulder for 5 minutes, then reduce the heat and simmer for 2 to 3 hours or until tender. Add water during the cooking if necessary. We like to serve the shoulder on a bed of stir-fried spinach and accompanied by steamed rice or a noodle soup.

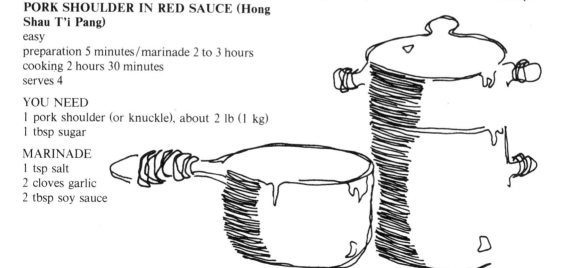

PORK WITH PEANUTS (Suan Ts'ai Hua Sheng Mi)

easy
preparation 10 minutes
cooking 4 minutes
serves 2 to 3

This is a typical family dish, usually served with steamed rice.

YOU NEED

¼ lb (150 g) minced pork
2½ oz (75 g) peanuts
2–3 cloves garlic
½ lb (250 g) sauerkraut (or Chinese pickled mustard greens)
4 oz (100 g) string beans fresh or frozen
1 tsp sugar
1 tbsp dry sherry
2 tbsp oil

THICKENING

1 tbsp cornflour
¼ tsp monosodium glutamate (optional)
¼ pint (⅛ litre) water

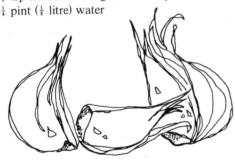

Cut the string beans on the diagonal into 1" lengths. (If fresh, pass them through boiling water for 5 minutes.) Mince the garlic finely. Prepare the thickening and set aside. In a frying pan, heat 1 tbsp oil. Stir-fry the sauerkraut (or pickled mustard greens), sprinkled with the sugar for 1 minute. Remove from the pan. Add 1 tbsp oil to the pan and re-heat until almost smoking. Stir-fry the garlic 30 seconds. Sprinkle with the sherry, then add the minced pork. Stir-fry for 2 minutes. Incorporate the string beans and stir-fry for 30 seconds. Add the sauerkraut (or pickled mustard greens) and stir and cook for 30 seconds. Pour in the thickening and stir and cook for 30 seconds (until thickened).

Incorporate the peanuts, stir and remove from the heat. Serve hot.

RED COOKED PIGS' FEET (Hong Men Chu Chiau)

easy
preparation 5 minutes
cooking 4 hours
serves 2 to 3

YOU NEED

2–3 pigs' feet
2 pints (1 litre) water

SEASONING

3–4 star anise
1 spring onion (or leek)
1 slice fresh ginger (or 1 good pinch powdered)
1 tbsp sugar
1 pinch pepper
1 tbsp dry sherry
3 tbsp soy sauce

THICKENING

½ tbsp cornflour dissolved in
1 tbsp water

Bring to the boil a large saucepan of water. Plunge the pigs' feet into the boiling water and cook for 5 minutes. Drain, discarding the water. Put the pigs' feet back into the saucepan and cover with the cold water. Add the seasoning ingredients. Leave the spring onion and ginger slice whole. Bring to the boil, reduce the heat and cover. Simmer 3 to 4 hours or until the pigs' feet are tender and falling apart. Bring back to the boil and cook rapidly until all liquid has been absorbed. Add the thickening and cook, stirring, for 30 seconds. Remove from the heat. Serve accompanied by stir-fried spinach.

RED COOKED PORK (Tsiang Jou)

easy
preparation 5 minutes
cooking 1 hour 5 minutes
serves 4

YOU NEED

1 hind loin or fillet of pork (or stewing beef), about 1½ lb (700 g)

2 tbsp hoisen sauce (or 1 tbsp each ketchup, soy
   sauce, and honey or sugar)
1 bunch Chinese or common parsley (or tinned
   cherries)

SEASONING
1–2 star anise
1 spring onion (or leek)
2 slices fresh ginger (or ⅓ tsp powdered)
1 tbsp honey
2 tbsp soy sauce
2 tbsp dry sherry
¼ pint (⅛ litre) water

Cut the pork (or beef) into 2 or 3 large pieces. In
a large, heavy saucepan, bring the seasoning
ingredients to a boil. The spring onion and
ginger slices should be whole. Add the pork,
bring back to the boil, reduce the heat and cover.
Simmer for 1 hour, adding a little water if
necessary, for there should be about ¼ pint (⅛
litre) liquid remaining at the end of the cooking.
Discard the fresh ginger, star anise and spring
onion. Incorporate the hoisen sauce, stir and
cook until thick, about 5 minutes. Remove from
the heat and allow to cool. Cut the pork (or beef)
into thin slices and arrange on a serving dish.
Cover with the sauce and garnish with parsley
or cherries. Serve warm or cold.

SESAME PORK (Tze Ma Jou)
easy
preparation 10 minutes/marinade 5 minutes
cooking 5 minutes
serves 2 to 3

YOU NEED
⅔ lb (300 g) lean pork
4 tbsp sesame seeds
1 tsp salt
½ tsp monosodium glutamate (optional)
2 egg yolks

2 tbsp cornflour
2 pints (1 litre) oil for frying

Cut the pork into even, bite-sized pieces, about
1" × 1" (2.5 × 2.5 cm). Sprinkle with the
monosodium glutamate and salt, then, set aside
for 5 minutes. Mix the egg yolks with the
cornflour. In a deep drying pan, heat the oil to
medium (365°). When a piece of bread, thrown
in, returns to the surface and browns in 60
seconds, the oil will be at the right temperature.
Dip each piece of pork into the egg/cornflour
mixture, then roll in the sesame seeds. Plunge
the pieces, one by one, into the hot oil. Fry for 4
to 5 minutes or until golden brown and done.
Drain on absorbent kitchen paper and serve hot.

STEWED LION'S HEAD (Hong Shau Shih Tze Tou)
easy
preparation 10 minutes
cooking 35 minutes
serves 4

This dish is greatly loved by the Chinese. There
are many different variations of it, but all have
in common the large pork balls which resemble
a lion's head.

YOU NEED
½ lb (250 g) minced pork
2 oz (50 g) shrimp (optional)
1 spring onion (or leek)
1 lb (500 g) cabbage (or Chinese cabbage)
2 tbsp water

SEASONING A
1 tbsp cornflour
½ tsp powdered ginger
1 pinch salt
1 egg

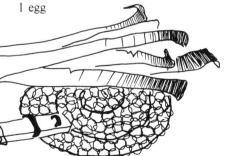

½ tbsp soy sauce
½ tbsp dry sherry

SEASONING B
1 tsp sugar
2 tbsp soy sauce
½ tbsp dry sherry
¼ pint (⅛ litre) chicken broth (1 broth cube)

THICKENING
1 tsp cornflour dissolved in
1 tsp water

Mince the shrimp finely. Mix together the minced pork, shrimp and seasoning A. Divide the mixture into 4 equal parts and form 4 large balls. Mince the spring onion (or leek) finely. Cut the cabbage into bite-sized pieces. In 2 bowls, prepare the seasoning B and the thickening. In a large, heavy saucepan, heat 2 tbsp oil until almost smoking. Brown the pork balls on all sides, about 4 minutes. Drain on absorbent kitchen paper. In the same saucepan, over high heat, stir-fry the spring onion. Add the cabbage and stir-fry for 10 seconds. Pour in the seasoning B and bring to the boil. Incorporate the pork balls, reduce the heat and cover. Simmer for 30 minutes. Add the thickening and cook until slightly thickened, about 1 minute. Remove from heat and serve.

STIR-FRIED PORK WITH AUBERGINE (Jou Hsiang Ch'ieh Tzu)
easy
preparation 15 minutes / marinade 10 minutes
cooking 25 minutes
serves 2 to 3

YOU NEED
¼ lb (250 g) lean pork
4 tbsp water
1 lb (500 g) aubergine
2 tbsp oil

MARINADE
1–2 cloves garlic
1 tbsp soy sauce
½ tsp salt
½ tsp sugar
1 tsp cornflour
1 generous pinch powdered ginger

1 generous pinch five-spice powder (optional)

Mince the garlic, then combine all the marinade ingredients. Cut the pork into ½" (1.5 cm) cubes and mix with the marinade. Marinate for 10 minutes. Peel the aubergine and cut it into ½" (1.5 cm) cubes. In a frying pan, heat 1 tbsp oil until almost smoking. Stir-fry the pork for 3 minutes. Sprinkle with the water, lower the heat and cover. Simmer for 10 minutes. Meantime, in another pan, heat 1 tbsp oil. Brown the aubergine 3 minutes, stirring constantly. Drain on absorbent kitchen paper, then add to the pork. Cover and cook for 10 minutes. Remove from heat. Serve at once, accompanied by steamed rice.

STIR-FRIED PORK WITH BEAN SPROUTS (Yin Ya Jou Szu)
easy
preparation 10 minutes
cooking 4 minutes
serves 2

YOU NEED
⅓ lb (150 g) lean pork (or rump steak or chicken)
½ lb (250 g) bean sprouts (or green pepper or cabbage)
½ tsp salt
1 tbsp dry sherry
½ pint (¼ litre) oil for frying

MARINADE
1 unbeaten egg white
1 tbsp water
1 tsp cornflour

THICKENING
2 tsp cornflour
½ tsp salt
2 tbsp water

In 2 bowls, prepare the marinade and the thickening. Cut the pork (or steak or chicken) against the grain into very thin strips. Mix with the marinade and set aside. Wash and drain the bean sprouts. (Cut the cabbage or green pepper

into thin strips). In a deep frying pan, heat the oil until almost smoking. Fry the slices of pork for 1 minute (or until half-cooked). Drain on absorbent kitchen paper. Leave only ½ tbsp oil in the pan and re-heat to the smoking point. Drop in the bean sprouts (or cabbage or green pepper) and sprinkle with the sherry and ½ tsp salt. Stir-fry for 1 minute, then remove from the pan. Add ½ tbsp oil to the pan. Stir-fry the pork (or steak or chicken) 1 minute. Return the bean sprouts (or cabbage or green pepper) to the pan and stir-fry 10 seconds. Pour in the thickening and cook, stirring, for 30 seconds (until thickened). Remove from heat and serve at once.

STIR-FRIED PORK WITH CAULIFLOWER (Hwa Ts'ai Ch'au P'ai Ku)
fairly easy
preparation 15 minutes / marinade 20 minutes
cooking 10 minutes
serves 2 to 3

YOU NEED
½ lb (250 g) lean pork
4 oz (100 g) button mushrooms, fresh or tinned
¼ cauliflower, about ¼ lb (300 g) (or broccoli)
2 sticks celery
1–2 cloves garlic
4 tbsp oil

MARINADE
2 tsp sugar
1 pinch pepper
1 tsp cornflour
2 tsp vinegar
2 tsp water
2 tsp dry sherry

SEASONING
¼ tsp salt
¼ tsp sugar
1 tsp dry sherry
1 tbsp soy sauce

THICKENING
1 tbsp cornflour dissolved in
1 tbsp water

Prepare the marinade. Cut the pork into even, bite-sized pieces. Mix with the marinade and set aside for 20 minutes. Meanwhile, bring to the boil a large saucepan of water. Separate the cauliflower (or broccoli) into small, equal florets. Drop into the boiling water for 1 minute. Drain and plunge into cold water. Cut the celery into matchstick-thin strips. Clean the mushrooms and slice. Mince the garlic. In 2 small bowls, prepare the seasoning and the thickening. In a deep frying pan, heat 2 tbsp oil until almost smoking. Brown the garlic for 10 seconds. Add the pieces of pork and stir-fry for 2 minutes (or until half-cooked). Remove from the pan. Add 2 tbsp oil to the pan and re-heat. Stir-fry the celery, mushrooms and cauliflower (or broccoli) for 30 seconds. Add the pork and stir-fry 30 seconds. Sprinkle with the seasoning and cook 4 to 5 minutes or until the pork is done and the cauliflower (or broccoli) crunchy-tender. Pour in the thickening and cook, stirring, for 30 seconds (or until thickened). Remove from heat and serve at once.

STIR-FRIED PORK WITH SPRING ONIONS (Ts'ung Pao Jou)
very easy
preparation 10 minutes / marinade 20 minutes
cooking 5 minutes
serves 2

YOU NEED
½ lb (250 g) lean pork (or rump steak)

8 spring onions (or leek)
½ tbsp dry sherry
1 tbsp cornflour
2 tbsp oil

MARINADE
½ tbsp dry sherry
1½ tbsp soy sauce

SEASONING
1 good pinch salt
1 tsp soy sauce

Prepare the marinade. Cut the pork (or steak) against the grain into very thin slices. Mix with the marinade and set aside for 20 minutes. Meanwhile, cut the spring onions (or leek) in 2" (5 cm) lengths. In a frying pan, heat 2 tbsp oil until almost smoking. Stir-fry the strips of pork 2 minutes. Sprinkle with ½ tbsp sherry and stir-fry 1 minute more. Add the spring onion and seasoning. Stir-fry another 2 minutes. Remove from heat and serve immediately.

STIR-FRIED PORK WITH WATER CHESTNUTS (Yu Hsiang Jou Szu)
fairly easy
preparation 15 minutes/marinade 5 minutes
cooking 6 minutes
serves 2 to 3

YOU NEED
⅔ lb (300 g) lean pork
8 water chestnuts
2 cloves garlic
1 chilli pod
5 'cloud ears' mushrooms (optional)
1 tbsp dry sherry
¼ pint (⅛ litre) oil for frying

MARINADE
1 tsp cornflour
1 tsp dry sherry
1 tbsp soy sauce

SEASONING
1 tsp cornflour
1 pinch each salt and pepper
1 tsp sugar
2 tbsp water
2 tbsp soy sauce
1 tbsp vinegar

Wash the cloud ears and soak in warm water 10 minutes or until soft. Drain, discarding the water, and cut into thin strips. In 2 bowls. prepare the marinade and seasoning. Cut the pork against the grain into matchstick-thin strips. Mix with the marinade and set aside for 5 minutes. Cut the water chestnuts into similar, matchstick-thin strips. Open and de-seed the chilli pod, then mince finely. Mince the garlic. In a deep frying pan, heat the oil until almost smoking. Fry the pork strips for 3 minutes (partially cooked). Drain on absorbent kitchen paper. Leave only 1 tbsp oil in the pan and re-heat. Stir-fry the garlic and chilli pod for 30 seconds. Add the water chestnuts, cloud ears and pork. Sprinkle with the dry sherry and stir-fry for 1 minute. Pour in the seasoning and cook, stirring, for 1 minute (until thickened). Remove from heat and serve at once.

SWEET AND SOUR PORK I (Ku Lau Jou)
fairly easy
preparation 15 minutes
cooking 6 minutes
serves 3 to 4

YOU NEED
1 lb (500 g) lean pork
4 medium-sized onions
1 clove garlic
1 carrot
1 green pepper
3 tbsp cornflour
1 tbsp dry sherry
2 pints (1 litre) oil for frying

MARINADE
1 tbsp dry sherry
2 tbsp soy sauce
2 tbsp vinegar

SEASONING
1 tbsp cornflour
3 tbsp sugar
2 tbsp vinegar
1 tsp soy sauce
4 tbsp ketchup

In 2 bowls, prepare the marinade and the seasoning. Cut the pork into even, bite-sized pieces, about 1" × 1" (2.5 cm × 2.5 cm). Mix with the marinade and set aside. Mince the garlic finely. Cut the onion and green pepper into even pieces the same size as the pork, and the carrot on the oblique in 1" (2.5 cm) lengths. In a deep frying pan, heat the oil to medium/high (375°). When a piece of bread thrown in returns to the surface and browns in 45 seconds, the oil will be at the right temperature. Sprinkle the pieces of pork with the cornflour. Plunge into the hot oil. Fry for 3 minutes, then turn the heat to high and fry for 1 minute more. Drain on absorbent kitchen paper. Fry for 10 seconds the onion, carrot and green pepper. Drain on absorbent kitchen paper. In another frying pan, heat 1 tbsp oil until almost smoking. Stir-fry the garlic for 30 seconds. Add the onion, green pepper and pork, then sprinkle with a tbsp sherry. Incorporate the seasoning and carrot. Cook until thick, about 1 minute. Remove from heat and serve at once.

SWEET AND SOUR PORK II (Ku Lau Jou)
fairly easy
preparation 20 minutes
cooking 7 minutes
serves 3 to 4

YOU NEED
1 lb (500 g) lean pork (or prawns or scampi)
1 tin pineapple in chunks, about 6 oz (150 g)
1 green pepper
1 carrot
1 spring onion (or leek)
2 egg yolks
3 tbsp cornflour
1 tbsp dry sherry
2 pints (1 litre) oil for frying

MARINADE
1 tsp salt
1 tbsp dry sherry
2 tbsp vinegar

SEASONING
4 tbsp sugar
½ tsp salt
1 tbsp cornflour
6 tbsp water
4 tbsp vinegar
2 tbsp ketchup
1 tsp soy sauce
1 tsp sesame oil (optional)

In 2 bowls, prepare the marinade and the seasoning. Cut the pork into even, bite-sized pieces, about 1" × 1" (2.5 cm × 2.5 cm). Mix with the marinade and set aside for 10 minutes. Cut the green pepper into pieces the same size as the pork. Cut the carrot on the oblique into 1" (2.5 cm) lengths and the spring onion (or leek) in 1" (2.5 cm) lengths. Beat the egg yolks. In a deep frying pan, heat the oil to medium/hot (375°). When a piece of bread, thrown in, returns to the surface and browns in 45 seconds, the oil is at the right temperature. Dip the pieces of pork into the egg yolk, then, roll in the cornflour. Plunge them into the hot oil and fry for 3 minutes. Turn the heat to high and fry for 1 minute more. Drain on absorbent kitchen paper. In another frying pan, heat 1 tbsp oil until almost smoking. Stir-fry the spring onion (or leek), carrot, green pepper and pineapple chunks for 1 minute. Pour in the seasoning and cook for

1 minute (until thickened). Incorporate the pork, stir and cook for 30 seconds more. Remove from the heat and serve.

SZECHWAN PORK WITH BEAN CURD (Ma P'o To Fu)
easy
preparation 10 minutes
cooking 6 minutes
serves 2 to 3

A very famous legend surrounds this delicious dish. Once upon a time there was a sweet and generous young girl from the region of Szechwan who married a poor merchant. In spite of the couple's humble circumstances, the young girl always found something to share with visiting friends. Her husband died very young, leaving her completely destitute. All the friends with whom she had previously been so generous gathered round her. One brought a little pork, another, some bean curd and so on. With these ingredients, she prepared a dish to share with everyone who had been so kind.

YOU NEED
5 oz (150 g) lean pork
¼ lb (250 g) bean curd
2 cloves garlic
2 spring onions (or leek)
1 tsp tabasco (or Chinese hot pepper oil)
3 tbsp oil
½ tsp salt
2 tbsp soy sauce

THICKENING
1 tbsp cornflour dissolved in
2 tbsp water

Finely mince the garlic and spring onions (or leek). Cut the bean curd into small bite-sized pieces. Cut the pork into similar, bite-sized pieces. Prepare the thickening and set aside. In a frying pan, heat the oil until almost smoking. Stir-fry the pork for 30 seconds. Add the garlic, tabasco, soy sauce and salt. Stir-fry for 1 minute. Incorporate the bean curd, stir gently and fry for 10 seconds. Cover the pan and cook for 3 minutes without touching. Pour in the thickening and cook for 30 seconds more or until thickened. Add the spring onion (or leek), stir and remove from the heat. Serve hot.

RICE (Mi Fan)

Rice is the basic food of two thirds of the vast land of China. There are many types and qualities of rice but the two most commonly available in the West are the long grain and the short grain. The Chinese generally prefer the long grain for preparing steamed, boiled and fried dishes, using the round grain for long-cooking soups, puddings and porridges such as Rice Congee.

Another variety, relatively unknown in the west and greatly appreciated by the Chinese, is 'glutinous' rice, sometimes called 'sweet' rice due to its frequent use in desserts. Its distinctive quality, however, is its stickiness, and not a sweet sweet flavour. It is also used in the preparation of such savoury dishes as Taiwanese Rice. Chalky in appearance, it only becomes gluey when cooked.

In China, prior to cooking, we wash rice thoroughly using several bowls of water. The rice-washing water is then given to the pigs and, when there is no pig in the family, a tub is placed in the garden where neighbours with pigs may have ready access to it. In fact, this practice is so widespread that today it is forbidden in the large cities. Notwithstanding Chinese custom, certain brands of rice, prepared and packaged for consumption in the United Kingdom, are pre-treated and do not need washing. Therefore, be sure to check the instructions on the package before washing your rice.

For cooking, a good heavy aluminium, non-stick or stainless steel saucepan with a tight fitting lid serves very well. Copper saucepans, on the other hand, are not recommended for they conduct the heat in such a way as to cause the rice to burn easily. The quantity of water to be used in the cooking of rice is dictated by both the quality of rice chosen and by personal preference. Two general rules: long grain rice requires more water than short grain, and slightly less water should be used in pre-cooking rice for stir-frying, so that it will not be too wet but will still absorb liquid seasonings. The quantities of water proposed in the recipes of this chapter are general guides and brand directions should always be followed.

STEAMED RICE (Ch'u Pai Fan)

very easy
preparation 1 minute
cooking 35 minutes
serves 3 to 4

YOU NEED

$\frac{1}{2}$ lb (250 g) rice, long or short grain
1 tsp salt
1 pint ($\frac{1}{2}$ litre) water for long grain rice ($\frac{3}{4}$ pint ($\frac{1}{3}$ litre) for short grain, see Tips & Tricks)

Wash the rice thoroughly and put it into a heavy saucepan. Add the salt and the appropriate amount of water, then bring to the boil. Lower the heat to medium and boil rapidly until the water is nearly absorbed, 5 to 10 minutes. Reduce the heat to low and cover tightly. Cook gently, without lifting the lid, for 20 minutes. Turn the heat off, leave tightly covered and let stand for 10 minutes. The rice will be tender and fluffy. Remove the rice from the saucepan with a wooden spatula so as not to crush the grains and serve hot.

TIPS & TRICKS

The quantities of water indicated above are intended to be a general guide and the quality of the rice as well as personal preference should be taken into consideration.

CANTONESE FRIED RICE (Shih Chin Ch'au Fan)

easy
preparation 15 minutes
cooking 8 minutes
serves 3 to 4

YOU NEED

$\frac{1}{2}$ lb (250 g) rice
3 oz (80 g) cooked chicken (see Tips & Tricks)
3 oz (80 g) shelled shrimp
3 oz (80 g) pork (or ham, sausage or bacon)
3 tbsp green peas (or green pepper)
1 spring onion (or leek or onion)
$\frac{1}{2}$ tsp soy sauce
$\frac{1}{2}$ tsp water
$\frac{1}{2}$ tsp dry sherry
2 eggs
1 pinch salt
2 tbsp oil

MARINADE (shrimp)

$\frac{1}{4}$ tsp salt
1 pinch pepper
$\frac{1}{4}$ tsp dry sherry

SEASONING

1 pinch pepper
$\frac{1}{4}$ tsp salt
2 tsp soy sauce
1 tbsp water

Steam or boil the rice, following the directions on the brand package or those given for steamed rice. Allow the cooked rice to cool. If possible, do this pre-cooking a day in advance, or use leftover rice. Cut the shrimp into small pieces, mix with the marinade and set aside. Dice the pork (or ham, sausage or bacon) and mix with the soy sauce. Dice the chicken and spring onion (or leek or onion) and green pepper if used. Prepare the seasoning and set aside. Beat the eggs with the sherry and water and a pinch of salt. In a frying pan, heat $\frac{1}{2}$ tbsp oil until almost smoking. Pour in half of the beaten egg, spreading thinly to make a fine omelette. Brown quickly on both sides, then remove from the pan. Add $\frac{1}{2}$ tbsp oil to the pan and re-heat. Repeat the same procedure with the remainder of the beaten egg. Roll the omelettes tightly and cut crosswise into thin strips. Add 1 tbsp oil to the pan and re-heat until almost smoking. Stir-fry the spring onion for 30 seconds. Add the pork (or ham, sausage or bacon) and stir-fry 2 minutes. Incorporate the shrimp, chicken and seasoning, stir, then add the rice. Stir-fry energetically for 3 minutes. Add the green peas (or green pepper) and strips of omelette. Stir-fry 1 minute more, then, remove from heat and serve.

TIPS & TRICKS

Fried Rice can be made exclusively with shrimp (or pork or chicken). In this case, increase the quantity of shrimp and omit the other meats. For additional seasoning, $\frac{1}{2}$ to 1 tbsp curry may be added to the frying pan at the same time as the spring onion. A good trick is to prepare fried rice in advance, freeze it, then re-heat in the oven, covering it well with aluminium foil. (Do not add any water or oil.)

CHINESE SAUSAGE RICE (La Chang Fan)

very easy
preparation 5 minutes
cooking 40 minutes
serves 3 to 4

YOU NEED
½ lb (250 g) rice
½ lb (250 g) Chinese sausage (or see Tips & Tricks)
1 spring onion (or chives)
1 tsp dry sherry
1 tsp salt
¼ pint (¼ litre) water for short grain rice (¾ pint (½ litre) for long grain)

Wash the rice thoroughly. In a heavy saucepan, cover it with the appropriate amount of water. Add the salt, sherry and sausage, then bring to the boil. Reduce the heat to medium and cook rapidly, uncovered, until the water is half absorbed, about 5 minutes. Reduce the heat to warm/low, cover tightly and cook gently until the water is completely absorbed, about 15 minutes. Turn off the heat and let stand, without lifting the lid, 15 minutes. Meanwhile, finely chop the spring onion (or chives). Remove the

sausages and slice them thinly on the diagonal. Garnish the rice with the spring onion (or chives) and slices of sausage. Serve hot or warm, sprinkled with several drops of sesame oil if so desired.

TIPS & TRICKS
Should you be unable to procure Chinese sausages (long, thin, bright red, spicy-sweet and available only in Chinese speciality shops) you may substitute the more brightly coloured, spicy pork sausages that are available in the supermarkets. In this case, however, be sure to serve with sesame oil, the touch which will impart an exotic bouquet and savour to the dish.

JADE RICE (Ts'ue Yü Fan)

easy
preparation 15 minutes / marinade 15 minutes
cooking 8 to 10 minutes
serves 3 to 4

YOU NEED
½ lb (250 g) rice
½ lb (250 g) spinach fresh or frozen
2 oz (60 g) ham
1 egg
½ tsp + 1 pinch salt
½ tsp monosodium glutamate (optional)
¼ tsp dry sherry
1–2 cloves garlic
2½ tbsp oil

Steam or boil the rice, following the directions on the brand package or those given for steamed rice. Allow the cooked rice to cool. If possible, do this pre-cooking a day in advance, or use leftover rice. Clean the spinach and chop. If frozen, let thaw. Sprinkle with ½ tsp salt and set aside for 15 minutes. Drain and squeeze out all excess water. Dice the ham and mince the garlic. Beat the egg with a pinch of salt and the sherry. In a frying pan, heat ½ tbsp oil until almost smoking. Pour in the beaten egg, rolling the pan to make a thin omelette. Brown quickly on both sides, then remove from the pan. Roll tightly, then cut crosswise into thin strips. Add 1 tbsp oil to the same pan and re-heat. Stir-fry the spinach 1 minute, then remove from the pan and drain well. Again add 1 tbsp oil to the pan and re-heat.

Stir-fry the garlic 30 seconds. Add the rice and monosodium glutamate, then stir-fry for 1 minute. Incorporate the ham, spinach and strips of omelette. Cook, stirring, for 2 minutes more. Remove from heat and serve.

PEARL RICE BALLS (Chen Chu Wan Tzu)
fairly easy
preparation 20 minutes/soaking 1 hour
cooking 22 minutes
makes about 20 rice balls

YOU NEED
4 oz (100 g) glutinous rice
8 oz (250 g) minced pork
4 oz (100 g) shelled shrimp
2 spring onions (or leek)
1 egg

SEASONING A
1 pinch powdered ginger (optional)
1 tsp salt
1 generous pinch pepper
2 tbsp cornflour
1 tsp dry sherry
1 tsp soy sauce

SEASONING B
1 tbsp dry sherry
2 tbsp water

You also need a steamer.

Wash the rice thoroughly and soak it in warm water for 1 hour. Drain, discarding the water. Meanwhile, prepare seasoning B and set it aside. Finely mince the shrimp and spring onions (or leek). Mix together the minced shrimp, pork, spring onions, egg and seasoning A. Form bite-sized balls with even portions of the mixture (about 1 tbsp). Roll the meatballs in the glutinous rice, covering each one well. Line the steamer basket with absorbent kitchen paper. Place the rice balls 1" (2.5 cm) apart in the basket. Bring to the boil the water in the steamer. Steam the rice balls for 10 minutes. Open the steamer and sprinkle the rice balls with seasoning B. Re-cover and continue to steam for 12 minutes. Serve the rice balls hot or warm.

RICE CONGEE (Nieu Jo Chou)
easy
preparation 10 minutes/marinade 10 minutes
cooking 2 hours 6 minutes
thick congee serves 3 to 4
thin congee serves 4 to 6

A very famous Chinese dish, congee is a creamy rice which resembles a thick porridge. There are many variations of congee and its consistency depends entirely upon personal preference.

Chinese partake of it at any time of the day, as a snack, a late-supper dish or with tea, but it is most frequently served for breakfast. In addition, congee makes an excellent meal for those who have a delicate stomach.

YOU NEED
½ lb (250 g) rice, preferably short grain
½ lb (250 g) steak (or chicken breast or fish fillet)
2 pints (1 litre) water for thick congee (or 3½ pints (2 litres) for thin congee
1 egg (optional)
1 spring onion (or leek or chives)

MARINADE A (rice)
1 tsp salt
2 tsp oil

MARINADE B (meat or fish)
1 pinch each salt and pepper
½ tsp soy sauce
1 tsp dry sherry

In 2 bowls, prepare the marinades. Wash the rice well, then, mix it with the marinade A. Set aside for 10 minutes. Cut the steak (or chicken or fish) against the grain into very thin strips. Mix with the marinade B and set aside. Put the rice into a heavy saucepan and cover with the appropriate amount of water. Bring to the boil. Reduce the heat to medium and boil, uncovered, for 20 minutes. Reduce the heat to medium/low and cook 15 minutes for a thick congee (45 minutes for a thin congee). Meantime, beat the egg and mince the spring onion (or leek). When the rice is cooked to the desired consistency, incorporate the steak and stir. Cook gently for 1 minute. Turn the heat to high and bring back to the boil. Pour in, in a slow steady stream, the beaten egg, stirring all the while. Add the spring onion (or leek). Turn off the heat, cover tightly and let stand for 5 minutes. Serve hot.

STEAMED RICE WITH PEANUTS (Shih Chin Cheng Fan)

easy
preparation 15 minutes
cooking 32 minutes
serves 3 to 4

YOU NEED
½ lb (250 g) rice
3 oz (80 g) pork (or chicken)
3 oz (80 g) shelled shrimp
2 oz (50 g) peanuts
1 stick celery (or bamboo shoots, cabbage or water chestnuts)
1 carrot
3 tbsp green peas (or green pepper)
1 spring onion (or leek)
1 dried Chinese mushroom (optional)
1 tbsp oil

MARINADE
½ tsp salt
1 pinch pepper
½ tsp dry sherry

SEASONING
½ tsp salt
1 pinch pepper

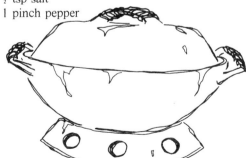

1 tsp soy sauce
¼ pint (⅛ litre) water for long grain rice (½ pint (⅓ litre) for short grain)

Wash the dried mushroom and soak it in warm water 10 minutes or until soft. Drain, remove the hard stalk and dice. If the shrimp are good-sized, cut into 2 or 3 pieces. Mix with the marinade and set aside. Dice the pork (or chicken), celery (or bamboo shoots, cabbage or water chestnuts), carrot and spring onion (or leek). Prepare the seasoning and set aside. In a heavy saucepan, heat the oil until almost smoking. Stir-fry the spring onion (or leek) for 30 seconds. Add the pork (or chicken) and stir-fry for 1 minute. Incorporate the shrimp and mushroom and continue to stir-fry for 1 minute. Add the rice, celery (or bamboo shoots, cabbage or water chestnuts) and carrot, stirring and frying for 30 seconds. Pour in the seasoning and bring to the boil. Reduce the heat, cover tightly and cook for 20 minutes without lifting the lid. Add the green peas (or green pepper, diced) and peanuts. Turn off the heat, cover tightly once again and let stand for 10 minutes. Serve hot.

STIR-FRIED RICE WITH CURRY (Ka Li Ch'au Fan)

very easy
preparation 5 minutes
cooking 5 minutes
serves 3 to 4

YOU NEED
½ lb (250 g) rice
4 oz (100 g) minced pork (or minced beef)
½–1 tbsp curry to taste
1 medium-sized onion
1 medium-sized carrot (optional)
2 tbsp dry sherry
½ tsp salt
2 tbsp oil

Steam or boil the rice, following the directions on the brand package or those given for steamed rice. Allow the cooked rice to cool. If possible, do this pre-cooking a day in advance, or use left-over rice. Dice the onion and carrot. In a deep frying pan, heat the oil until almost smoking. Stir-fry the onion, 1 minute. Add the curry powder and stir-fry 30 seconds. Sprinkle with the sherry and stir-fry 30 seconds. Add the mince and salt, then stir-fry 1 minute. Incorporate the carrot and rice, stirring energetically. Cook, stirring, for 3 minutes or until the grains of rice are hot and well separated. Remove from heat and serve.

TAIWANESE RICE (Taiwan Nuo Mi Fan)
easy
preparation 10 minutes/soaking 1 hour

cooking 22 minutes
serves 3 to 4

YOU NEED
$\frac{1}{2}$ lb (250 g) glutinous rice
$\frac{1}{2}$ pint ($\frac{1}{4}$ litre) water
3 oz (80 g) lean pork
3 oz (80 g) shelled shrimp
1 dried Chinese mushroom (optional)
1 small onion
$\frac{1}{2}$ tsp salt
1 tbsp soy sauce
1 tbsp dry sherry
$\frac{1}{5}$ pint ($\frac{1}{10}$ litre) oil (or $\frac{1}{20}$ pint ($\frac{1}{20}$ litre) each sesame and cooking oil)

Wash the rice and soak it in warm water for 1 hour. Wash the dried mushroom and soak it in warm water 10 minutes or until soft. Drain, remove the hard stalk and cut into matchstick-thin strips. Cut the pork into very thin strips. Finely chop the onion. In a heavy saucepan, heat the oil until almost smoking. Stir-fry the onion for 1 minute. Add the pork, mushroom and shrimp. Stir-fry energetically for 1 minute. Sprinkle with soy sauce and sherry, stir, then incorporate the rice. Stir, season with salt and pour in the water. Bring to the boil, cover and reduce the heat. Cook until the rice is done, about 20 minutes. Serve hot or cold.

TIPS & TRICKS
Cooked, warm Taiwanese Rice may be formed into little, bite-sized balls and served with cocktails or tea or even carried on picnics.

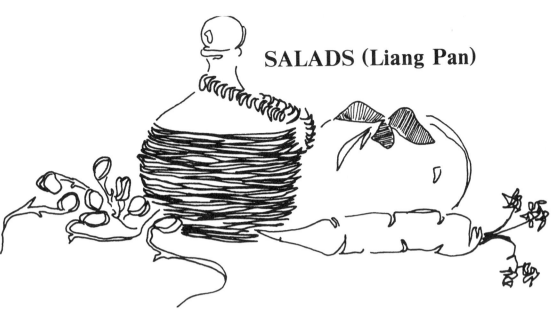

SALADS (Liang Pan)

We Chinese are very partial to cold vegetables served in salads, à la vinaigrette or marinated. We eat them as a first course, condiment or just simply with tea. Some large salads are a whole meal in themselves and make exotic summertime repasts. (See Mixed Noodle Salad, and Chinese Mixed Salad I)

All of our salads may be prepared in advance, their dressings added just before serving. This is, moreover, the method used in China where it was once necessary to scald all vegetables which could not be peeled in boiling water. Only recently, due to modern sanitary systems, have we begun to eat raw vegetables, western-style. However, we continue to blanche and marinate our vegetables for these processes intensify colour and texture, render the ingredients more digestible and, above all, impart the savoury results that you will discover when you try the following recipes.

AUBERGINE SALAD (Liang Pan Chieh Tzu)
easy
preparation 10 minutes
cooking 10 minutes
serves 3 to 4

YOU NEED
1 lb (500 g) aubergine
2 cloves garlic
½ tsp salt
2 tsp soy sauce
1 tsp vinegar (or lemon juice)
2 tsp sesame oil (optional)

You also need a steamer.

Bring the steamer water to the boil. Peel the aubergine, leaving it whole. Steam 8 to 10 minutes or until tender. Meantime, finely chop the garlic and prepare the dressing. Remove the aubergine from the steamer and cut into even, bit-sized pieces. Mix with the dressing and serve hot or cold.

CABBAGE À LA VINAIGRETTE (Liang Pan Pao Hsin Ts'ai)
very easy
preparation 10 minutes/marinade 10 minutes
serves 3 to 4

YOU NEED
1 lb (500 g) cabbage (or Chinese celery cabbage)
1 onion
1 chilli pod (optional)

MARINADE
2 tsp salt

2 tsp vinegar

DRESSING
1 tsp vinegar
2 tsp sesame oil (or other)

Remove the outer leaves and tough stalks of the cabbage. Shred coarsely. Mix with the marinade ingredients and set aside for 10 minutes. Meantime, cut the onion in half, then in thin strips. Open the chilli pod, de-seed and cut into thin strips. Prepare the dressing. Drain the cabbage, squeezing out any excess water. Combine the cabbage, onion and chilli pod with the dressing. Mix well and serve at once.

DRESSING
1 tsp sugar
1 tbsp soy sauce
1 tbsp vinegar (or lemon juice)
1 tsp sesame oil (or other)
1 dash tabasco (optional)

Remove the outer leaves and tough stalks of the cabbage. Shred coarsely. Sprinkle with salt and set aside for 10 minutes. Meanwhile, prepare the dressing. Drain the cabbage, squeezing out any excess water. Mix with the dressing and serve.

TIPS & TRICKS
Asparagus can also be prepared by this recipe. Cut on the diagonal into ½" (1.5 cm) lengths, then pass through boiling water for 2 minutes. Plunge immediately into cold water, drain well and mix with the dressing.

CANTONESE SALAD (Kuang Tong P'ao Ts'ai)
very easy
preparation 15 minutes/marinade 12 hours
cooking 1 minute
serves 4

YOU NEED
2–3 turnips (or radish)
½ lb (250 g) cabbage
2 chilli pods (or tabasco or Chinese hot pepper oil)
1 carrot
1 cucumber
1 tsp salt

DRESSING
4 tbsp vinegar
4 tbsp water
1 tbsp whisky

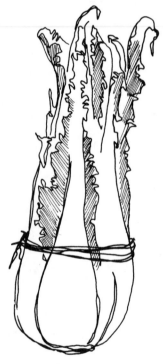

CABBAGE WITH RED DRESSING (Yi Fen Sa La)
very easy
preparation 5 minutes/marinade 10 minutes
serves 2 to 3

YOU NEED
¼ lb (250 g) cabbage (or spinach, lettuce, celery, Chinese celery cabbage or see Tips & Tricks)
½ tsp salt

3 oz (80 g) sugar
10 black peppercorns (or Szechwan pepper)

In a small saucepan, combine the marinade ingredients and bring to the boil. Stir, remove from heat and set aside to cool. Peel and cut into very thin slices the carrot and the turnips. Peel the cucumber, cut it open lengthwise and de-seed. Cut into very thin slices. Remove the outer leaves and tough stalk of the cabbage. Cut into bite-sized pieces. Open and de-seed the chilli pods, then cut into shreds. Sprinkle with salt the turnip, cabbage and cucumber. Set aside for 10 minutes. Drain without rinsing. Put all the vegetables, well mixed, in a tightly covered container. Pour in the marinade, close tightly and shake until all the ingredients are well covered with the marinade. Place in the refrigerator overnight. (Shake or stir from time to time.) Serve cold as a first course, salad or condiment.

CELERY SALAD (Liang Pan Ch'in Ts'ai)
very easy
preparation 10 minutes
cooking 1 to 2 minutes
serves 3 to 4

YOU NEED
1 small head celery

DRESSING
1 tbsp soy sauce
1 pinch salt
1 tbsp sesame oil (or other)
1 pinch monosodium glutamate (optional)

Bring to the boil enough water to cover the celery. Clean the celery and cut on the diagonal into matchstick-thin 2" (5 cm) lengths. Drop into the boiling water 1 to 2 minutes (depending upon the tenderness of the celery). Drain, then,

plunge into cold water. Prepare the dressing. Drain well the celery and mix with the dressing. Chill and serve cold.

CHICKEN SESAME SALAD (Chi See Hwang Kua)
easy
preparation 20 minutes
cooking 2 to 3 minutes
serves 3 to 4

YOU NEED
$\frac{1}{2}$ lb (250 g) cooked chicken (or turkey-breast steak)
1 medium-sized cucumber
1 chilli pod

DRESSING
4 tbsp sesame seeds
1 tsp sugar
2 tbsp soy sauce
1 tsp sesame oil (or other)
$\frac{1}{2}$ tsp salt
$\frac{1}{2}$ tsp monosodium glutamate (optional)

If the chicken (or turkey) is uncooked, simmer in gently boiling water for 15 minutes or until done, reserving the water for a soup base. Peel the cucumber and cut it open lengthwise. De-seed, then, cut into 2" (5 cm) lengths. Plunge into cold water and set aside. Open the chilli pod, de-seed and cut into shreds. Add the chilli pod shreds to the cold water. Cut the chicken (or turkey) into shreds and arrange prettily on a serving dish. Heat a small, unoiled frying pan. Toast the sesame seeds, stirring continually, until golden brown, 2 to 3 minutes. Crush the seeds by passing them through a blender or

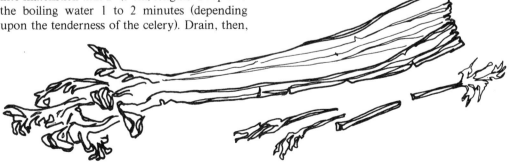

using a mortar and pestle, or a rolling pin, first pouring the seeds into a plastic bag. Combine the powder obtained with all other dressing ingredients. Drain the cucumber and chilli pod and place on top of the chicken. Add the dressing just before serving.

TIPS & TRICKS
Although not truly authentic, this salad is sometimes served on lettuce leaves, a pretty touch adopted by certain Chinese restaurants.

CHINESE MIXED SALAD I (Liang Pan Shih Chin)

easy
preparation 20 minutes
cooking 4 minutes
serves 3 to 4

YOU NEED
½ lb (250 g) cooked chicken (or turkey-breast steak)
4 oz (100 g) ham
½ lb (250 g) bean sprouts
1 small cucumber
2 eggs
1 pinch salt
½ tsp dry sherry
2 tsp oil

(Choose one of the following)

DRESSING I
2 tbsp sugar
½ tsp salt
2 tsp prepared mustard
1 tbsp soy sauce
3 tbsp vinegar (or lemon juice)

DRESSING II
¼ tsp salt
½ tbsp prepared mustard
2 tbsp sesame paste (or peanut butter)
2 tbsp water
1 tbsp sesame oil
½ tsp monosodium glutamate (optional)
1½ tbsp soy sauce

If the chicken (or turkey) is uncooked, simmer in gently boiling water for 15 minutes or until done, reserving the water for a soup base. Bring to the boil enough water to cover the bean sprouts. Pass the sprouts in the boiling water 30 seconds, then drain. Plunge immediately into cold water and set aside. Peel the cucumber, cut it open lengthwise and de-seed. Cut into 2" (5 cm) lengths and plunge into cold water. Coarsely shred the ham and chicken. Beat the eggs with a pinch of salt and the sherry. In a small frying pan, heat 1 tsp oil until almost smoking. Pour in half of the beaten egg, spreading to make a thin omelette. Brown quickly on both sides and remove from the pan. Add 1 tsp oil to the pan and re-heat. Repeat the same procedure with the remainder of the beaten egg. Roll the omelettes tightly and cut crosswise into thin strips. Prepare one of the two dressings indicated above. Drain the cucumber and bean sprouts. Arrange prettily on a serving dish the chicken (or turkey), ham, cucumber and omelette strips. Add the dressing just before serving.

CHINESE MIXED SALAD II (Liang Pan Shih Chin)

easy
preparation 20 minutes
cooking 4 minutes
serves 3 to 4

YOU NEED
½ lb (250 g) ham (or cooked pork, beef, turkey or chicken)
1 small cucumber
2 eggs
1 carrot
½ tsp dry sherry
1 pinch salt
2 tsp oil

DRESSING
1 clove garlic
1 tsp salt
1 tsp sesame oil (or other)
1 tsp whisky
1 tsp monosodium glutamate (optional)
1½ tbsp soy sauce
1½ tbsp vinegar (or lemon juice)

Peel cucumber, cut it open lengthwise and de-seed. Cut into 2" (5 cm) lengths and plunge into cold water. Coarsely shred the carrot and ham (or pork, beef, turkey or chicken); plunge the carrot into the cold water. Mince the garlic. Prepare the dressing. Beat the eggs with a pinch of salt and the sherry. In a small frying pan, heat 1 tsp oil until almost smoking. Pour in half of the beaten egg, spreading thinly to make a fine omelette. Brown quickly on both sides and remove from the pan. Add 1 tsp oil to the pan and re-heat. Repeat the same procedure with the remainder of the beaten egg. Roll the omelettes tightly, then, cut crosswise into thin strips. Drain the cucumber and carrot. Arrange prettily on a serving dish the cucumber, carrot, meat and strips of omelette. Add the dressing just before serving.

CUCUMBER SALAD (Liang Pan Hwang Kua)

very easy
preparation 10 minutes/marinade 10 minutes
serves 2 to 3

YOU NEED
1 cucumber
1 chilli pod (or tabasco to taste)

DRESSING
$\frac{1}{2}$ tsp salt
1 tbsp sesame oil (or other)
1 tsp whisky
$\frac{1}{2}$ tsp monosodim glutamate (optional)

Peel the cucumber, cut it open lengthwise and de-seed. Cut into bite-sized pieces, about 1" × 1" (2.5 cm × 2.5 cm). Open and de-seed the chilli pod, then, cut into 4 to 6 pieces. Prepare the dressing. Combine the dressing, chilli pod and cucumber, mixing well. Chill in the refrigerator for 10 minutes. Serve cold.

GOLD AND SILVER SALAD (Liang Pan Chin Yin Szu)

easy
preparation 20 minutes
cooking 4 minutes
serves 2 to 3

YOU NEED
6–8 oz (200 g) cooked chicken (or turkey)
$\frac{1}{2}$ lb (250 g) bean sprouts
2 eggs
1 small onion
1 pinch salt
$\frac{1}{2}$ tsp dry sherry
2 tsp oil

DRESSING
$\frac{1}{2}$ tsp salt
1 clove garlic
1 tbsp lemon juice
1 tsp mustard
1 tsp sesame oil (or other)
$\frac{1}{2}$ tsp tabasco (optional)

Bring to the boil enough water to cover the bean sprouts. Pass the sprouts through the boiling water for 30 seconds, then, drain and plunge into cold water. Cut the onion in half, then into very thin strips and add to the cold water. Cut the chicken into shreds. Mince the garlic. Prepare the dressing. Beat the eggs with a pinch of salt and the sherry. In a small frying pan, heat 1 tsp oil until almost smoking. Pour half of the beaten egg into the pan, spreading thinly to make a fine omelette. Brown quickly on both sides, then remove from the pan. Add 1 tsp oil to the pan and reheat. Repeat the same process with the remainder of the beaten egg. Roll the

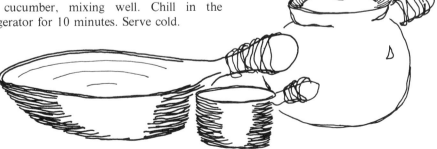

omelettes tightly like a cigarette, then cut crosswise into strips and set aside. Drain the bean sprouts and onion strips. Arrange prettily on a serving dish the bean sprouts, chicken (or turkey) and omelette strips. Garnish with the onion. Add the dressing just before serving.

GREEN PEPPER SALAD (Yien Ch'in Chiao)
very easy
preparation 5 minutes/marinade 30 minutes
serves 2 to 4

YOU NEED
2–3 green peppers
2–3 tomatoes (optional)
1 tsp salt

DRESSING
½ tsp sugar
1 tbsp soy sauce
1 tbsp vinegar (or lemon juice)
1 tbsp sesame oil (or other)

Cut the green peppers in half and de-seed. Cut each half into 4 pieces. Sprinkle with salt and set aside for 30 minutes. Prepare the dressing. Cut the tomatoes into very thin slices. Drain the

green pepper. Arrange the tomato slices on a serving plate and top with the green peppers. Add the dressing just before serving.

LION'S TOOTH SALAD (Jo Szu La P'i)
easy
preparation 15 minutes
serves 3 to 4

YOU NEED
6 oz (200 g) ham (or cooked chicken, turkey or pork)
5 rice galettes
1 small cucumber
1 slice fresh ginger (or 1 good pinch powdered)
2 cloves garlic

DRESSING (or one of the dressings for mixed noodle salad)
½ tsp salt
1 tbsp sugar
2 tbsp soy sauce
2 tbsp lemon juice (or vinegar)
4 tbsp water
4 tbsp sesame paste (or peanut butter)
1 tbsp sesame oil
1 tsp tabasco (or Chinese hot pepper oil)

Bring to the boil a large saucepan of water. Place the galettes in a drainer, being careful not to break them. Pour the boiling water over the galettes and drain well. Cut the galettes into 2" (5 cm) lengths, then, transfer to a serving dish. Prepare the dressing. Cut the ham (or chicken, turkey or pork) into strips the same size as the strips of galette. Finely chop the garlic and fresh ginger. Peel the cucumber and cut in half lengthwise. De-seed, then slice thinly. Arrange the cucumber and ham on top of the galettes. Garnish with the ginger and garlic. Add the dressing and serve.

PICKLED AUBERGINE (Chiang Ch'ieh Tzu)
very easy
preparation 10 minutes/marinade 3 hours
serves 3 to 4

YOU NEED
1 lb (500 g) aubergine
1 tsp salt

½ chilli pod (optional)
1 tsp sesame oil (optional)

MARINADE

1 pinch salt
1 tbsp prepared mustard
2 tbsp soy sauce
2 tbsp sugar
3 tbsp vinegar (or lemon juice)
½ tsp monosodium glutamate (optional)

Peel the aubergine and cut it in half, then, into strips. Sprinkle with the salt and set aside for 30 minutes. Meanwhile, de-seed the chilli pod and chop it finely. Prepare the marinade. Drain the strips of aubergine, squeezing out any excess water. Pat dry with absorbent kitchen paper. Put the aubergine and the chilli pod in a tightly covered container. Pour in the marinade, stir, and close tightly. Marinate for 3 hours or overnight. Serve cold, sprinkled with sesame oil if desired.

PICKLED RADISHES (Chiang Lo Po)
easy
preparation 15 minutes / marinade 3 hours
cooking 2 to 3 minutes
serves 3 to 4

YOU NEED

1 bunch radishes (or celery, cucumber or courgette, (See Tips & Tricks)
2 tbsp sesame seeds (optional)

MARINADE

1 tbsp sugar
3 tbsp soy sauce
2 tbsp vinegar
2 tbsp sesame oil (or other)

In a small saucepan, combine the marinade ingredients and bring to the boil. Stir until the sugar is dissolved, then, remove from heat and allow to cool. Meanwhile, clean the radishes and cut into paper-thin slices. This may be done with a potato peeler. Mix the radish slices with the marinade and put into the refrigerator for 3 hours. Heat a small, unoiled frying pan. Toast the sesame seeds, stirring frequently, until golden brown, 2 to 3 minutes. Sprinkle the radishes with the toasted sesame seeds and serve as a first course, salad or condiment.

TIPS & TRICKS
Cut the courgettes or de-seeded cucumber diagonally into thin slices, the celery into thin strips. Pass the courgettes through boiling water for 1 minute before mixing with the marinade.

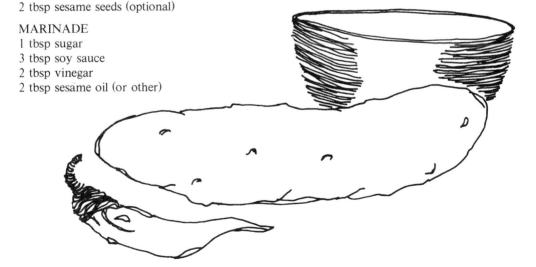

SALAD OF THREE COLOURS (Liang Pan Sen Seh)

very easy
preparation 15 minutes
cooking 10 minutes
serves 2 to 3

YOU NEED

2 tomatoes
2 hard boiled eggs
½ lb (250 g) bean sprouts (or string beans)

DRESSING

1 pinch each salt and pepper
½ tsp sugar
2 tbsp vinegar
2 tbsp sesame oil (or other)
½ tsp tabasco (or Chinese hot pepper oil)

Hard boil the eggs, cool and shell. Bring to the boil enough water to cover the bean sprouts (or string beans). Drop the sprouts into the boiling water for 30 seconds, drain, then plunge into cold water. Cut into thin slices the tomatoes and the hard boiled eggs. Prepare the dressing. Drain the bean sprouts and place them on a serving dish. Arrange the slices of tomato and egg on top of the sprouts. Add the dressing and serve immediately.

SPINACH SALAD (Chieh Pan Po Ts'ai)

very easy
preparation 15 minutes
cooking 30 seconds
serves 2 to 3

YOU NEED

1 lb (500 g) fresh spinach (or endive)

DRESSING

1 tbsp prepared mustard
2 tbsp dry sherry
½ tsp salt
½ tsp vinegar
½ tsp monosodium glutamate (optional)

Bring to the boil a large saucepan of water. Clean the spinach, then pass through the boiling water 30 seconds. Drain, squeezing out any excess water. Cut into thin strips and place in a serving dish. Prepare the dressing. Combine the spinach and dressing, mixing well. Serve warm or cold.

SZECHWAN CUCUMBERS (La Hwang Kua)

very easy
preparation 10 minutes/marinade 5 hours
serves 3 to 4

YOU NEED

2 cucumbers
1½ tsp salt

MARINADE

3–4 cloves garlic
1 tsp sugar
½ tbsp vinegar (or lemon juice)
1 tsp tabasco (or Chinese hot pepper oil)
2 tbsp sesame oil (or other)
1 tbsp soy sauce

Peel the cucumber and cut it open lengthwise. De-seed, then, cut into strips about 1½" × ½" (4 cm × 1.5 cm). Sprinkle with the salt and set aside for 2 hours. Meanwhile, shred the garlic. Prepare the marinade in a large bowl. Rinse the cucumber, then drain well. Mix with the marinade and set aside for 3 hours. Serve cold.

TIPS & TRICKS
Szechwan cucumbers may be kept in the refrigerator up to 2 weeks.

SZECHWAN SALAD (Szu Ch'uan P'au Ts'ai)
very easy
preparation 15 minutes / marinade 12 hours
cooking 1 minute
serves 4

YOU NEED
2–3 turnips (or radish)
¾–1 lb (500 g) cabbage
1–2 carrots
1 small cucumber

DRESSING
3–4 chilli pods
10 black peppercorns (or Szechwan pepper)
1½ pints water
2 tbsp whisky (or gin)
2 tbsp salt
4 slices fresh ginger (or ½ tsp powdered)

Open the chilli pods, de-seed and cut each into 4 pieces. In a small saucepan, bring to the boil the marinade ingredients. The slices of fresh ginger should be whole. Stir, remove from heat and set aside to cool. Peel the turnips and carrot, then, cut into thin slices. Peel the cucumber, cut it open lengthwise and de-seed. Cut into thin slices. Remove the outer leaves and thick stalks of the cabbage. Cut into bite-sized pieces. Put the turnips, carrot and cabbage into a tightly closing container. Pour in the marinade and stir until all the vegetables are well covered. Place in the refrigerator and marinate overnight, shaking or stirring from time to time. Serve cold as a first course, salad or condiment.

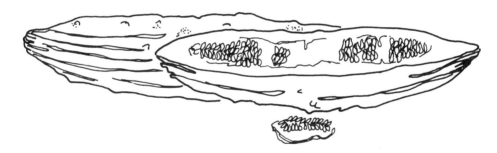

SOUPS (T'ang)

We do not serve our soups at the beginning of the meal as is done in western cultures but, rather, at the same time or following the main or 'salty' dishes. There are clear, light soups to help the digestion, sweet soups to create contrast, and very thick soups which are often in themselves main dishes. Certain thick noodle soups are served for special celebrations and holidays, at lunchtime, before the beginning of the long evening banquet. You will find recipes for these in the noodle chapter because we consider them noodles served in a little soup rather than soups containing a little noodle.

Soup stocks can be prepared in advance and the vegetables added at the very last moment.

The Chinese housewife always keeps a saucepan of water on the stove into which she tosses shrimp shells or chicken or pork bones, a little spring onion, a slice of ginger. Conveniently, stock cubes and other prepared stocks offer a perfectly adequate substitute for the eternal Chinese stock pot.

The thickness of Chinese soups depends to a certain degree upon personal preference and availability of ingredients. Moreover, for western palates, their consistancy often seems more stew-like than soup-like. Therefore, extra water or stock may be added to clarify any of the following soups to taste.

ASPARAGUS SOUP (Lu Sun Ch'au Ku Ch'in T'ang)
easy
preparation 10 minutes
cooking 4 minutes
serves 3 to 4

YOU NEED
4 oz (100 g) asparagus tinned or frozen
4 oz (100 g) button mushrooms fresh or tinned
4 oz (100 g) lean pork
1 small carrot
1 small cucumber
2 pints (1 litre) chicken stock (or 1 broth cube)

MARINADE
1 tbsp cornflour

1 generous pinch salt
1 unbeaten egg white
½ tsp dry sherry

SEASONING
1 pinch pepper
1 tsp salt
½ tbsp dry sherry
½ tsp soy sauce
¼ tsp monosodium glutamate (optional)

Prepare the marinade. Cut the pork against the grain into thin strips. Mix with the marinade and set aside for 10 minutes. Clean the mushrooms and slice thinly. Peel the cucumber and cut it open lengthwise. De-seed, slice thinly, then plunge it into cold water. Cut the carrot diagonally into thin slices and add them to the cold water. Cut the asparagus on the diagonal in 1" (2.5 cm) lengths. Prepare the seasoning and set aside. Bring to the boil a saucepan of water, about 2 pints (1 litre). Plunge in the pork strips and boil rapidly until they return to the surface, about 2 minutes. Drain, discarding the water. Bring the chicken stock to the boil. Add the seasoning, mushrooms, asparagus and pork. Boil for 1 minute. Drain the carrot and cucumber and add them to the soup. Bring back to the boil, remove from heat and serve at once.

CHICKEN SOUP (Suan Kua Chi T'ang)
very easy
preparation 5 minutes
cooking 14 minutes
serves 3 to 4

YOU NEED
2 chicken breasts (or thighs or leftover chicken, see Tips & Tricks)
4 oz (100 g) dill pickles (or Chinese pickled mustard greens)
1 tsp salt
1½ pints (1 litre) water

SEASONING
¼ tsp soy sauce
2 tbsp dry sherry
1 tsp monosodium glutamate (optional)

Bring the water to the boil. Plunge in the chicken breast (whole) and season with salt. Bring back to the boil and skim. Cook rapidly 10 to 12 minutes or until done. Remove the chicken, reserving the stock in the saucepan. Cut the chicken into even, bite-sized pieces, about 1" × 1" (2.5 cm × 2.5 cm). Thinly slice the pickles on the diagonal. Bring the chicken stock back to the boil. Add the seasoning ingredients and boil for 30 seconds. Incorporate the pieces of chicken and the pickles. Cook for 1 minute. Remove from the heat and serve.

TIPS & TRICKS
If leftover chicken is used, omit the pre-cooking, reduce slightly the quantity of water and flavour with 1 chicken broth cube. This soup is an excellent complement to all stir-fried, deep-fried and noodle dishes.

CHICKEN SOUP WITH CUCUMBER (Wu Ts'ai T'ang)
easy
preparation 15 minutes
cooking 10 minutes
serves 3 to 4

YOU NEED
1 chicken breast
4 oz (100 g) ham
1 small cucumber
1 egg
1 spring onion (or leek)
1 slice fresh ginger (optional)
1 pinch salt
½ tbsp dry sherry
2 tsp oil
2 pints (1 litre) water

SEASONING
1 tsp salt
½ tbsp dry sherry
1 pinch pepper
½ tsp sesame oil (optional)
½ tsp monosodium glutamate (optional)

Bring the water to the boil. Plunge in the chicken breast and boil gently for 5 minutes. Remove the chicken, reserving the water, and shred coarsely. Peel the cucumber and cut it open lengthwise. De-seed and cut into 2" (5 cm) long, thin strips. Cut the spring onion into 2" (5 cm) lengths and the ham into 2" (5 cm) long strips. Beat the egg with a pinch of salt and the sherry. In a frying pan, heat 1 tsp oil until almost smoking. Pour in the beaten egg, rolling the pan to make a very thin omelette. Brown quickly on both sides, remove from the pan and roll tightly. Cut the omelette crosswise in thin strips and set aside. In a heavy saucepan, heat 1 tsp oil until almost smoking. Stir-fry the spring onion (or leek) and ginger (the ginger slice should be whole) for 30 seconds. Pour in the chicken broth which you have reserved. Bring to the boil, then discard the fresh ginger slice and spring-onion. Incorporate the ham, chicken, cucumber and seasoning. Bring back to the boil and cook rapidly for 3 minutes. Add the strips of omelette and remove from the heat. Serve immediately.

CHINESE SHRIMP SOUP (Jou Szu T'ang)
easy
preparation 15 minutes
cooking 7 to 8 minutes
serves 2 to 3

YOU NEED
4 oz (100 g) lean pork
1 oz (25 g) dried shrimp (or 4 oz (100 g) fresh or frozen shelled shrimp)
1 carrot
3 rice galettes (or 4 oz (100 g) rice noodles)
1 spring onion (or leek)
½ tsp salt
1 pinch pepper
4–5 sprigs Chinese or common parsley (or celery leaves)

1½ pints (1 litre) water (including the dried shrimp soaking water)
2 tbsp oil

Rinse the dried shrimp and cover with ½ pint (¼ litre) warm water to soak for 10 minutes or until soft. Drain, reserving the soaking water which you will add to the stock. Bring to the boil a large saucepan of water to pour over the galettes (or rice noodles). Place the galettes (or noodles) in a drainer, being careful not to break them. Pour the boiling water over the galettes (or rice noodles). Drain, then, cut into strips. Cut equally into strips the pork, carrot and spring onion. Coarsely chop the parsley. In a heavy saucepan, heat 2 tbsp oil until almost smoking. Stir-fry the spring onion, pork, and shrimp for 2 minutes. Season with salt and pepper, then pour in the water (including the shrimp soaking water). Bring to the boil, add the carrot strips and boil for 5 minutes. Incorporate the rice galettes and parsley, stir and remove from heat. Serve at once, sprinkled with nuoc mam or Chinese fish sauce, if desired.

CRAB SOUP (Hsiah Jou T'ang)
easy
preparation 5 minutes
cooking 18 minutes
serves 3 to 4

YOU NEED
4 oz (100 g) crab meat (or scallops or shrimp)
1 tomato
1 egg
1 spring onion (or leek)
1 generous pinch salt
1 slice fresh ginger (optional)

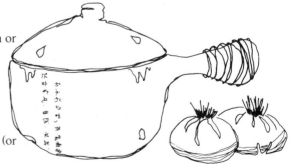

1 tsp oil
1 dash sesame oil (optional)
1½ pints (1 litre) chicken stock (1 stock cube)

MARINADE
½ tsp dry sherry
½ tsp powdered ginger

SEASONING
1 pinch pepper
1 tbsp dry sherry
1 tbsp soy sauce

Prepare the marinade. Mix the crab meat (or scallop or shrimp) with the marinade and set aside for 10 minutes. Coarsely chop the tomato and mince the spring onion (or leek). Beat the egg with the seasoning. In a heavy saucepan, heat the oil until almost smoking. Stir-fry the ginger and salt for 10 seconds, then discard the ginger. Add the crab meat (or scallop or shrimp) and tomato and stir-fry for 3 minutes. Pour in the chicken stock and bring to the boil. Lower the heat and simmer for 10 minutes. Pour in the beaten egg in a slow steady stream, stirring constantly. Add the spring onion (or leek) and simmer for 3 minutes more. Remove from the heat and sprinkle with sesame oil, if desired. Serve at once.

EGG FLOWER SOUP I (Chin Tzen T'ang)

very easy
preparation 5 minutes
cooking 4 minutes
serves 2 to 3

YOU NEED
3 eggs
1 spring onion (or chives)
1 pinch salt to taste
1 tsp soy sauce
1 dash sesame oil (optional)
1½ pints (1 litre) chicken stock (1 stock cube)

Bring the stock to the boil. Meanwhile, beat the eggs. Finely mince the spring onion (or chives). Pour the beaten eggs into the boiling broth in a slow steady stream, stirring constantly. Season with soy sauce and salt. Stir and remove from heat. Garnish with the spring onion and a dash of sesame oil, if desired. Serve at once.

EGG FLOWER SOUP II (Fan Chieh Tan Hau T'ang)

very easy
preparation 4 minutes
cooking 4 minutes
serves 2 to 3

YOU NEED
1 tomato
2 large lettuce leaves
1 egg
1½ pints (1 litre) chicken stock (1 stock cube)

SEASONING
1 tsp salt
1 tsp dry sherry
½ tsp soy sauce

THICKENING
½ tbsp cornflour dissolved in
½ tbsp water

Bring the chicken stock to the boil. Meanwhile, cut the lettuce leaves into thin strips and plunge into cold water. Cut the tomato into thin slices. Beat the egg. Prepare the thickening and set aside. Add the seasoning to the boiling stock. Cook rapidly for 30 seconds. Incorporate the thickening and boil for 30 seconds. Pour in the beaten egg in a slow steady stream, stirring constantly. Drain the lettuce and add it to the soup. Stir, then add the tomato. Stir again, remove from heat and serve immediately.

FLOATING CLOUD SOUP I (Niu Nau T'ang)

easy
preparation 15 minutes
cooking 4 minutes
serves 2 to 3

YOU NEED

5 oz (120 g) (lamb's) brain
1 egg white
2 tsp dry sherry
1 slice fresh ginger (or 1 good pinch powdered)
1 spring onion (or chives)
½ tsp monosodium glutamate (optional)
1 pinch each salt and pepper to taste
1½ pints (1 litre) chicken (1 stock cube)

Under cold running water, and with the aid of a toothpick, remove the membrane which covers the brain. Mince finely and mix with the sherry. Mince the fresh ginger and spring onion. Bring the chicken stock to the boil. Add the brain and stir. Bring back to the boil. Pour the egg white into the boiling soup in a slow steady stream, stirring constantly. Bring back to the boil. Incorporate ginger, salt, pepper and mono-sodium glutamate. Stir and remove from heat. Garnish with the spring onion (or chives) and serve at once.

FLOATING CLOUD SOUP II (Tong Ku Niu Nau T'ang)

easy
preparation 15 minutes
cooking 12 minutes
serves 2 to 3

YOU NEED

5 oz (120 g) (lamb's) brain
5 dried Chinese mushrooms (or button mush-
    rooms)
1 tsp dry sherry
½ tsp salt
1 spring onion (or chives)
1 pinch pepper
½ tsp monosodium glutamate (optional)
1½ pints (1 litre) water (including mushroom
    soaking water)

Wash the dried mushrooms and cover with ½ pint (¼ litre) warm water to soak for 10 minutes or until soft. Drain (reserving the water), remove the hard stalks and cut in strips. Under cold running water, and with the aid of a toothpick, remove the membrane which covers the brain. Cut the brain into 1" (2.5 cm) pieces. Mince the spring onion (or chives). Bring to the boil 1½ pints (1 litre) water (including the mushroom soaking water). Incorporate the brain and mushrooms and cook for 10 minutes. Add the sherry, salt, pepper and monosodium glutamate. Stir, garnish with the spring onion and remove from heat. Serve immediately.

TIPS & TRICKS

This soup, both elegant and nourishing, makes an excellent first course for highly seasoned and deep fried dishes as well as those rich in soy sauce.

FUKIEN SOUP (Hsieh Hwang Ts'ai Sin)

easy
preparation 15 minutes
cooking 6 minutes
serves 3 to 4

YOU NEED

4 oz (100 g) crab meat
¼ lb (250 g) spinach
2 spring onions (or leek)
4 egg yolks
1 slice fresh ginger (or 1 pinch powdered)
1 tbsp cornflour
2 tsp oil
1½ pints (1 litre) water

SEASONING A

½ tsp salt
½ tsp dry sherry
1 tbsp water

SEASONING B

1 tsp salt
1 good pinch pepper
1 tsp dry sherry
1 tsp sesame oil (optional)

Mince the spring onions (or leek) and fresh ginger. Clean the spinach and cut the leaves on the diagonal into thin strips. Dissolve the cornflour in the water. In 2 bowls, prepare seasonings A and B. Beat the egg yolks. In a heavy saucepan, heat 1 tsp oil until almost smoking. Stir-fry the spinach for 1 minute. Add the seasoning A and stir-fry for 2 minutes. Remove the spinach from the pan and place it in a deep serving dish. To the same saucepan, add 1 tsp oil and heat until almost smoking. Stir-fry the ginger and spring onions (or leek) for 30 seconds. Incorporate the crab meat and seasoning B. Stir-fry for 30 seconds. Add the water/cornflour mixture and bring to the boil. Pour in the beaten egg yolks in a slow steady stream, stirring constantly. Cook for 30 seconds, then pour the soup over the spinach. Serve at once.

JADE SOUP (Po Ts'ai Muo Ku T'ang)

very easy
preparation 15 minutes
cooking 3 minutes
serves 3 to 4

This is a delicate and light soup which makes a perfect first course for dinners composed of very rich dishes.

YOU NEED
⅓ lb (150 g) fresh spinach
4 oz (100 g) button mushrooms fresh or tinned
½ tsp salt to taste
1 pinch pepper
1 tsp monosodium glutamate (optional)
2 pints (1 litre) chicken stock (2 stock cubes)

Clean the spinach and cut the leaves on the diagonal into thin strips. Clean the mushrooms and slice thinly. Bring the chicken stock to the boil. Incorporate the salt, pepper and monosodium glutamate. Boil for 30 seconds. Add the mushrooms and spinach. Boil for 2 minutes. Remove from heat and serve at once.

MANDARIN SOUP (Hsia Jen Po Ts'ai T'ang)

easy
preparation 20 minutes
cooking 18 minutes
serves 4

YOU NEED
6 oz (150 g) fresh or frozen shrimp (or minced pork or minced beef)
4 oz (100 g) spinach
4 cabbage leaves
1 stick celery (or water chestnuts)
1 spring onion (or leek)
1 small carrot
1 egg
½ tsp salt to taste
2 pints (1 litre) chicken stock (1 stock cube)

MARINADE
1 unbeaten egg white
½ tsp salt
1 pinch powdered ginger
1 tsp dry sherry

THICKENING
1 tbsp cornflour dissolved in
2 tbsp water

Prepare the marinade. Shell the shrimp and remove veins, then, mince finely. Mix with the marinade and set aside. Clean the spinach leaves and chop coarsely. Coarsely chop the cabbage leaves. Mince the spring onion (or leek). Dice the celery (or water chestnut) and carrot. Beat the egg. Prepare the thickening and set aside. Bring the chicken stock to the boil. Add the cabbage, celery or carrot and salt. Cook gently for 10 minutes. Incorporate the thickening and boil for 1 minute (or until thickened). Add the shrimp (or meat) gradually, stirring constantly. Cook for 5 minutes. Add the spring onion (or leek) and spinach. Pour in the beaten egg slowly; stirring constantly. Cook for 1 minute more, then remove from the heat. Serve at once.

PIGS' FEET SOUP (Yin Ya T'i Hua T'ang)

very easy
preparation 5 minutes
cooking 2½ to 3 hours
serves 4

YOU NEED

2 pigs' feet
1 spring onion (or leek)
2 slices fresh ginger (or ⅓ tsp powdered)
½ lb (250 g) bean sprouts (or cabbage sliced thinly)

SEASONING

1 pinch pepper
2 tsp salt

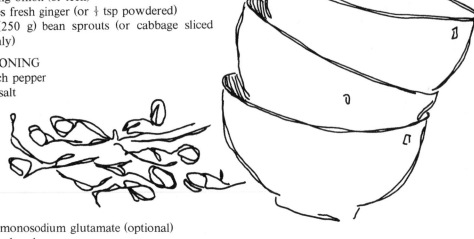

1 tsp monosodium glutamate (optional)
1 tbsp dry sherry

If possible, ask your butcher to cut the pigs' feet into little pieces. Mince the fresh ginger. Wash the pigs' feet well and place in a heavy saucepan. Cover with water and bring to the boil. Add the ginger. Lower the heat and simmer for 2½ hours or until the pigs' feet are very tender. Meanwhile, mince the spring onion (or leek). Rinse the bean sprouts (or cabbage). Add the spring onions (or leek) and sprouts (or cabbage) to the soup. Cook for a further 10 minutes. Add all seasoning ingredients and stir. Serve hot.

SCALLOP SOUP (San Szu Kan Psi T'ang)

easy
preparation 10 minutes
cooking 5 minutes
serves 2 to 3

YOU NEED

4 oz (100 g) scallops (or crab or shrimp)
2 spring onions (or leek)
1 medium-sized onion
1 small carrot
1 egg (optional)
½ tsp sugar
½ tbsp dry sherry
1 tbsp oil
1½ pints (1 litre) water

SEASONING

1 pinch pepper
1 good pinch powdered ginger
½ tsp salt
1 tsp soy sauce
½ tbsp dry sherry
½ tsp sesame oil (optional)

THICKENING

½ tbsp cornflour dissolved in
1 tbsp water

Tear the scallops (or crab or shrimp) into shreds. Cut into shred-like strips the spring onions, carrot and onion. Beat the egg with the sherry. In 2 bowls, prepare the seasoning and the thickening. In a heavy saucepan, heat the oil until almost smoking. Stir-fry for 30 seconds the spring onions (or leeks) sprinkled with the sugar. Add the carrot, onion and scallops (or crab or shrimp). Stir-fry for 1 minute. Incorporate the seasoning and stir and cook for 1 minute. Pour in the water and bring to the boil. Add the seasoning, stir and cook until slightly thickened, about 1 minute. Pour in, in a slow steady stream, the beaten egg, stirring constantly. Cook for 30 seconds, then remove from heat. Serve immediately.

SOUP OF SIX COLOURS (Su Ts'ai T'ang)

easy
preparation 20 minutes
cooking 7 minutes
serves 3 to 4

YOU NEED

4 oz (100 g) lean pork
4 oz (100 g) ham
4 oz (100 g) spinach
4 oz (100 g) button mushrooms fresh or tinned
1 spring onion (or leek)
1 small carrot
1 small cucumber
2 pints (1 litre) chicken stock (1 stock cube)

MARINADE

1 unbeaten egg white
1 pinch salt
1 tbsp cornflour
$\frac{1}{2}$ tsp monosodium glutamate (optional)
$\frac{1}{2}$ tsp dry sherry

SEASONING

1 good pinch powdered ginger
1 tbsp cornflour
1 tsp salt
$\frac{1}{2}$ tsp soy sauce
1 tbsp dry sherry
1 pinch pepper

Prepare the marinade. Cut the pork against the grain into thin slices, about 1" × 2" (2.5 cm × 5 cm). Mix with the marinade and set aside. Mince the spring onion (or leek). Clean the mushrooms and slice thinly. Cut the carrot on the diagonal into thin slices and the ham into strips 1" × 2" (2.5 cm × 5 cm). Peel the cucumber and cut it open lengthwise. De-seed, then slice thinly. Clean the spinach and cut the leaves on the diagonal into strips. Prepare the seasoning and set aside. Bring to the boil a saucepan of water (about 2 pints). Plunge the pork piece by piece into the boiling water. Boil rapidly until the pieces return to the surface, about 2 minutes, then drain. Discard the water. Bring the chicken stock to the boil. Incorporate the seasoning, cucumber and carrot. Cook rapidly for 3 minutes. Add the pork, ham, spinach and mushrooms. Cook for 2 minutes more, then remove from heat. Serve at once.

SOUP OF TWO FLAVOURS (Hwang Kua Jou P'ien T'ang)

very easy
preparation 5 minutes
cooking 6 minutes
serves 2 to 3

YOU NEED

4 oz (100 g) rump steak (or lean pork, shrimp or fish fillet)
1 small cucumber
1$\frac{1}{2}$ pints (1 litre) chicken stock (1 stock cube)

SEASONING

$\frac{1}{2}$ tbsp soy sauce
1 pinch each salt and pepper to taste
1 good pinch monosodium glutamate (optional)

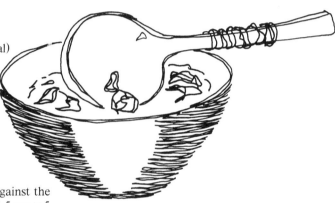

Remove fat and gristle from the meat, then put it into the freezer for 15 minutes or until half-frozen. Peel the cucumber and cut it open lengthwise. De-seed and slice thinly. Cut the (half-frozen) meat into paper-thin slices. Bring the stock to the boil and add the seasoning. Stirring, drop in the slices of meat. Cook rapidly for 3 minutes. Incorporate the slices of cucumber and cook for 3 minutes more or until the cucumber becomes translucent. Remove from the heat and serve at once.

SOUR AND PUNGENT SOUP (Suan La T'ang)

easy
preparation 10 minutes
cooking 12 minutes
serves 3 to 4

YOU NEED

4 oz (100 g) lean pork
4 oz (100 g) bamboo shoots (or water chestnuts or bean sprouts)
4 dried Chinese mushrooms (or cloud ears or button mushrooms)
6 oz (150 g) bean curd (or 1 oz (25 g) *fenszu*)
1 spring onion (or chives)
1 egg
1 tbsp oil
2 pints (1 litre) chicken stock including the dried mushroom soaking water (2 stock cubes)

SEASONING

$\frac{1}{2}$ tsp salt
2 tbsp cornflour
2 tbsp dry sherry
2 tbsp vinegar
1 tsp soy sauce
1 pinch dried red pepper (or 1 dash tabasco)

Wash the dried mushrooms (or cloud ears) and cover with $\frac{1}{2}$ pint ($\frac{1}{4}$ litre) warm water to soak for 10 minutes or until soft. Drain (reserving the water of the dried Chinese mushrooms for the stock), remove the hard stalks of the mushrooms and cut into strips. If using *fenszu*, soak 1 to 2 minutes in warm water, then drain and cut into 3 or 4 lengths. Cut the pork against the grain into thin strips. Cut into thin strips, the bamboo shoots (or water chestnuts or bean sprouts) and bean curd (or *fenszu*). Mince the spring onion (or chives). Beat the egg. Prepare the seasoning and

set aside. In a heavy saucepan, heat the oil until almost smoking. Stir-fry the pork for 1 minute. Add the mushrooms, stir and pour in the chicken stock. Bring to the boil, lower the heat and simmer for 10 minutes. Incorporate the bean curd (or *fenszu*), bamboo shoots (or water chestnuts or bean sprouts) and seasoning. Cook, while stirring, 2 minutes or until thickened. Pour in slowly the beaten egg, stirring constantly. Remove from heat, garnish with the spring onion (or chives) and serve at once.

TIGER LILY SOUP (Chin Tzen T'ang)

very easy
preparation 5 minutes
cooking 1$\frac{1}{2}$ hours
serves 2 to 3

YOU NEED

1 oz (25 g) dried tiger lilies
$\frac{1}{2}$ lb (250 g) stewing beef (or chicken or pork)
1 tsp salt
2$\frac{1}{2}$ pints (1$\frac{1}{4}$ litre) water

Bring to the boil 2 pints (1 litre) water. Meanwhile, wash the tiger lilies and cut off the hard ends. Cover with $\frac{1}{2}$ pint ($\frac{1}{4}$ litre) warm water and set aside to soak. Cut the meat into even, bite-sized pieces. Plunge the pieces of meat into the boiling water. Bring back to the boil, lower the heat and skim. Cover and simmer for 1 hour or until the meat is tender. Add the tiger lilies and their soaking water. Cook for 30 minutes more. Season with salt and stir. Serve hot.

WATERCRESS SOUP (Hsi Yang Ts'ai T'ang)

easy
preparation 15 minutes/marinade 5 minutes
cooking 12 minutes
serves 3 to 4

YOU NEED

½ lb (250 g) watercress (or cabbage or courgettes)
4 oz (100 g) pork
1–2 slices fresh ginger (or 1 good pinch powdered)
1 tsp salt to taste
1 tsp oil
2 pints (1 litre) water

MARINADE

½ tbsp soy sauce
½ tsp sugar
1 tsp cornflour
1 pinch pepper

Prepare the marinade. Cut the pork against the grain into thin strips. Mix with the marinade and set aside for 5 minutes. Wash the watercress (or cabbage) and chop coarsely. (Cut the courgettes into very thin slices.) Mince the fresh ginger finely. In a heavy saucepan, heat the oil until almost smoking. Stir-fry the ginger and salt 30 seconds. Pour in the water and bring to the boil. Drop in the pork piece by piece and bring back to the boil. Cook rapidly for 5 minutes. Add the watercress (or cabbage or courgettes), lower the heat and cover. Simmer for 5 minutes more. Remove from the heat and serve at once.

VEGETABLES (SuTs'ai)

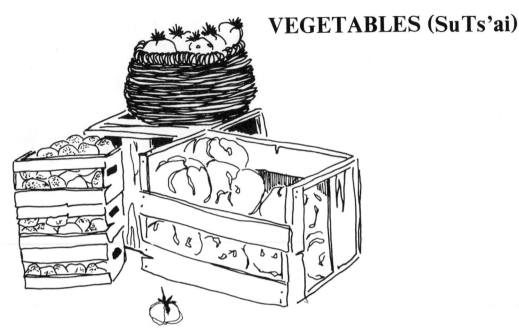

There is hardly a Chinese dish which does not contain at least one vegetable, if not several. It could be said the vegetable is the preferred food of the Chinese. In fact, vegetarianism is very widespread in China.

Through the centuries a superlative technique for the cooking of vegetables has been developed, one which enhances all of their inherent qualities: taste, colour, texture and vitamin content. This is the stir-fry method, now being adopted throughout the world. Success depends upon the use of very little oil and the pan being heated to the smoking point before the vegetable is added. While being stirred energetically with a spatula, the vegetable is sautéed until its colour intensifies and it becomes tender yet still crunchy. As a general rule, this takes from one to three minutes. The vegetable is then removed from the pan and immediately served.

BRAISED CABBAGE (Suh Pao Shin Ts'ai)
very easy
preparation 4 minutes
cooking 12 minutes
serves 2 to 3

YOU NEED
1 lb (500 g) cabbage (or Chinese cabbage)
1 pinch pepper
1 tsp salt
1 tsp sesame oil (optional)
1 tbsp oil
¼ pint (⅛ litre) water

Clean cabbage, removing the coarse outer leaves and thick stems. Tear or cut into bite-size pieces about 1½'' (3 cm) square. In a deep frying pan, heat the oil until almost smoking. Stir-fry the cabbage 1 minute. Add salt, pepper and water. Lower the heat and let simmer 10 minutes

uncovered. Remove from heat and sprinkle with sesame oil. Serve at once.

BRAISED PUMPKIN (Chien Na Kua)
very easy
preparation 10 minutes
cooking 12 minutes
serves 2 to 3

YOU NEED
1 lb (500 g) pumpkin (or winter marrow)
1 spring onion (or leek)
2 tbsp oil

SEASONING
$\frac{1}{2}$ tsp soy sauce
1 pinch pepper
$\frac{1}{4}$ tsp salt
$1\frac{1}{2}$ tsp sugar
$\frac{1}{4}$ pint ($\frac{1}{8}$ litre) chicken broth (1 broth cube)

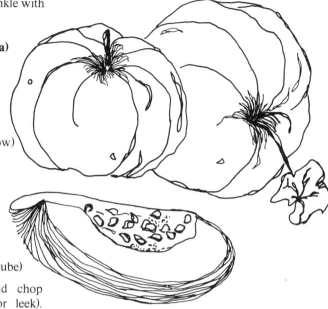

Peel the pumpkin (or marrow) and chop coarsely. Mince the spring onion (or leek). Prepare the seasoning and set aside. In a frying pan, heat the oil until almost smoking. Stir-fry the pumpkin for 2 minutes. Add the spring onion (or leek) and seasoning, then reduce the heat. Let simmer for 10 minutes. Remove from heat and serve.

COURGETTES WITH GINGER (Ch'au Szu Kua)
very easy
preparation 5 minutes
cooking 3 to 4 minutes
serves 2 to 3

YOU NEED
2 medium-sized courgettes, about 1 lb (500 g)
1 slice fresh ginger (or $\frac{1}{4}$ tsp powdered)
$\frac{1}{2}$ tsp salt
3 tbsp water
$\frac{1}{2}$ tbsp oil

Peel the courgettes and cut on the diagonal into very thin slices. Mince finely the fresh ginger. In a frying pan, heat the oil until it is almost smoking. Stir-fry the ginger 30 seconds (powdered 10 seconds). Add the slices of courgette and stir fry for 30 seconds. Sprinkle with the water and salt. Continue to cook over high heat until all liquid is absorbed, 2 to 3 minutes. Remove from heat and serve at once.

COURGETTES WITH SESAME SEEDS (Chih Ma Ch'au Chin Kua)
very easy
preparation 4 minutes
cooking 2 to 3 minutes
serves 2 to 3

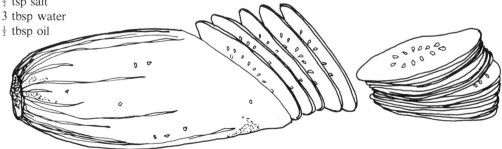

YOU NEED

2 medium-sized courgettes about 1 lb (500 g)
½ tbsp sesame seeds
½ tsp salt
1 pinch pepper
1 tbsp oil

Peel the courgettes and cut into strips about 2" (5 cm) long and ½" (1.25 cm) wide. In a frying pan, heat the oil until almost smoking. Stir-fry the courgettes for 30 seconds. Sprinkle with salt, pepper and sesame seeds. Stir-fry until crunchy-tender, 1 to 2 minutes. Remove from heat and serve at once.

MUSHROOMS BRAISED IN SOY SAUCE (Ch'au Hsiang Ku)

easy
preparation 10 minutes
cooking 13 minutes
serves 2 to 3

These mushrooms are usually served as a first course.

YOU NEED

20 dried Chinese mushrooms (or ½ lb (500 g) fresh button mushrooms)
1 tsp sesame oil (optional)
2 tbsp oil

SEASONING

1 tbsp sugar
1 tsp dry sherry
2 tbsp soy sauce
¼ pint (⅛ litre) water (or mushroom soaking water)

Wash the dried mushrooms and cover with warm water to soak 10 minutes or until soft. Drain (reserving the water) and remove the hard stalks. (If using fresh mushrooms, clean and cut in half.) Prepare the seasoning and set aside. In a frying pan, heat the oil. Stir-fry the mushrooms for 3 minutes. Pour in the seasoning and bring back to the boil. Lower heat and let simmer, uncovered, 25 minutes (10 minutes for the fresh mushrooms). Remove from heat, sprinkle with sesame oil and serve warm or cold.

TIPS & TRICKS

An ancient Chinese belief held that dried Chinese mushrooms contributed to a long life. And, modern scientific research has proved that, in fact, this is true for they contain an element which diminishes cholesterol!

MUSHROOMS WITH NUOC MAM (Hau Yu Hsien Ch'au Ku)

easy
preparation 15 minutes
cooking 5 minutes
serves 2 to 3

YOU NEED

½ lb (250 g) fresh button mushrooms
½ lb (250 g) fresh spinach (or romaine or Chinese cabbage)
4 tbsp water
1 tbsp oil

SEASONING A

½ tsp salt
1 tsp dry sherry
1 tsp water

SEASONING B

2 tbsp nuoc mam (or Chinese fish sauce)
1 tsp lemon juice
1 tsp sesame oil (optional)
½ tsp monosodium glutamate (optional)

THICKENING

1 tbsp cornflour dissolved in
1 tbsp water

Bring to the boil enough water to cover the mushrooms. Clean and wash the mushrooms, and, if they are large, cut them in half. Drop in the boiling water for 1 minute. Drain and plunge into a basin of cold water. Clean and wash the spinach (or cabbage), then, cut the leaves diagonally in strips. In 3 small bowls, prepare the seasonings and thickening. In a deep frying pan, heat the oil until almost smoking. Stir-fry the spinach for 30 seconds. Sprinkle with seasoning A and stir-fry 2 minutes. Remove the spinach from the pan and set aside. In the same pan, bring the water to the boil. Drain the mushrooms and drop in the pan. Add seasoning B and bring once again to the boil. Incorporate the seasoning and let thicken, about 1 minute. Return the spinach (or cabbage) to the pan, stir and remove from heat. Serve at once.

RED COOKED AUBERGINE (Hung Shao Ch'ieh)

very easy
preparation 5 minutes
cooking 31 minutes
serves 2 to 3

YOU NEED

1 lb (500 g) aubergine (or turnip or radish)
$\frac{1}{2}$ tsp salt
1 tsp sugar
2 tsp sesame oil (optional)
1 tbsp oil

SEASONING

1 tsp dry sherry
2 tsp vinegar
3 tsp soy sauce
$\frac{1}{4}$ pint ($\frac{1}{8}$ litre) water

Prepare the seasoning and set aside. Peel the aubergine and cut into $\frac{1}{2}$" (1.25 cm) cubes. In a deep frying pan, heat 1 tbsp oil. Drop the aubergine into the pan and immediately sprinkle with sugar and salt. Stir-fry for 1 minute. Pour in the seasoning, lower heat and simmer, uncovered, for 30 minutes or until the liquid is reduced to a scant $\frac{1}{4}$ pint ($\frac{1}{8}$ litre). Add the sesame oil, stir and remove from heat. Serve hot.

RED COOKED CABBAGE (Hung Shao Pau Shin Ts'ai)

very easy
preparation 10 minutes
cooking 7 minutes
serves 2 to 3

YOU NEED

1 lb (500 g) cabbage (or Chinese cabbage)
1 slice fresh ginger (or 1 good pinch powdered)
1 pinch salt
1 tbsp oil
4 tbsp water

SEASONING

1 chicken broth cube
4 tbsp water
2 tsp soy sauce
2 tsp sugar

Clean cabbage, removing the coarse outer leaves and thick stems. Tear or cut into bite-size pieces about $1\frac{1}{2}$" (3 cm) square. Mince finely the fresh ginger. In a small saucepan, bring the water to the boil. Dissolve the chicken broth cube, then, add the sugar and soy sauce. Stir, remove from heat and set aside. In a deep frying pan, heat the oil until almost smoking. Sauté the ginger for 10 seconds. Add the cabbage and a pinch of salt. Stir-fry until the cabbage is well covered with oil, about 1 minute. Pour in the seasoning, reduce heat and cover. Let simmer for 5 minutes. Remove from heat and serve at once.

RED COOKED SOY BEANS (Hung Shao Hwang Tou)

easy
preparation 5 minutes/soaking 2 hours or
    overnight
cooking 3 hours
serves 3 to 4

In China, red cooked soy beans are often carried on outings or served simply with tea.

YOU NEED
½ lb (250 g) dried soy beans (or dried white haricots)
4 tbsp soy sauce
2 spring onions (or shallot)
2 tbsp sugar
2 pints (1 litre) water

The night before cooking, cover the beans with warm water to soak. Or, 2 hours before cooking, put the beans in a large saucepan, cover with water and bring to the boil. Turn off the heat and let soak 2 hours. Drain the soy beans. The soaking water of the dried white haricot beans may be used for cooking. In a large saucepan, bring water, sugar and soy sauce to the boil. Add the beans and bring back to the boil. Lower heat and simmer, uncovered, until the beans are tender, about 3 hours (1½ to 2 hours for the dried white haricots). Add boiling water if need be for there should be about ¼ pint (⅛ litre) sauce remaining at the end of the cooking. Serve the beans warm or cold, garnished with chopped spring onion (or shallot). Sprinkle with sesame oil, tabasco or hot chilli sauce, if you so desire.

STEAMED AUBERGINE (Cheng Ch'ieh)
easy
preparation 10 minutes
cooking 10 minutes
serves 2 to 3

YOU NEED
1 lb (500 g) aubergine
2 slices fresh ginger (or ⅓ tsp powdered)
2 spring onions (or leek)
2 cloves garlic
2 tsp soy sauce
½ tsp salt
2 tsp sesame oil (optional)

You also need a steamer.

Put the steamer water to heat. Meanwhile, finely chop spring onion (or leek), garlic and fresh ginger. Peel the aubergine and cut into ½" (1.25 cm) cubes. In an oven proof bowl which will fit into the steamer, mix the aubergine with all other ingredients. Steam for 10 minutes or until the aubergine is tender. Serve hot or cold.

STIR-FRIED AUBERGINE (Hsiang Ch'ieh Tzu)
very easy
preparation 10 minutes
cooking 5 minutes
serves 2 to 3

YOU NEED
1 lb (500 g) aubergine
3 slices fresh ginger (or ½ tsp powdered)
3 spring onions (or leek)
1 clove garlic
1 tbsp dry sherry
1 tbsp oil

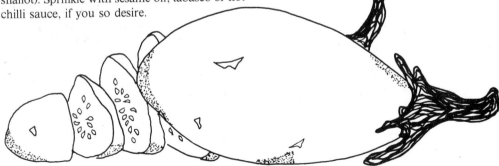

SEASONING
1 tsp sugar
3 tbsp soy sauce
½ tbsp vinegar
1 tbsp water
½ tbsp sesame oil (optional)

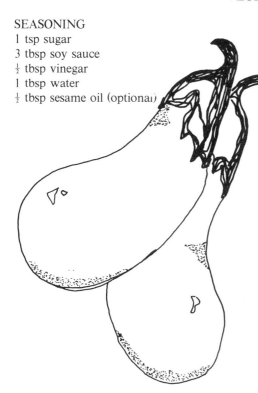

YOU NEED
½ lb (250 g) bean curd
1 spring onion
1 tbsp oil

SEASONING
1 tbsp soy sauce (or oyster sauce)
½ tsp sugar
¼ pint (⅛ litre) water

Cut the bean curd into bite-sized pieces about 1" (2.5 cm) square. Finely chop the spring onion. Prepare the seasoning and set aside. In a frying pan, heat the oil to a medium temperature. Brown the pieces of bean curd on all sides, about 5 minutes. Pour in the seasoning and bring to the boil. Cook over medium heat until the liquid has been reduced to a fine sauce, 4 to 5 minutes. Garnish with the spring onion and serve at once.

TIPS & TRICKS
Here is an even easier variation. Brown the pieces of bean curd on all sides in the hot oil, then remove from heat and serve immediately accompanied by, for dipping, small dishes of oyster sauce, nuoc mam or soy sauce mixed with several dashes of tabasco.

Mix the seasoning ingredients in a small bowl. Finely chop the spring onion (or leek), garlic and fresh ginger. Peel the aubergine and cut into strips about ½" (1.25 cm) thick, then plunge into cold water. In a frying pan, heat the oil until almost smoking. Stir-fry for 1 minute spring onion (or leek), garlic and ginger. Drain the aubergine and add to the pan. Sprinkle with the sherry and stir-fry for 1 minute. Pour in the seasoning and cook until the aubergine is tender, 2 to 3 minutes. Remove from heat and serve at once.

STIR-FRIED BEAN CURD (Hau Yiu Tou Fu)
very easy
preparation 5 minutes
cooking 10 to 12 minutes
serves 3 to 4

Stir-fried bean curd may be served as a first course although it is considered a vegetable and usually served as such on Chinese tables.

STIR-FRIED BROCCOLI (Ch'au Hua Yeh Ts'ai)
very easy
preparation 5 minutes
cooking 5 to 6 minutes
serves 2 to 3

YOU NEED
1 lb (500 g) broccoli
1 tsp salt
1 tbsp dry sherry
1 tbsp water
2 tbsp oil

Wash and drain the broccoli, then break into equal-sized florets including the small stems. Peel the large stems and cut into 1" (2.5 cm) pieces. In a frying pan, heat the oil until almost smoking. Add the broccoli and stir-fry for 30 seconds. Sprinkle with salt, sherry and water. Stir-fry until crunchy-tender and jade green, 4 to 5 minutes. Remove from heat and serve at once.

STIR-FRIED CAULIFLOWER (Ch'au Ts'ai Hua)
very easy
preparation 6 minutes
cooking 5 to 6 minutes
serves 2 to 3

YOU NEED
1 lb (500 g) cauliflower
2 spring onions (or leek)
1 tsp salt
1 tbsp dry sherry
1 tbsp water
2 tbsp oil

Divide the cauliflower into small, equal-sized florets, then, wash and drain. Finely chop the spring onions (or leek). In a frying pan, heat the oil until almost smoking. Stir-fry the spring onion (or leek) 10 seconds. Add the cauliflower and stir-fry for 30 seconds. Season with salt, then sprinkle with the sherry and water. Stir-fry until the cauliflower is crunchy-tender, 4 to 5 minutes. Remove from heat and serve at once.

STIR FRIED CELERY (Ch'au Chin Ts'ai)
very easy
preparation 5 minutes
cooking 3 to 4 minutes
serves 2 to 3

YOU NEED
1 small head celery (see Tips & Tricks)
1 tsp salt
1 tbsp dry sherry
2 tbsp oil

Wash and clean celery. Cut into thin strips about 2" (5 cm) long. In a frying pan, heat the oil until almost smoking. Add the celery and salt, then, stir and sprinkle with sherry. Stir-fry until crunchy-tender, 3 to 4 minutes. Remove from heat and serve immediately.

TIPS & TRICKS
This is the basic recipe for all stir-fried vegetables. We prepare in the same manner bean sprouts, spinach, mustard greens, cabbage (shredded), onions and so forth. Often we mix in equal quantities, two vegetables such as celery/onions, bean sprouts/onions, etc.

STIR-FRIED COURGETTES (Ch'au Chin Kua)
easy
preparation 5 minutes
cooking 5 minutes
serves 2 to 3

YOU NEED
2 medium-sized courgettes (or tomato), about 1 lb (500 g)
1–2 cloves garlic

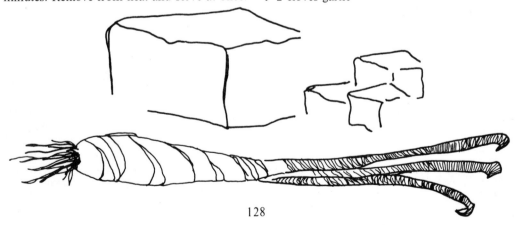

½ tsp salt
½ tsp soy sauce (or vinegar)
1 tbsp dry sherry
½ tsp sesame oil (optional)
1 tbsp oil

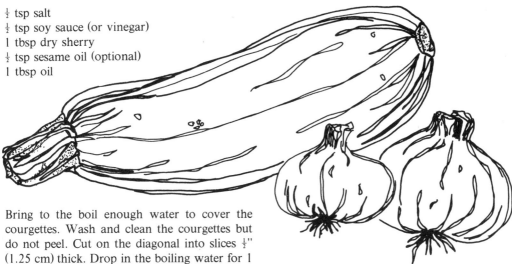

Bring to the boil enough water to cover the courgettes. Wash and clean the courgettes but do not peel. Cut on the diagonal into slices ½" (1.25 cm) thick. Drop in the boiling water for 1 minute, then, drain. Finely mince the garlic. In a frying pan, heat the oil until almost smoking. Stir-fry the garlic 10 seconds. Add the courgette and stir-fry until well covered with oil, about 1 minute. Sprinkle with sherry and salt, lower heat and cover the pan. Let cook until crunchy-tender, 2 to 3 minutes. Sprinkle with soy sauce and sesame oil, stir and remove from heat. Serve hot.

STIR-FRIED FROZEN SPINACH WITH PORK (Ch'au Hsüeh Li Hung)

very easy
preparation 5 minutes
cooking 5 minutes
serves 2 to 3

YOU NEED
10–12 oz (400 g) frozen spinach (or mustard greens)
4 oz (100 g) lean pork (or ham or bacon)
1 chilli pod
1 tsp vinegar
½ tsp salt
1 tbsp dry sherry
1 tbsp oil

Thaw spinach and drain well, squeezing if necessary, to extract excess water. Sprinkle with vinegar and set aside. Dice the pork (or ham or bacon). Open and de-seed the chilli pod, then cut into 4 pieces. In a frying pan, heat the oil until almost smoking. Stir-fry the chilli pod for 1 minute. Add the pork (or ham or bacon) and stir-fry 2 minutes. Incorporate spinach (or mustard greens), sherry and salt. Stir-fry 2 minutes more. Remove from heat and serve at once.

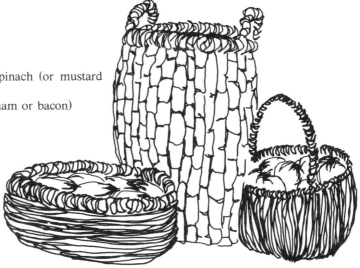

STIR-FRIED MIXED VEGETABLES
(Ch'au Shih Chin Ch'in Ts'ai)
easy
preparation 15 minutes
cooking 3 minutes
serves 2 to 3

YOU NEED
1 lb (500 g) bean sprouts (or see Tips & Tricks)
1 medium carrot
1 large green pepper
1 large onion
1 chilli pod (optional)
2 tbsp oil

SEASONING
1 pinch pepper
$\frac{1}{2}$ tsp salt
1 tbsp sugar
1 tbsp dry sherry
2 tbsp soy sauce
1 tbsp vinegar

Open and de-seed the chilli pod and green pepper. Cut both, as well as the carrot and onion, into matchstick-thin strips about 2" (5 cm) long. Wash and drain the bean sprouts. Prepare the seasoning and put aside. In a frying pan, heat the oil until almost smoking. Stir-fry carrot, green pepper, chilli pod and onion for 2 minutes. Add the bean sprouts and seasoning. Cook, stirring continually, for 1 minute or until all the vegetables are well coated with the seasoning. Remove from heat and sprinkle with sesame oil if you so desire.

TIPS & TRICKS
We also prepare this recipe using 4 ounces of *fenszu* in the place of the bean sprouts. Before cooking, soak the *fenszu* for 1 to 2 minutes in warm water, then drain and cut into segments about 2" (5 cm) long. Proceed with the cooking as indicated above.

STIR-FRIED SPINACH WITH HAM (Yang Huo T'ue Po Ts'ai)
easy
preparation 10 minutes
cooking 3 minutes
serves 2 to 3

YOU NEED
1 lb (500 g) spinach (or asparagus, cabbage or courgette)
½ lb (250 g) ham
1 clove garlic (optional)
½ tsp salt
½ tsp sugar
4 tbsp oil

Cut the ham and garlic in very thin strips. Clean the spinach (or asparagus, cabbage or courgettes) and cut on the diagonal in thin strips. In a deep frying pan, heat 2 tbsp oil and the salt. Stir-fry the spinach (or asparagus, cabbage, or courgettes) 2 minutes. Remove from the pan and let drain. Add 2 tbsp oil to the same pan and reheat until almost smoking. Stir-fry the garlic and ham for 1 minute. Return the spinach to the pan and sprinkle with the sugar. Stir-fry for 20 seconds. Remove from heat and serve at once.

SWEET AND SOUR CABBAGE (T'ien Suan Pao Hsin Ts'ai)
easy
preparation 10 minutes
cooking 4 minutes
serves 2 to 3

YOU NEED
1 lb (500 g) cabbage (or Chinese cabbage)
2 cloves garlic
2 chilli pods
2 tbsp oil

SEASONING A
½ tsp dry sherry
1 tbsp water

SEASONING B
2 tbsp sugar
½ tsp salt

1 tbsp soy sauce
1 tbsp vinegar (or lemon juice)

THICKENING
2 tsp cornflour dissolved in
1 tbsp water

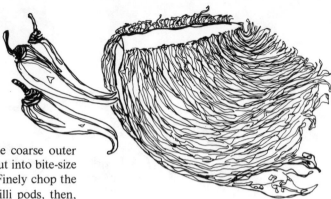

Clean the cabbage, removing the coarse outer
leaves and thick stems. Tear or cut into bite-size
pieces about 1½" (4 cm) square. Finely chop the
garlic. Open and de-seed the chilli pods, then,
cut each into 4 pieces and cover with ice-cold
water. In 3 small bowls, prepare the seasonings
and thickening. In a deep frying pan, heat the oil
until almost smoking. Stir-fry the garlic and
drained chilli pods 30 seconds. Remove from
pan and set aside. Keeping the pan over a high
heat, drop in the cabbage. Sprinkle with
seasoning A and stir fry for 2 minutes.
Incorporate seasoning B, garlic and chilli pods.
Stir-fry for 1 minute. Pour in the thickening and
cook until thickened, about 30 seconds. Remove
from heat and serve immediately.

TURNIPS BRAISED IN SOY SAUCE (Chien Ta Tou Ts'ai)

very easy
preparation 10 minutes
cooking 15 minutes
serves 2 or 3

This vegetable dish is a delicious accompani-
ment for roast and stir-fried meats.

YOU NEED
3–4 medium-sized turnips
2 spring onions (or leek)
½ tbsp soy sauce
1 pinch pepper
2 tbsp oil

SEASONING
½ tsp salt
1 tsp dry sherry
¼ pint (⅛ litre) water

Peel the turnips and slice very thinly. Finely
chop the spring onions (or leek). Prepare the
seasoning and set aside. In a frying pan, heat the
oil. Stir-fry the slices of turnip for 2 minutes.
Pour in the seasoning and bring back to the boil.
Lower the heat and let simmer for 10 minutes.
Add the soy sauce, pepper and spring onion (or
leek). Cook for 3 minutes more. Remove from
heat and serve.

WHITE COOKED CABBAGE (Pai Ch'au Pao Shin Ts'ai)

very easy
preparation 10 minutes
cooking 7 minutes
serves 2 to 3

YOU NEED
1 lb (500 g) cabbage (or Chinese celery cabbage
  or celery)
1 slice fresh ginger (or 1 good pinch powdered
  or 1 clove garlic)

1 pinch salt
1 tbsp oil

SAUCE
1 pinch pepper
2 tsp sugar
1 chicken broth cube
3 tbsp water
6 tbsp milk

Clean cabbage (or celery), removing the coarse outer leaves and thick stems. Tear or cut into bite-size pieces about $1\frac{1}{2}$" (3 cm) square. Finely mince the fresh ginger (or garlic). In a small saucepan, bring the water to the boil. Dissolve the chicken broth cube, then, add the sugar and pepper. Stir, remove from heat and incorporate the milk. Set aside. In a deep frying pan, heat the oil until almost smoking. Stir-fry the ginger (fresh or powdered) 10 seconds. Add the cabbage (or celery) and a pinch of salt. Stir-fry until it is well covered with oil, about 1 minute. Pour in the seasoning, reduce heat and cover. Let simmer for 5 minutes. Remove from heat and serve immediately.

DESSERTS (T'ien Tan)

Chinese rarely eat desserts, except at banquets where small, sweet delicacies appear on the table between salty courses. At home, seasonal fruit is usually served toward the end of the meal. In fact, fruit has always played an important role in the Chinese diet, as illustrated by a famous and very old story concerning the lichee. The Empress Yang of the Tang Dynasty adored this fruit and obliged the people to send her the best of their harvest, still warm with the sun. In order to deliver the perishable fruit as quickly as possible to the demanding Empress, a pony express system was developed which crossed half of China in one day! Lichees, today conserved in tins and distributed throughout the world by the most modern methods of transportation, convey a special flavour to any Chinese meal. Serve them with the biscuits or creams for which you will find the recipes in this chapter.

ALMOND BISCUITS (Tau Su)
easy
preparation 20 minutes
cooking 25 minutes
makes 24 almond biscuits

YOU NEED
10 oz (300 g) flour
5 oz (150 g) castor sugar
8 oz (250 g) lard (or generous $\frac{1}{4}$ pint ($\frac{1}{8}$ litre) oil)
4 tbsp powdered almonds
$\frac{1}{2}$ tsp baking powder
$\frac{1}{2}$ tsp salt
1 egg
1 tsp almond essence (or 1 tbsp Kirsch)
24 blanched almonds

GLAZE
1 egg yolk
2 tsp water

Pre-heat your oven to a moderate temperature (electricity 350°, gas regulo 4). Grease a flat biscuit pan. Prepare the glaze, beating together the egg yolk and water, then, set aside. Sieve together the flour, baking powder, sugar and salt. Work in the lard. Add the egg, powdered almonds and almond essence. Mix well. The dough should be firm but manageable; if it is too difficult to work, add several drops of water. Between the palms of your hands, roll the dough, 1 tsp at a time, into small balls. Place the balls on the biscuit pan, spacing them about 2"

(5 cm) apart. Press a blanched almond half-way down into each ball. Brush the top of each with the glaze. Bake the biscuits 20 to 25 minutes or until golden brown. Cool and serve.

TIPS & TRICKS

Conserve these biscuits in a tightly closed container. If, however, they become a bit damp, put them in a very slow oven (electricity 250°, gas regulo 1) for 20 minutes. This will restore all the savour of their first baking.

ALMOND CREAM JELLY (Hsing Jen Tou Fu)

very easy
preparation 10 minutes/refrigeration 2 hours
serves 4 to 6

You will often find this jelly on oriental restaurant menus for it is well known the world over as an especially light and delicate complement to a rich Chinese meal.

YOU NEED

¼ pint (⅛ litre) milk
¾ pint (½ litre) water
1½ tbsp castor sugar to taste
1 oz (20 g) gelatine (or 3 oz (80 g) agar-agar)
1 tsp almond essence (or 1 tbsp Kirsch)
1 tin mixed fruit salad (or cherries)

To dissolve the agar-agar, see instruction in the glossary. Bring to the boil ½ pint (¼ litre) water. Meantime, in an 8" (20 cm) mould (square if possible) soften the gelatine with ¼ pint cold water. Pour the boiling water over the gelatine

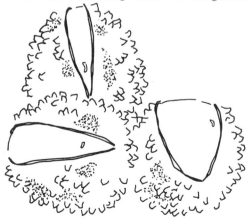

and stir until completely dissolved. Add the sugar and stir until dissolved. Incorporate the milk and almond essence. Stir and mix well, then, put the jelly into the refrigerator for 2 hours or until very firm. Cut into squares or triangles and serve in individual bowls garnished with the fruit salad.

ALMOND CREAM PUDDING (Hsing Jen Ch'a)

easy
preparation 5 minutes
cooking 40 to 45 minutes
serves 3 to 4

YOU NEED

3–4 tbsp castor sugar to taste
3 oz (80 g) blanched almonds
2 tbsp rice
1 pint (½ litre) water
1 tsp vanilla essence
1 pinch salt

You also need a blender.

In a blender, combine almonds, rice and ½ pint (¼ litre) water. Blend until you have obtained a well-ground, creamy mixture. Pour into a small saucepan and add ½ pint (¼ litre) water. Bring to the boil. Boil rapidly for 10 minutes. Reduce the heat and simmer until thick and smooth, 20 to 30 minutes. Add the vanilla essence, sugar and salt. Bring back to the boil, stir until the sugar is dissolved, then, remove from heat. Serve hot or cold.

ALMOND TEA CREAM (Hsing Jen Ch'a)

very easy
preparation 2 minutes
cooking 7 minutes
serves 3 to 4

This delectable cream is frequently served at the great banquets between the 'salty' dishes. For these occasions, it is prepared with additional water so that it may be drunk as a sweet soup or, as the Chinese call it, a 'sweet tea'.

YOU NEED

3 oz (80 g) castor sugar to taste
¼ pint (⅛ litre) milk
¼ pint (⅛ litre) water
1–2 drops almond essence (or 1 tbsp Kirsch)

THICKENING

5 tbsp cornflour dissolved in
¼ pint (⅛ litre) water

Prepare the thickening and set aside. In a small saucepan, bring to the boil ¼ pint (⅛ litre) water. Add the sugar and cook, while stirring, for 2 minutes Incorporate the almond essence and stir. Pour in the thickening, continuing to stir, and bring back to the boil. Cook, stirring, for 3 minutes. Add the milk and bring back to boil. Stirring, cook until thick and smooth, 2 to 3 minutes. Remove from heat and serve warm or cold.

CARAMEL TEA (Mein Ch'a)
easy
preparation 2 minutes

cooking 10 to 12 minutes
serves 2

Caramel tea is a charming and unusual sweet drink which is especially pleasing to children and may be served to them when the older guests are taking cocktails or after-dinner liqueurs.

YOU NEED

4 tbsp flour
4 tbsp sugar
1 tsp lard (or oil)

Heat a small, unoiled frying pan over a moderate flame. Pour in the flour and stir until it begins to brown. Reduce the heat to its very lowest temperature and continue stirring until the flour is caramel-coloured, about 8 minutes. Add the lard and stir energetically to prevent lumps from forming for 1 minute. Remove from the heat and divide between two cups. Add 2 tbsp sugar to each cup. Top with boiling water and stir well. Serve hot or warm.

TIPS & TRICKS

The flour/lard/sugar mixture may be kept in an airtight container for several weeks.

CHINESE SPONGE CAKE (Cheng Tan Kau)
fairly easy
preparation 20 to 25 minutes
cooking 30 minutes
serves 4 to 6

This cake is served during the Chinese New Year's 15-day-long celebration for it symbolises the hope that business affairs and property may 'puff up' like the cake.

YOU NEED

6 eggs
4 oz (100 g) cake flour
6 oz (150 g) castor sugar
½ tsp baking powder
1 pinch salt
½ tsp vanilla (or lemon or almond) essence

You also need a steamer.

Oil a deep pudding or soufflé mould which will fit into the steamer. Prepare the water in the steamer and bring to the boil while mixing the batter. Sieve together the flour, baking powder and salt, then, set aside. Separate the yolks from the egg whites. Beat the whites until very stiff. Slowly, spoonful by spoonful, incorporate the sugar, beating well after each addition. Beat for 5 minutes. Add the vanilla essence and beat for 1 minute. Slightly beat the egg yolks, then gently add to the whites, continuing to beat all the while. Incorporate, little by little, the sieved, dry ingredients. Beat 1 minute more. Pour the batter into the mould. Place the mould into the steamer and a towel between it and the lid to catch any condensation. Steam for 30 minutes over high heat. Open the steamer and carefully remove the cake which will shrink slightly. Unmould and cut into small pieces. Serve warm or cold.

TIPS & TRICKS
This sponge cake can be re-heated easily, either in the steamer (10 minutes) or, if well wrapped in aluminium foil, in a moderate oven (10 minutes). Serve the cake with tea and accompanied by seasonal or tinned fruit.

EIGHT TREASURES RICE PUDDING (Ba Bau Fan)
difficult
preparation 30 minutes
cooking 1 hour 25 minutes
serves 4 to 6

YOU NEED
6 oz (200 g) glutinous rice (or pudding rice)
4 oz (100 g) dates (or red bean paste)
4 oz (100 g) variety candied fruits
5 oz (150 g) castor sugar
1 oz (25 g) raisins
1 oz (25 g) blanched almonds
6 pitted prunes (or dates)
2 tbsp sherry
1 tbsp lard (or oil)
1½ pints (¾ litre) water

SAUCE
1 tbsp castor sugar
1 tbsp cornflour
¼ pint (⅛ litre) water

You also need a steamer.

Wash the rice thoroughly, put in a heavy saucepan and cover with 1 pint water. Bring to the boil, cover tightly and cook slowly until the rice becomes quite sticky, about 25 minutes. Incorporate the sherry and the sugar. Re-cover and cook for 15 minutes more. If you are using red bean paste, omit the following step. Wash the dates, put in a saucepan and cover with ½ pint (¼ litre) water. Bring to the boil and cook rapidly until all liquid is absorbed, about 20 minutes. Remove from the heat and allow to cool. Skin and pit the dates (or prunes), then, pass through a blender or Mouli to obtain a thick paste. Add the lard (or oil) to the dates (or prunes) and mix well. Oil a pudding mould or heat-resistant bowl which will fit into the steamer. At the bottom and on the sides of the mould, create a pretty design using the prunes, raisins, candied fruits and almonds. Gently pack the rice on top of the fruit, leaving a hole in the middle. Fill this hole with the date (or red bean) paste. Bring to the boil the water in the steamer. Steam the pudding for 20 minutes. Meanwhile, in a small saucepan, bring to the boil the sauce ingredients. Simmer, stirring, until the sauce

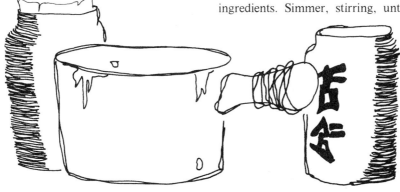

thickens and becomes translucent, about 5 minutes. Remove the pudding from the steamer and unmould. Cover with the sauce and serve warm or cold.

FORTUNE COOKIES (Chien Ping)
Fairly easy
preparing 5 minutes
cooking 3 minutes per cookie
makes 24 fortune cookies

Enclosed in each of these cookies is a tiny piece of paper upon which is written the 'fortune' of the person to whom it is served. Fortune cookies were actually created by Chinese restaurateurs in the United States, to the great enchantment of their clients, and add an exotic and delightful touch to any Chinese meal.

YOU NEED
2 egg whites
4 tbsp brown sugar
2 tbsp cornflour
2 tbsp flour
$\frac{1}{4}$ tbsp oil

$\frac{1}{2}$ tsp almond essence (or lemon essence or orange flower water)
$1\frac{1}{2}$ tbsp water

Write 'fortunes' or Chinese proverbs (see below) on 24 pieces of paper $1\frac{1}{2}$" × $\frac{1}{2}$" (4 cm × 1.25 cm). Whisk until frothy, about 1 minute, the egg whites and brown sugar, Sieve the flour and cornflour, then combine with the egg whites. Beat well, then add the water, oil and almond essence (or lemon essence or orange water). Beat for 1 minute more. Heat over a medium flame, a very lightly oiled crêpe or scone pan. Pour 1 tbsp of the batter into the pan. Working quickly with the back of a spoon, spread the batter thinly and evenly into a 3" to 4" (8 cm to 10 cm) round. Cook until set and lightly brown, about 2 minutes, then turn over. Flatten with the spatula and brown on the other side, about 1 minute. Remove from the pan. Using cooking gloves for easy handling, lay the 'fortune' in the middle of the biscuit and fold the biscuit in half. Bend the folded biscuit over the edge of a bowl, pressing the two points down against the sides of the bowl. Hold in this position until the biscuit has cooled slightly and keeps its shape, about 30 seconds. Set the biscuit aside to cool completely, about 30 minutes. Repeat the procedure until all the batter is used.

TIPS & TRICKS
These biscuits should be very crisp. However, due to insufficient heat or cooking, they sometimes remain rather limp. This can be easily remedied by placing them in a slow oven

(electricity 200°, gas regulo ½–1) for 5 minutes or until crisp. Keep the biscuits in an airtight container.

Chinese Proverbs for Fortune Cookies

The fool in a hurry drinks his tea with his chopsticks.

Great talents mature slowly.

Truth does not need to yell.

Patience brings peace.

If you bow down, bow low.

Good sees good; wisdom sees wisdom.

Once a fruit is eaten, the tree is forgotten.

Good takes 3 years to learn; evil one day.

Too much is as bad as too little.

With money and wine, you will always have friends.

A good son makes a good father.

One tree does not make a forest.

The family which lives in harmony succeeds in everything.

With rules, there is no perfection.

Plant melons, harvest melons; plant beans, harvest beans.

The heart of the just man does not fear thunder.

No matter which profession a man undertakes, he will find fault with it.

It is better to perfect a little talent than to accumulate a big fortune.

If you wish to attract the south wind, open the north window.

One cannot have both fish and bear's paws.

Dragons beget dragons; phoenix beget phoenix.

Three men make a tiger.

Eyes do not see their lashes.

Gold is tested by fire, men by gold.

A trip of a thousand miles begins with a single step.

When one drinks with a true friend, a thousand glasses are too few.

Paper cannot wrap fire.

It is a thousand times easier to destroy than to build.

It is easier to release a tiger than to catch it.

Early up three mornings, a day gained.

Work is longer than life.

After the wine is poured, the truth flows.

True gold does not fear fire.

The rich never have enough money, the poor never enough sleep.

There is no egg under an upside down nest.

It is the fishman who profits, when the oyster and the heron fight.

The older the ginger, the hotter it is.

Peaches and plums are silent but paths are worn beneath their branches.

It's the old horse that knows the road.

A long night is full of dreams.

PEANUT CANDY (Hua Sheng Tang)
very easy
preparation 5 minutes
cooking 12 minutes
makes about 20 pieces

Chinese merchants shave this candy into large curly leaves which children adore. In the United Kingdom it is sold in oriental shops in the form of rectangles or squares. In addition, peanut candy is very easy to prepare at home and all the more delicious. Offer it as a perfect sweet for the end of a large Chinese meal.

YOU NEED
4 oz (100 g) peanuts
4 tbsp sesame seeds (see Tips & Tricks)

8 tbsp brown sugar
8 tbsp honey (or corn syrup)
½ tbsp oil

Cover an 8" (10 cm) flan ring or unbreakable plate with aluminium foil. Grease with ½ tbsp oil. Coarsely chop the peanuts, if large. Heat a small, unoiled frying pan. Roast the sesame seeds, shaking the pan or stirring, 2 to 3 minutes. Mix the roasted seeds with the peanuts and set aside. In a saucepan, bring to the boil the brown sugar and honey. Lower the heat and, stirring frequently, boil gently for 10 minutes or until the candy reaches the hard ball stage. To test, drop a little of the candy into a cup of cold water: if it forms a hard ball it is done and if not, continue cooking until it reaches this stage. Remove from the heat and add the peanuts and sesame seeds, mixing well. Pour the candy on to the aluminium foil and spread fairly thinly. Allow to cool and harden, then break into pieces.

TIPS & TRICKS
The sesame seeds may be omitted and the quantity of peanuts increased. Likewise, the candy can be made exclusively of sesame seeds. In either case, the amount of peanuts or sesame seeds used depends upon personal preference.

PEANUT CREAM PUDDING (Tze Ma Hua Sheng Lu)
fairly easy
preparation 15 minutes
cooking 8 to 10 minutes
serves 3 to 4

YOU NEED
3 tbsp peanut butter (or 2 oz (50 g) peanuts)
1 tbsp sesame seeds
2 tbsp milk
3 tbsp sugar
¼ pint (⅛ litre) water

THICKENING
2 tbsp cornflour dissolved in
2 tbsp water

You also need a blender.

Prepare the thickening and set aside. Heat a small, unoiled frying pan. Roast the sesame seeds, while stirring or shaking the pan, until browned, 2 to 3 minutes. Remove from the heat. Blend the roasted sesame seeds, peanut butter and water. Pour the mixture into a small saucepan. Add the sugar and bring to the boil. Cook, stirring continually, until thick and smooth, about 3 minutes. Incorporate the thickening, stir and cook 2 minutes more. Add the milk, stir well and remove from the heat. Serve warm or cold.

SESAME CREAM PUDDING (Tze Ma Hu)
easy
preparation 5 minutes/soaking 12 hours
cooking 15 minutes
serves 3 to 4
This little cream is not only delightful to eat but we also believe that it bestows a beautiful complexion on he who partakes of it.

YOU NEED
4–6 tbsp sugar to taste
3 tbsp sesame seeds
2 tbsp rice

1 pint ($\frac{1}{2}$ litre) water

2 oz (50 g) flaked toasted almonds (optional)

You also need a blender.

Wash the rice, then, cover it with $\frac{1}{2}$ pint ($\frac{1}{4}$ litre) water to soak overnight. The next day, heat a small, unoiled frying pan. Roast the sesame seeds, stirring or shaking the pan, until they are well browned, 2 to 3 minutes. Remove from heat. Blend the rice, its soaking water and the roasted sesame seeds. Pour this mixture into a small saucepan and add $\frac{1}{2}$ pint ($\frac{1}{4}$ litre) water. Bring to the boil and cook over medium heat, stirring frequently, until thick, 10 to 15 minutes. Incorporate the sugar and continue to stir and cook until it is completely dissolved, about 2 minutes. Remove from the heat and garnish with the flaked toasted almonds. Serve warm or cold.

SPECIALITIES (Ch'a Ta)

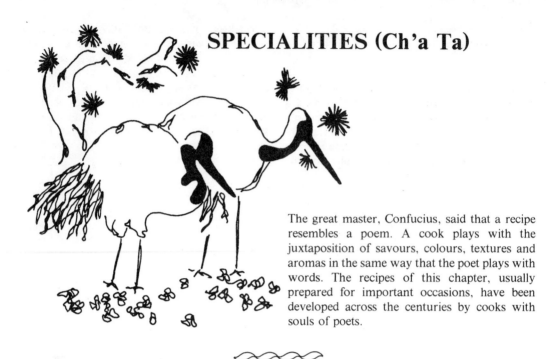

The great master, Confucius, said that a recipe resembles a poem. A cook plays with the juxtaposition of savours, colours, textures and aromas in the same way that the poet plays with words. The recipes of this chapter, usually prepared for important occasions, have been developed across the centuries by cooks with souls of poets.

CANTONESE ROAST DUCK (Shau Ya)
difficult
preparation 20 minutes / drying 1–3 hours
cooking 1 hour 45 minutes to 2 hours
serves 3 to 4

The skin of this duck is very crisp, its meat perfumed and moist.

YOU NEED
1 duck weighing 2–4 lb (1–2 kg)
1 tsp salt

SEASONING
3 star anise
2 tbsp sugar
¼ pint (⅛ litre) soy sauce

MARINADE
4 tbsp honey
2 tbsp vinegar
1 tbsp soy sauce
4–6 drops red food colouring (optional)

You also need a baking pan with a rack.

Tightly tie or sew closed the neck opening of the duck. Pass a string under its wings and around its body, then hang it in the fresh air for 1 to 3 hours. This dries the skin, rendering it crisp. Pre-heat your oven to very hot (electricity 475°, gas regulo 8–9). Rub the duck inside and out with the salt. Prepare the marinade and set aside. Combine the seasoning ingredients in a small saucepan. Bring to the boil, lower the heat and simmer for 10 minutes. Remove from the heat. Holding the duck by its legs, pour the seasoning inside the cavity. Sew up the opening with strong linen thread. Place the duck, on its back, on the baking pan rack. Bake for 20 minutes. Baste with the marinade and lower the oven temperature to hot (electricity 425°, gas regulo 7). Roast for 10 minutes, then baste again with the marinade. Lower the oven temperature to medium/hot (electricity 375°, gas regulo 5–6) and roast for 30 minutes, basting frequently. Lower the oven temperature to moderate (electricity 350°, gas regulo 4). Roast for 30 minutes, continuing to baste frequently. Lower the oven temperature to cool (electricity 275°, gas regulo 1–2) and roast for 15 minutes or until done, basting as necessary. Remove from the oven and cut into bite-sized pieces. Serve hot.

CHINESE CONDIMENT I (La Fan Ch'ieh Chiang)

very easy
preparation 3 minutes
serves 2 to 3

This condiment is especially enjoyed with such dishes as spring rolls, egg rolls and egg fu yung.

YOU NEED
1 tbsp soy sauce
1 tbsp ketchup
1 tsp sesame oil
1 dash tabasco (or hot pepper oil)

Combine all ingredients and mix well. Serve the sauce in small individual bowls for dipping.

CHINESE CONDIMENT II (called sate) (Sha Ch'a)

fairly easy
preparation 15 minutes
serves 4 to 6

Sate is served with Chinese Hot Pot and other such specialities.

YOU NEED
2 oz (50 g) peanuts
1 tbsp coriander seeds

2 spring onions (or chives)
2 tbsp soy sauce
1 good pinch pepper
1 clove garlic
1 dash tabasco (or hot pepper oil)
2 tbsp lemon juice
1 tbsp brown sugar

You also need a blender or Mouli.

Blend, mincing finely, the peanuts, coriander seeds and spring onions (or chives). Add the remaining ingredients and blend until a smooth mixture is obtained. Serve this condiment in small individual bowls for dipping.

CHINESE HOT POT (Sha Ch'a Huo Kuo)

very easy
preparation 30 minutes
individual cooking
serves 4

YOU NEED
2 chicken breasts
½ lb (250 g) pork (or rump steak)
1 lb (500 g) squid (or prawns or fish fillet)
½ lb (250 g) chicken livers (optional)
½ lb (250 g) fresh spinach (or watercress, lettuce, mange-tout or Chinese celery cabbage)
½ lb (250 g) cauliflower (or broccoli, tomatoes or courgettes)
4 oz (100 g) button mushrooms
6 oz (200 g) bamboo shoots
4 oz (100 g) *fenszu* (optional)
2 spring onions (or leek)
½ lb (250 g) bean curd (optional)
2 pints (1 litre) chicken stock (or water)

CONDIMENT
1 raw egg per person mixed with Chinese Condiment II, or with soy sauce, to taste.

You also need a fondue pot, electric saucepan, oriental hot pot or a soup pot set on an electric hot plate.

Cover the *fenszu* with warm water to soak for 1 to 2 minutes. Drain and cut into 2 or 3 sections. Cut into thin strips: the meat, chicken liver and squid (or fish). Clean and wash the vegetables, then drain well. Separate the cauliflower (or broccoli) into small, even florets. Drop the watercress into boiling water for 30 seconds to remove its bitter taste. Cut into thin slices mushrooms, tomatoes, courgettes, bamboo shoots. Cut the spring onions into 1" (2.5 cm) lengths, and the bean curd into 1" (2.5 cm) cubes. Arrange all these ingredients on a large serving dish which you will place on the table within the reach of your guests. Break a raw egg into each of 4 bowls and mix with a small amount of condiment or allow each guest to mix his own to taste. On the stove, bring the chicken stock to the boil, then transfer it to the tables where it should be kept boiling on a hot-plate. Add the bean curd to the stock. Each guest with his chopsticks, will dip the vegetables and meat into the boiling soup until done to taste, then into the condiment. The *fenszu* should be added to the soup toward the middle of the meal for it will absorb a certain amount of the liquid. At the end of the meal each guest may pour some of the soup into his bowl and enjoy its delicious flavour.

TIPS & TRICKS
The quantities of the ingredients given above are general indications and depend upon personal preference. Serve Chinese Hot Pot with steamed rice and a simple dessert.

CHOP SUEY (Ba Bau Ts'ai)
fairly easy
preparation 30 minutes
cooking 6 minutes
serves 3 to 4

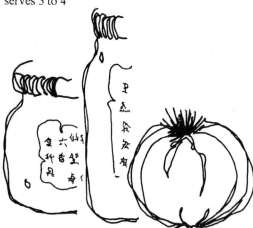

YOU NEED
⅓ lb (150 g) lean pork (or rump steak)
4 oz (100 g) shelled shrimp (fresh or frozen)
4 oz (100 g) mange-tout (or string beans)
1 lb (500 g) squid (optional)
1 carrot
1 small cucumber (or bamboo shoots)
1 green pepper
½ lb (250 g) cabbage
2 spring onions (or leek)
1 tsp sugar
1 clove garlic
2 tbsp oil

MARINADE A (pork)
2 tbsp cornflour
2 tbsp soy sauce
1 tsp dry sherry
½ tsp sesame oil (optional)
1 egg yolk

MARINADE B (shrimp)
1 unbeaten egg white
½ tsp salt

SEASONING
1 pinch pepper
½ tsp vinegar
1 tsp soy sauce
½ tsp salt
½ pint (¼ litre) water

THICKENING
1 tbsp cornflour dissolved in
1 tbsp water

In 2 bowls, prepare the marinades A and B. Cut the pork (or steak) against the grain into thin strips. Mix with marinade A and set aside for 15 minutes. Mix the shrimp with marinade B and marinate for 15 minutes. Clean the squid, then cut the tentacles into 2" (5 cm) lengths and the body into even, bite-sized pieces. Peel the cucumber, de-seed and slice thinly. Cut the carrot on the diagonal into thin slices; the spring onions into 1" (2.5 cm) pieces, and the cabbage into bite-sized pieces. Finely mince the garlic. In a deep frying pan, heat the oil until almost smoking. Stir-fry for 30 seconds the spring onions (or leek) sprinkled with the sugar. Add the meat and stir-fry for 2 minutes. Incorporate the shrimp, squid, carrot and garlic, stir-frying 1 minute. Add the cabbage and seasoning, bring to the boil and cook 1 minute. Add the cucumber, green pepper and mange-tout. Stir and simmer for 1 minute. Pour in the thickening and cook 1 minute or until thickened. Remove from heat and serve at once with steamed rice.

TIPS & TRICKS
The quantity of any one vegetable may be increased to replace another.

CRAB IN PUNGENT SAUCE (Sheng Ch'au Hsieh)

easy
preparation 30 minutes / marinade 30 minutes
cooking 2 minutes (27 minutes for an uncooked crab)
serves 3 to 4

YOU NEED
1 fresh crab, about 2 lb (1 kg)
2 chilli pods
1 clove garlic
½ tbsp flour
½ tbsp cornflour
½ tbsp dry sherry
2 tbsp oil

MARINADE
½ tsp salt
1 good pinch powdered ginger
½ tsp dry sherry

SEASONING
1 tsp cornflour
½ tsp sugar
½ tsp monosodium glutamate (optional)
2 tbsp water
1 tbsp soy sauce
½ tsp sesame oil (optional)

If your crab is live, plunge it into boiling water for 20 to 25 minutes or until red. Carefully pick the crab meat from the shell in as large pieces as possible. Mix with the marinade and set aside for 30 minutes. Meanwhile, prepare the seasoning and set aside. Open and de-seed the chilli pods. Mince the chilli pods and the garlic. Sprinkle the crab meat with the cornflour and flour. In a frying pan, heat 1 tbsp oil until almost

smoking. Sauté the crab meat, stirring gently, for 30 seconds. Remove from the pan. Add 1 tbsp oil to the pan and re-heat. Stir-fry the garlic and chilli pod for 30 seconds. Sprinkle with the sherry. Add the crab and seasoning. Cook for 30 seconds or until thickened. Serve immediately.

TIPS & TRICKS
Another method of preparing the crab, greatly enjoyed by the Chinese, is to pass it, shell and all, through very hot deep-frying oil before stir-frying it in the sauce. The crab is then served, still in its shell and its meat picked out with the fingers, a rather greasy experience!

CHRYSANTHEMUM FLOWERS WITH CHICKEN (Chou Keh Song)

difficult
preparation 20 minutes
cooking 6 to 8 minutes
serves 3 to 4

YOU NEED
4 oz (100 g) *fenszu*
2 chicken breasts (or turkey-breast steak)
1–2 chicken livers
1½ oz (25 g) chicken fat
1 head romaine lettuce (or lettuce or batavia)
2 slices fresh ginger (or ⅓ tsp powdered)
2 spring onions (or onion)
1 tbsp dry sherry
8 water chestnuts
1 tsp cornflour

2 egg yolks
1 pint (½ litre) oil for frying

SEASONING
1 tsp salt
1 tsp soy sauce
1 tsp sugar
1 tsp sesame oil (optional)
¼ tsp pepper

THICKENING
2 tbsp cornflour dissolved in
2 tbsp water

With scissors, cut the dry *fenszu* into 1½" (3 cm) lengths. To prevent its scattering about, cut it inside a large paper bag. Mince the fresh ginger, spring onions (or onion), chicken breasts, liver and fat. Crush the water chestnuts with the flat side of a cleaver. Mix together the cornflour, livers, water chestnuts, chicken fat and egg yolks. Wash and pat dry the lettuce, separating the leaves and place on a serving dish. In a deep frying pan, heat the oil until a piece of *fenszu*, thrown in, returns immediately to the surface and puffs up. Drop the *fenszu* into the hot oil by little handfuls and fry 10 to 20 seconds or until puffed up like little flowers. Drain on absorbent kitchen paper. Arrange the *fenszu* 'flowers' on a serving dish and keep warm. In another frying pan, heat 1 tbsp oil until almost smoking. Stir-fry the ginger and spring onions (or onions) for 30 seconds. Add the minced chicken and stir-fry for 2 minutes. Sprinkle with the sherry and stir-fry 30 seconds. Add the minced liver and cook, without stirring, for 30 seconds. Incorporate the seasoning ingredients and stir. Cook for 1 minute. Pour in the thickening and cook for 1 minute more. Remove from the heat and serve at once. Each guest will place a spoonful of chicken pâté on a lettuce leaf, add a *fenszu* 'flower', then roll the leaf. It may be eaten with the fingers.

EGG ROLLS (Ch'un Chüan)
difficult
preparation 25 minutes
cooking 6 minutes
serves 4

YOU NEED
½ lb (250 g) shelled shrimp fresh or frozen
½ lb (250 g) lean pork (or rump steak or chicken)
1 lb (500 g) bean sprouts (or cabbage)
5 spring onions (or leek or onion)
1 tsp cornflour
8–10 galettes (or prepared eggroll wrappers)
1½ pints (¾ litre) oil for frying (see Tips & Tricks)

MARINADE A (shrimp)
1 pinch salt
1 unbeaten egg white
1 tsp dry sherry

MARINADE B (pork)
1 tsp cornflour
½ tsp soy sauce
1 egg yolk

SEASONING
1 generous pinch each salt and pepper
1 tsp soy sauce
1 tsp monosodium glutamate (optional)
1 tbsp cornflour
1 tsp sesame oil (or other)

In 3 bowls, prepare the seasoning and the marinades A and B. Mix the shrimp with marinade A and set aside for 10 minutes. Cut the pork into matchstick-thin strips and mix with marinade B. Marinate for 10 minutes. Coarsely shred the spring onions (or cabbage). In a frying pan, heat 2 tbsp oil until almost

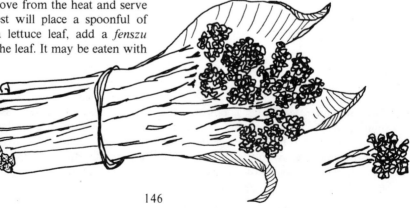

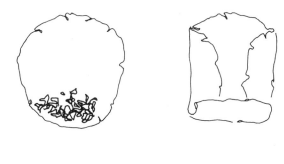

Egg roll

½ lb (250 g) bean sprouts (or green pepper, aubergine or other vegetables of preference)
4 sticks celery
½ pint (¼ litre) oil

SAUCE
1 pinch salt
3 star anise (optional)
1 tbsp sugar
½ pint (¼ litre) soy sauce
3–4 cloves garlic
¼ pint (⅛ litre) sherry
1½ pints (¾ litre) water

You also need a hibachi or electric frying pan.

smoking. Sprinkle the shrimp with the cornflour. Stir-fry the pork 2 minutes. Add the shrimp and spring onion (or leek). Stir-fry for 1 minute. Incorporate the bean sprouts and seasoning. Cook 1 minute more, then remove from the pan. Allow to cool, about 10 minutes. Bring to the boil enough water to dampen the rice galettes. Place the galettes in a drainer, being careful not to break them. Pour the boiling water over the galettes and drain. Spread an even portion (about 4 tbsp) of the pork/shrimp mixture over one-third of each galette. Fold the two sides of the galette toward the centre, then, roll tightly. In a deep frying pan, heat the oil until almost smoking. Gently slip the rolls into the hot oil and fry until brown, 3 to 4 minutes. Drain on absorbent kitchen paper and serve hot.

TIPS & TRICKS
Egg rolls may also be pan-fried, a method often preferred for home cooking. Heat 2 tbsp oil until almost smoking, then, lightly brown the rolls on all sides.

MONGOLIAN GRILL (Monku Kau Jou)
very easy
preparation 30 minutes
individual cooking
serves 4

YOU NEED
½ lb (250 g) meat per person, either rump steak or lamb
½ lb (250 g) watercress
½ lb (250 g) fresh spinach
½ lb (250 g) leek (or onion or spring onion)

Mince the garlic. Combine the sauce ingredients in a saucepan and bring to the boil. Stir until the sugar is dissolved, then remove from heat. Strain the sauce to remove the garlic and star anise. Divide the sauce equally between 5 bowls, one for each guest and one for the cooking. Cut the meat against the grain into paper-thin slices. Wash and drain the vegetables. Cut the leek (or onion) celery and spinach into 2" (5 cm) lengths. Arrange the vegetables and meat on a serving platter. Place the hibachi (or electric frying pan) in the middle of the table with one bowl of sauce nearby. Place the platter of vegetables and meat within the reach of everyone. The fuel in the hibachi (either wood or charcoal) should be brought to a white heat. If using an electric frying pan, heat

to the highest temperature. Place a fine mesh grate or iron griddle on top of the hibachi. Oil the grate or frying pan lightly. Each guest, with his chopsticks, will dip the pieces of meat and vegetables into his bowl of sauce, then cook to taste. The meat and vegetables being grilled may be sprinkled with the sauce.

TIPS & TRICKS

The quantities of vegetables given above are general indications and depend on personal preference. Place tabasco (or hot pepper oil) and sesame oil on the table so that each guest may season his sauce to taste. Serve with steamed rice and simple dessert.

PEKINESE ROAST DUCK (Shau Ya)

easy

preparation 10 minutes/marinade 1 hour/
    drying 1 to 3 hours
cooking 1½ hours to 1 hour 45 minutes
serves 3 to 4

This crispy and succulent roast duck is quite easy to prepare.

YOU NEED

1 duck weighing 2–4 lb (1–2 kg)
½ tbsp salt
½ tbsp five-spice powder (optional)
4 tbsp hoisen sauce (or ketchup)
1 tsp sesame oil (optional)

MARINADE

¼ pint (⅛ litre) soy sauce
4 tbsp dry sherry
4 tbsp honey
4 slices fresh ginger (or¼ tsp powdered)
4–6 drops red food colouring (optional)

You also need a baking dish with rack.

Prepare the marinade. Wash the duck under cold running water and pat dry. Place it in a shallow dish and cover with the marinade. Marinate for 1 hour, turning from time to time. Drain the duck (preserving the marinade). Tie a string under its wings and around its body, then hang the duck in the fresh air for 1 to 3 hours. The longer the better, for this dries the skin and makes it crisp. Pre-heat your oven to moderate-warm (electricity 325°, gas regulo 3). Sprinkle

inside the duck with the salt and five-spice powder. Place the duck, on its back, on the baking dish rack. Roast for 45 minutes. Turn the duck over and roast for 45 to 60 minutes more until done. Meanwhile, in a small saucepan, mix the remaining marinade with the hoisen sauce. Bring to the boil, lower heat and cook gently for 5 minutes, or until thickened, stirring frequently. Remove from heat and add the sesame oil. Cut the duck into bite-sized pieces and serve hot, accompanied by the sauce for dipping.

PUNGENT CHINESE MUSTARD (Chieh Muo Chiang)

very easy
preparation 5 minutes
serves 2 to 3

We Chinese like a pungent and very liquid mustard.

YOU NEED

1 tbsp powdered mustard
1½ tbsp water
¼ tsp lemon juice (or vinegar)

Combine the lemon juice and water. Dissolve the mustard in the lemon water. Mix well, then cover and set aside for 2 to 3 minutes. This is the trick which makes the mustard so savoury. Serve in small, individual bowls for dipping.

MILD CHINESE MUSTARD (Chieh Muo Chiang)

very easy
preparation 5 minutes
serves 2 to 3

This variation is for those who prefer a milder mustard.

YOU NEED

1 tbsp prepared mustard
2 tsp water
¼ tsp powdered mustard
¼ tsp lemon juice

Combine the lemon juice and water. Dissolve the powdered mustard in the lemon water, then add the prepared mustard. Mix well, cover and set aside for 2 to 3 minutes. This develops the full flavour of the mustard. Serve in small, individual bowls for dipping.

SHRIMP TOAST (Hsia Jen Tu Se)

fairly easy
preparation 15 minutes
cooking 3 minutes per canapé
makes about 24 canapés

YOU NEED
¼ lb (250 g) unshelled shrimp
4 oz (100 g) water chestnuts
1 oz (20 g) ham (optional)
6–8 slices white sandwich bread
1 spring onion (optional)
1 egg
½ tsp salt
1 tbsp cornflour
½ pint (¼ litre) oil for frying

CONDIMENT (optional)
2 tsp salt
½ tsp black peppercorns
1 pinch monosodium glutamate (optional)

To prepare the condiment, heat a small, unoiled frying pan. Roast the salt and peppercorns, stirring constantly (4 to 5 minutes). Using a mortar and pestle, or blender, grind into a powder. Sieve the powder and add the monosodium glutamate. Pour into a small serving dish (or individual salt dishes) and set aside. Shell the shrimp and remove the veins, then wash and pat dry. Mince the shrimp and

ham. Crush the water chestnuts with the flat side of a cleaver. Mix together the shrimp, ham, water chestnuts, egg, salt and cornflour. Finely mince the spring onion. Toast the slices of bread. Cut each slice into triangles or squares (about 1" (2.5 cm) per side). Spread the shrimp paste on each triangle. Garnish with the spring onion. In a deep frying pan, heat the oil until almost smoking. Gently slip the canapés, shrimp-side down, into the hot oil. Fry for 2 minutes, then turn over and fry for 1 minute more or until the canapés are golden brown. Drain on absorbent kitchen paper. Serve hot or cold, accompanied by the roasted salt for dipping.

TIPS & TRICKS
These canapés can be made in advance, frozen, then re-heated in the oven without pre-thawing.

SPRING ROLL I (San See Fen Chaun)

difficult
preparation 30 minutes
cooking 10 minutes
serves 4

YOU NEED
8–10 rice galettes
½ lb (250 g) lean pork (or chicken livers)
4 oz (100 g) shelled shrimp fresh or frozen
1 lb (500 g) bean sprouts (or bamboo shoots)
1 leek
3 dried Chinese mushrooms (optional)
3 tbsp oil

SEASONING
¼ tsp sesame oil (optional)
1 tsp salt
1 generous pinch pepper
2 tbsp water

THICKENING
1 tbsp cornflour dissolved in
1 tbsp water

You also need a steamer.

Wash the dried mushrooms and cover with warm water to soak for 10 minutes or until soft. Drain, remove the hard stalks and cut into thin strips. If the shrimps are rather large, cut them in half. Cut the leek into 1" (2.5 cm) lengths. Cut into thin strips the pork or liver and bamboo shoots). Rinse and drain the bean sprouts. In 2 bowls, prepare the seasoning and thickening. In a frying pan, heat the oil until almost smoking. Stir-fry the pork 2 minutes. Add the bean sprouts, mushrooms and shrimp. Stir, then sprinkle with the seasoning. Cook and stir for 3 minutes. Pour in the thickening and cook 30 seconds (or until thickened). Remove from the pan and allow to cool, about 10 minutes. Bring to the boil enough water to dampen the rice galettes. Place the galettes in a drainer, being careful not to break them. Pour the boiling water over them and drain. Place an equal portion (about 3 tbsp) of the pork/vegetable mixture on each galette. Roll the galettes tightly without closing the ends, then cut each roll into 3 or 4 pieces. Arrange the pieces on a heat-resistent plate which will fit inside the steamer. Steam for 3 minutes. Serve hot, accompanied by Chinese Condiment I, or nuoc mam.

SPRING ROLL II (Jou Szu La Pi)
difficult
preparation 30 minutes
cooking 10 minutes
serves 4

YOU NEED
½ lb (250 g) lean pork
½ lb (250 g) bean sprouts
4 oz (100 g) mange-tout (optional)
4 oz (100 g) peanuts
½ lb (250 g) cabbage (or Chinese celery cabbage)
4 oz (100 g) celery (or water chestnuts or bamboo shoots)

Spring rolls I and II

½ lb (250 g) shelled shrimp fresh or frozen
1 leek
1 carrot
2 eggs
1 pinch salt
½ tsp dry sherry
4 tbsp oil
8–10 rice galettes

SEASONING A
¼ tsp salt
1 pinch pepper
1 tbsp dry sherry
1 tbsp soy sauce

SEASONING B
1 pinch salt
½ tbsp dry sherry

Grind peanuts to a fine powder in a blender or Mouli. Coarsely shred the cabbage, carrot, pork and celery. Cut the leek into 2" (5 cm) lengths and, if large, cut the shrimp in half. In 2 bowls, prepare the seasonings A and B. Beat the eggs with the salt and the sherry. In a frying pan, heat ½ tbsp oil until almost smoking. Pour in half of the beaten egg, spreading to make a thin omelette. Brown quickly on both sides, then remove from the pan. Add ½ tbsp oil to the pan, re-heat and repeat the same procedure with the rest of the beaten egg. Roll the omelettes tightly, then cut crosswise into thin strips. Add 2 tbsp oil to the pan and re-heat until almost smoking. Stir-fry the pork, shrimp, cabbage and carrot for 1 minute. Sprinkle with seasoning A and stir-fry for 2 minutes. Remove the ingredients from the pan, leaving the liquid. Toss in the celery and mange-tout; bring to the boil, then remove. Add 1 tbsp oil to the pan and re-heat. Stir-fry the leek and bean sprouts for 30 seconds. Sprinkle with seasoning B and stir-fry for 2 minutes. Remove from the pan. Bring to the boil enough water to dampen the rice galettes. Place the galettes in a drainer, taking care not to break them. Pour the boiling water over the galettes and drain. Spread an even portion of the pork/cabbage and leek/bean sprout mixtures as well as the omelette strips over one-quarter of each galette. Sprinkle generously with the powdered peanuts. Fold the two sides of each galette toward the middle then roll tightly. Serve cold, accompanied by the Chinese Condiment I, or nuoc mam.

TIPS & TRICKS

The quantity of any one vegetable may be increased to replace another or any vegetable of personal preference used instead of those indicated.

SWEET AND SOUR CRAB (Tsu Liu Hsieh)

easy
preparation 30 minutes/marinade 30 minutes
cooking 3 minutes (28 minutes for an uncooked crab)
serves 3 to 4

YOU NEED

1 fresh crab, about 2 lb (1 kg)
1 spring onion
1 clove garlic
1 chilli pod
2 tsp dry sherry
½ tbsp flour
½ tbsp cornflour
2 tbsp oil

MARINADE

1 good pinch powdered ginger
1 good pinch each salt and pepper
2 tsp soy sauce
2 tsp dry sherry

SEASONING

3 tbsp sugar
1 good pinch salt
1 tsp cornflour
3 tbsp vinegar
3 tbsp water
2 tsp soy sauce
¼ tsp sesame oil (optional)

If the crab is alive, plunge it into boiling water for 20 to 25 minutes or until red. In 2 bowls, prepare the marinade and the seasoning. Carefully pick the crab meat from the shell in as large pieces as possible. Mix with the marinade and set aside for 30 minutes. Meanwhile, cut the spring onion into 2" (5 cm) lengths. Open and de-seed the chilli pod, then mince finely. Mince the garlic. Sprinkle the crab meat with the flour and the cornflour. In a frying pan, heat 1 tbsp oil

until almost smoking. Sauté the crab meat for 30 seconds, stirring gently. Remove from the pan. Add 1 tbsp oil to the pan and re-heat. Stir-fry the spring onion, garlic and chilli pod for 1 minute. Sprinkle with the sherry and stir. Incorporate the crab and seasoning. Cook until thickened, about 1 minute. Remove from the heat and serve at once.

TOMATOES STUFFED WITH SHRIMP (Niang Fen Ch'ieh)

difficult
preparation 20 minutes
cooking 10 minutes
serves 4

YOU NEED

½ lb (250 g) shrimp fresh or frozen (or minced pork)
½ lb (250 g) spinach (or green pepper)
4 firm tomatoes (or green pepper)
1 egg yolk
2 tsp cornflour
2 tbsp water
½ tsp salt
1 tbsp dry sherry
1½ tbsp oil

SEASONING

2 spring onions (or leek)
½ tsp salt
1 tsp dry sherry
1 unbeaten egg white
2 tbsp cornflour

THICKENING

1 tsp cornflour and 1 pinch salt dissolved in 1 tsp water

Mince the shrimp (or pork) and spring onions (or leek). Mix the minced shrimp with the seasoning. Clean the spinach and cut on the diagonal into strips. Halve the tomatoes (or peppers) on the diagonal and scrape out the seeds, reserving the juice. With absorbent kitchen paper, dry the halves, then sprinkle the inside of each with ¼ tsp cornflour. Fill with the shrimp. Brush with the slightly beaten egg yolks. Prepare the thickening and set aside. In a frying pan, heat ½ tbsp oil until almost smoking. Toss in the spinach and season with the salt.

Stir-fry for 1 minute, then remove from the pan. Place in a serving dish and keep warm. Add ¼ tbsp oil to the pan and re-heat over a medium/ hot flame. Carefully slide the tomatoes into the pan, shrimp-side down. Sprinkle with 1 tbsp water. Cover and cook for 3 minutes. Sprinkle again with 1 tbsp water, re-cover and cook for 3 minutes. Repeat once again the same procedure, so that the tomatoes will have cooked a total of 9 minutes (15 minutes for the pork stuffing). Remove from the pan and arrange on top of the spinach. In a small saucepan, bring to the boil ¼ pint (⅛ litre) juice from the tomatoes (or water). Incorporate the thickening and cook for 1 minute or until thickened. Pour the sauce over the tomatoes and serve hot.

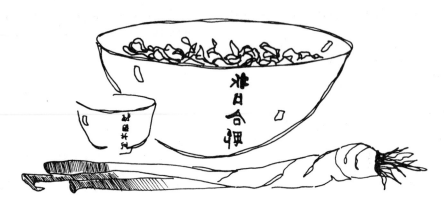

GLOSSARY OF CHINESE INGREDIENTS

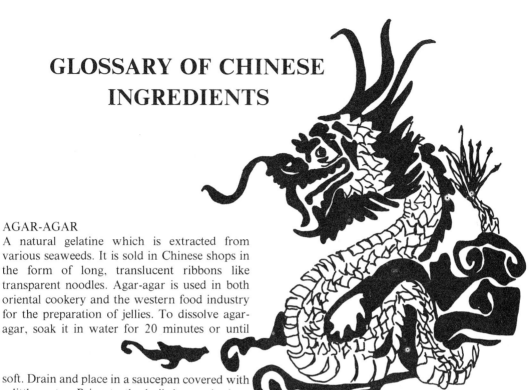

AGAR-AGAR

A natural gelatine which is extracted from various seaweeds. It is sold in Chinese shops in the form of long, translucent ribbons like transparent noodles. Agar-agar is used in both oriental cookery and the western food industry for the preparation of jellies. To dissolve agar-agar, soak it in water for 20 minutes or until

soft. Drain and place in a saucepan covered with a little water. Bring to the boil, lower the heat and cook gently until completely dissolved. Then use according to recipe instructions. It is not necessary to refrigerate agar-agar for solidification. It becomes very firm at room temperature and does not liquefy. It can be replaced by any powdered gelatine. Well wrapped, agar-agar may be kept in the cupboard for an indefinite length of time.

BAMBOO SHOOTS

There are many varieties of bamboo shoots, coming from all corners of China and harvested nearly the year round. Bamboo shoots are valued in Chinese cookery not only for their texture but also for their ivory colour which creates a striking contrast with other

ingredients. Bamboo shoots must be used in cooked dishes. After opening the tin, they should be rinsed and placed in the refrigerator in a tightly closed container filled with water. If the water is changed every three days, the bamboo shoots will keep for a month or longer.

BEAN CURD

Also called 'Tou Fu' or 'Dow Foo', it resembles, in appearance, a soft, white cheese. The curd is made from crushed soy beans and water. Its method of preparation was conceived in 164 BC by Lord Hui Am of Huai-Nam. Today, it is recognized as one of the world's most complete foods, due to its high content of proteins, vitamins and minerals. There are as many varieties of bean curd as there are ways of preparing it. The vegetarians call it the 'meat of the fields' and Buddhists, in particular, prefer a certain type which they name 'Buddha's chicken'. Bean curd is especially savoury when prepared in highly seasoned dishes. To conserve

153

it, place the bean curd in the refrigerator in a tightly closed container filled with water. If the water is changed every day, the bean curd will keep up to two weeks.

BEAN SPROUTS

Sprouts of the mung (green soja) bean, which are eaten when they reach a length of 2" to 3" (5 cm to 8 cm). The thin green skin which covers the head of the sprout should be removed and discarded. Many cooks also remove the tip of the little root. Cabbage and lettuce hearts, coarsely shredded, may be substituted in cooking, but bean sprouts are very easy to grow at home. There are several methods for sprouting mung beans, the easiest being to use a 'sprouter', a special container designed for this purpose and which is available in health food shops. A second method consists of using a

towel. First soak the mung beans in warm water for several hours or overnight. Then, wet the towel and fold it in half lengthwise. Starting 4" (10 cm) from one end of the folded towel, sprinkle the seeds across an area 4" (10 cm) wide. Fold the towel over the seeds and repeat

the procedure until all the seeds have been sprinkled on the towel and the towel folded over upon itself several times. Place the towel on a drainer and sprinkle with water several times a day so that it remains damp. In 5 or 6 days the seeds will be ready to harvest. A third sprouting method is to pierce several holes in the metal lid of a large glass jar. After having soaked the beans, place them in the jar and close it. Keep the jar in a dark place, rinsing the beans several times every day so that they remain damp. The sprouts will be ready to eat in 4 to 5 days. Both towel and jar should be disinfected with household bleach after sprouting. Four tablespoons of dry beans will produce a harvest of about 1½ pound (500 g) of sprouts. The harvested sprouts may be kept in the refrigerator for 4 to 5 days.

BLACK FUNGUS

Also called 'cloud ears', it is sold by weight in oriental groceries. Black fungus is a coal-black shrivelled-up mushroom which, when soaked, triples or quadruples in volume and takes on the shape of an ear, whence its name. Also with

soaking, its colour lightens, causing it to be designated at times as 'brown fungus'. The water in which the black fungus is soaked, must not be used for cooking. Black fungus is greatly appreciated for its glutinous yet crunchy texture. In its dried form, it will keep indefinitely in the pantry or cupboard.

CHINESE CABBAGE

Also called 'Bok Choy', Chinese cabbage has thick white stems and dark-green leaves, closely resembling Swiss Chard. It can be kept in the refrigerator up to one week. Chinese cabbage is

used in cooked dishes and can be replaced by green or white cabbage.

CHINESE CELERY CABBAGE

Also called 'Siu-Choy', it has rather curly, light green leaves and resembles romaine lettuce in form. Very delicate, with a taste similar to that of celery, Chinese celery cabbage can be used in salads or stir-fried. It should be firm and tightly

closed when bought and can be kept in the refrigerator up to one week. Green or white cabbage, spinach or celery may be substituted for it.

CHINESE MUSTARD GREENS AND PICKLED MUSTARD GREENS

Also called 'Gai Choy', with large, apple-green leaves and thick white stalks, it can be bought fresh or tinned, under the name 'Salted Pickled Mustard Greens'. Mustard greens are most frequently used in stir-fried dishes and soups. The tinned mustard greens are similar in taste to dill pickles and sauerkraut, both of which make excellent substitutes. Fresh, it will keep in the refrigerator up to 5 days. Tinned, it should be

placed in another container after opening and covered with vinegar-water or brine. It can be conserved in this way for several weeks. Before using the pickled mustard greens, rinse well, then cut into thin strips.

CHINESE PARSLEY

Known by the name of 'coriander', it is sold fresh and can also be grown in any kitchen herb garden. Its leaves are light green and very

tender, its flavour rather bitter and more pungent than that of common parsley. It is particularly used in soups and as garnish for fried dishes. Chinese parsley may be kept in the refrigerator for 4 to 5 days.

CHINESE SAUSAGES

Also called 'Lop Cheong', they can be found in certain Chinese shops hung in bunches or under plastic wrap. Deep-red in colour, these sausages are made of pork and spices. Their aroma is

most agreeable. Usually steamed with rice, the sausage fat becomes translucent when cooked (about 30 minutes). They can be kept for several months if well wrapped and placed in the refrigerator.

DRIED CHINESE MUSHROOMS

Sold by weight in oriental groceries, these mushrooms must be soaked before using. Through soaking, they become fleshy and

155

velvety. They are favoured for their delicate aroma and bouquet which has given them the name in French of 'perfumed mushrooms'. The water in which the Chinese mushrooms are

soaked may be used in cooking and serves to heighten the exotic flavour of all Chinese dishes. Indeed, these mushrooms can be added to almost any Chinese dish with the exception of those which are sweet. Button and other varieties of fresh mushrooms can be used as substitutes but will not replace the special fragrance and savour of Chinese mushrooms.

DRIED CHINESE SHRIMP
Amber coloured, their flavour is very pronounced. Dried shrimp are sold by weight in oriental shops. They must be rinsed and soaked before using and should be added to any dish only in very small quantities. Half an ounce (10 g) of dried shrimp replaces about four oz (100 g) of fresh shrimp. They are used primarily in soups to which they impart a most exotic savour and aroma. Dried shrimp may be kept in a closed container for several months.

FENSZU
Called Chinese vermicelli or transparent noodles, *fenszu* resembles very thin nylon cord. It is made from the mung bean (green soja) and starch. Its outstanding quality is to absorb the flavours of the seasonings with which it is cooked. If it is to be prepared in a sauce, *fenszu* must be first soaked 1 to 2 minutes in warm

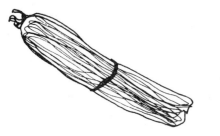

water. Be careful not to oversoak for it quickly becomes swollen with water. Dry, *fenszu* can be fried in very hot, deep-frying oil in which it will puff up and form curly, crunchy nests resembling chrysanthemum flowers. *Fenszu* cannot be replaced by any other noodle but it is readily available in oriental shops.

FIVE-SPICE POWDER
A powdered mixture of five different spices which include star anise, fennel, cinnamon, cloves and Szechwan pepper. It can be substituted by allspice which is available in all supermarkets or even prepared at home from the following spices: $\frac{1}{4}$ tsp powdered ginger; $\frac{1}{4}$ tsp allspice; $\frac{1}{4}$ tsp powdered anise (or nutmeg); $\frac{1}{2}$

tsp powdered cinnamon; 1 generous pinch powdered cloves. This mixture represents the equivalent of 2 tsp of five-spice powder. In a closed container, five-spice powder will keep indefinitely.

GARLIC
Garlic, both fresh and dried, plays such a large role in Chinese cooking that it has been called the 'prince of condiments'. Contrary to the

French method of slowly sautéeing garlic in butter, the Chinese brown it quickly in very hot oil, stirring energetically all the while. After several seconds of stir-frying, another ingredient is added to the pan, thus lowering the temperature of the oil and preventing the garlic from burning. Or else, as soon as the oil is seasoned and the garlic well browned, it will be removed and discarded. Therefore, when using garlic in Chinese cooking, be sure to employ the Chinese method of frying it in order to obtain the best results.

GINGER

A tubular root which is sold fresh and is also widely available in powdered form. Scrape or peel the thin skin which covers the fresh ginger

before preparing it for cooking. Fresh ginger may be kept in the refrigerator, unwrapped, for 3 to 4 weeks. To conserve for a longer period of time, place it, peeled, in a container which can be tightly closed and cover it with dry sherry. The sherry, which will absorb a ginger flavour, can later be used in cooking. Ginger adds a very special flavour to Chinese dishes.

GLUTINOUS RICE

Its chalky-white colour distinguishes it from all other rice. After cooking, it becomes extremely glutinous, whence its name. Due this sticky quality, glutinous rice is only used in very special dishes, sweet or salty, which are moulded or formed into balls.

HOISEN SAUCE

A reddish-brown, thick sauce, made from chilli pods, soy beans, sugar and flour. Hoisen sauce is the Chinese equivalent of ketchup and can be used in similar ways, either in cooking or as a condiment. To substitute, mix equal quantities of ketchup, soy sauce and honey or sugar. Bring to the boil and cook gently for 5 minutes, or until thickened, then remove from the heat. Keep hoisen sauce in the refrigerator, tightly closed.

LICHEE

A small, round fruit with a hard, rough, red-coloured shell. The flesh of the lichee is white and plump. It may be bought fresh or tinned.

After opening the tin, lichees may be kept in the refrigerator for about one week.

LONGAN

Also called 'dragon's eyes', this is a small fruit about the size of a cherry. Sold in tins in Chinese shops, longans can be used in soups or in desserts. They may be substituted by white, seedless raisins which are similar in taste. After the opening tin, place the longans in the refrigerator where they can be kept for about a week.

LOTUS SEEDS

The lotus is a very beautiful variety of water lily from which the seeds are extracted. These seeds are white and almond shaped and have a very delicate taste of nuts. In fact, blanched almonds may be used as a substitute for them. They are added to both sweet and salty dishes. In China,

lotus seeds are sold dried and require long, slow cooking. However, in the United Kingdom they are sold tinned, ready to be eaten or incorporated into cooked dishes. Lotus seeds are the symbol of fertility and as such are served at wedding banquets to signify the desire for 'successive births of sons'.

MONOSODIUM GLUTAMATE

Monosodium glutamate, formerly extracted from seaweed, has been used by the Chinese for centuries to enhance the natural flavour of foods. Today, it is a product of various vegetable sources, notably beet, corn and wheat. It has been widely adopted by the American public where a great controversy has arisen over its excessive use in Chinese restaurants. According to its critics, M.S.G. has caused an outbreak of allergies, called the 'Chinese restaurant syndrome'. However, there has been no scientific evidence justifying these claims in spite of intensive research. Since monosodium glutamate serves to enhance and bring out the flavour of old or tasteless food, its usage is purely optional.

NUOC MAM

A Vietnamese fish brine which is the equivalent of Chinese fish sauce. The finest quality of these fish sauces will have marinated for at least 10 years but the usual aging period for commercial use is 6 months. Nuoc Mam and Chinese fish sauce are very rich in nitrogen, albuminoids and vitamins, and therefore considered as much a tonic as a condiment. For those who do not care for the strong, unique flavour of such fish sauces, soy sauce may be used instead.

OYSTER SAUCE

A thick, brown sauce, used in cooking or as a condiment. Oyster sauce can be kept in the refrigerator. To obtain a substitute very similar in taste and appearance, soy sauce and ketchup may be combined with oyster juice. However, nuoc mam, Chinese fish sauce or soy sauce may be used in its place.

RED BEAN PASTE

A paste made from red soy beans, it is primarily used in the preparation of sweets. Once opened, it can be kept in a tightly closed container in the refrigerator for several months.

RICE GALETTES

In the shape of a transparent pancake, very thin and breakable, rice galettes are sold in oriental shops. They are used primarily as 'skins' for spring and egg rolls in the place of egg roll wrappers. Rice galettes must be dampened

before using. In their dry form and well wrapped, they may be kept in the cupboard or pantry indefinitely.

RICE NOODLES

Made from rice, these noodles come in many different widths. They can be prepared in

sauces, after having first been soaked, or, in their dry form, deep-fryed in oil until crisp. Rice noodles have no substitute.

SESAME OIL

A thick oil which is extracted from sesame seeds, it adds a very special savour and 'perfume' to Chinese delicacies. Its flavour has no substitute. Only in its quality as an oil can it be replaced by other oils.

SESAME PASTE

Obtained from finely ground, lightly roasted sesame seeds, sesame paste resembles a thick cream and keeps perfectly in the refrigerator. Peanut butter is a common and much used substitute for sesame paste. However, the peanut butter should be mixed with sesame oil to .achieve the same consistancy and taste. Sesame paste is used primarily in sauces and dressings.

SESAME SEEDS

Small seeds which come in two colours, black and ivory. The ivory-coloured seeds are those which are the most frequently found. They are used in both sweet and salty dishes. To enhance their flavour, they should be lightly roasted in an unoiled pan. Since ancient times, the Chinese have believed that sesame seeds contributed to good health, good memory and beauty. Today,

these beliefs have been confirmed by scientific evidence proving that they contain elements specifically recommended for the nervous system. In a humidity-free container, sesame seeds may be kept for an indefinite period of time.

SOY BEANS
There exist numerous varieties of these beans, the most commonly available in the United Kingdom being the yellow soy bean. Soy beans require a long soaking period (usually overnight) before cooking. They are one of the world's most complete natural foods, rich in fats, amino acids, proteins and minerals. Most vegetarians consume great quantities of soy beans which insures them excellent health. The Chinese make many different products from the soy bean, the most well known of which are bean curd and soy bean milk. In fact, it is the soy bean milk which replaces cow's milk in the Chinese diet. Well wrapped, dried soy beans may be kept in the cupboard for an indefinite period of time.

SOY SAUCE
A brown, liquid, salty sauce made from soy beans, wheat flour, salt and water, then fermented with yeast. Tightly closed, soy sauce can be kept in the cupboard for an indefinite period.

SPRING ONION
Well-known member of the onion family, the spring onion is much loved and used by Chinese

cooks. The white bulb and about 6" (15 cm) of its green stem are eaten. The spring onion serves in Chinese cookery both as a condiment and as a vegetable. It is widely available throughout the United Kingdom, but can be replaced by the leek and the onion when used as a vegetable and by shallots and chives in its seasoning role. Spring onions will keep in the refrigerator for up to a week.

STAR ANISE
Also called 'badiane', star anise is a spice which originated in China but is today commonly used in France in the preparation of anise liqueurs, notably anisette. Star anise resembles an eight-pointed star, dark brown in colour and about 1"

(2.5 cm) in diameter. It is sold in Chinese shops but can be replaced by anise, preferably in powdered form, or by cinnamon. In a tightly closed container, star anise will keep indefinitely.

SZECHWAN PEPPER
This peppercorn which comes from the province of Szechwan resembles in form the common black peppercorn. Reddish-brown in colour, its taste is stronger and more piquant than the black peppercorn which can, however, replace it.

TIGER LILY
Yellow-brown in colour, tiger lilies symbolise money for the Chinese. They are sold dried, by weight, in oriental shops. Pre-soaking is essential. These flowers bring a distinct and

slightly sweet bouquet to the dishes in which they are cooked. Well wrapped, in their dry form, they can be kept in the cupboard for an indefinite period.

VINEGAR

Red, black or colourless, Chinese vinegar is made from rice. The colourless and black vinegars are used in cooking, while the red is served at table as a condiment and dip. Common red wine and cider vinegars can replace the Chinese varieties perfectly well.

WATER CHESTNUTS

The aquatic 'roots' or bulbs of a vegetable which grows in irrigated fields, water chestnuts are valued for their crunchy texture and white colour. Widely adopted by the American public for oriental and non-oriental dishes alike, they are most especially used in salads and stir-fried dishes. Water chestnuts may be replaced by celery. After opening the tin, the chestnuts

should be rinsed and placed in a container filled with water which should be changed every two days. In the refrigerator, they will keep up to one month.

GENERAL INDEX

NOTES

NOTES